BOOKS BY FRED W. FRIENDLY

See It Now (with Edward R. Murrow)
Due to Circumstances Beyond Our Control . . .
The Good Guys, the Bad Guys and the First Amendment
Minnesota Rag

MINNESOTA RAG

MINNESOTA RAG

FRED W. FRIENDLY

The Dramatic Story
of the Landmark
Supreme Court Case
That Gave
New Meaning to
Freedom of the Press

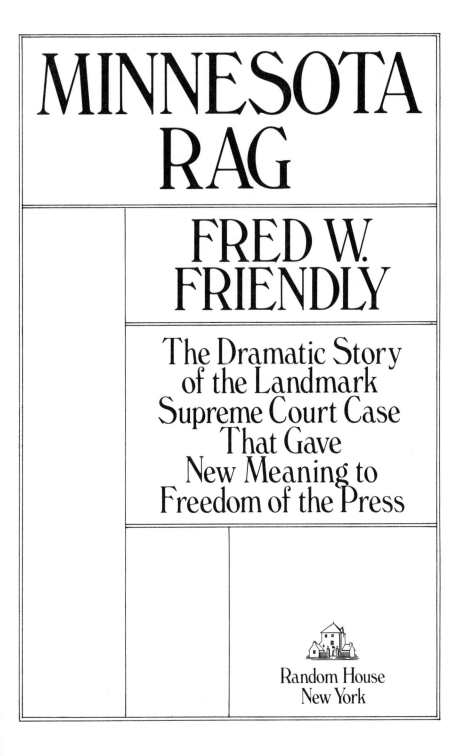

Random House
New York

*Grateful acknowledgment is made to the following for permission
to reprint previously published material:*

Minnesota Historical Society: Reproduction of the *Saturday Press*
issue for October 15, 1927. *Saturday Press,* exhibit in Hennepin
County District Court case #272132, Near vs. Minnesota, Minnesota
State Archives, Minnesota Historical Society.

Library of Congress Cataloging in Publication Data

Friendly, Fred W
Minnesota rag.

Bibliography: p.
Includes index.
1. Near, Jay M.   2. Saturday press (Minneapolis)
3. Liberty of the press—Minnesota.   4. Liberty of the
press—United States.   I. Title.
KF228.N35F73   342.73′0853   80–6018
ISBN 0-394-50752-5

Manufactured in the United States of America

98765432

FIRST EDITION

*For Paul A. Freund, who has raised the teaching of
constitutional law to an art;
for Ruth W. Friendly, who radiates on her own special frequency; and
for our six children, who have picked up that signal*

"*The Bill of Rights is worth no more than the statutes of Hammurabi*"

Here was the most noble opportunity that the Supreme Court in all its history faced. It had a chance to do something, perhaps transiently unpopular, that would be of more value to human liberty in this world than a dozen bogus wars to save democracy. How did it meet the challenge? If you want to find out . . . go read the dissenting opinions of the war years and immediately thereafter—that is, go read the opinions of those justices [Brandeis and Holmes] who stood out for the Bill of Rights in the face of all pressure and uproar and were defeated only by the votes of their illustrious colleagues.

In those minority opinions, chiefly by Justices Brandeis and Holmes, there is much melancholy history. And in that history lie the roots of the evil esteem in which the courts are held today . . . but few Americans . . . can escape the conclusion that some way to improve them is needed and that it must be found.

—H. L. MENCKEN
January 17, 1926

Contents

MINNESOTA RAG

Chapter 1
The Trail from Rip-saw

There ought to be a law against
such scandalous sheets.

—SENATOR GEORGE LOMMEN, *1925*

"**W**ILD women infest Superior! Read all about it. Wild women infest Superior!" shouted Iz Cohen. Though the eleven-year-old newsboy had no idea what the headline meant, he kept hawking his copies of the Duluth *Rip-saw*. Wearing knickers and a visor cap, he paced up and down that Saturday morning in 1924 in front of the old St. Louis County State Bank, making his sales pitch for the five-cent paper until a banker came out, grabbed his papers and chased him away.

That crude act of censorship only affected Isadore Cohen and the *Rip-saw*'s street circulation; the next act would have all the force of the Minnesota Legislature. Eventually the trail from *Rip-saw* would stretch all the way to the Supreme Court in Washington. By the time it was settled in 1931, the role of that Minnesota rag in this constitutional drama would be all but forgotten.

Saturday mornings were special in Duluth because that was when John L. Morrison's *Rip-saw* hit the street. It was a ragtag scandal sheet in which blazing headlines told of lurid peccadilloes, bootleggers and pols in cahoots with thugs. Outraged at the "unholy and undesirable alliance" between the underworld and officialdom in Duluth, Morrison had decided to resurrect the weekly four-sheeter he had briefly published in Crete, Nebraska. "There is a great wealth of unwritten history lying loose around Duluth," wrote Morrison in the lead editorial of the first issue on March 24, 1917. "The daily papers are so crammed with advertising that they have no space for it . . . Then there are a lot of old deadheads sticking in the mud of the old millpond. Right now seems a fitting time to rip them open and see whether they are sound or rotten." Morrison announced that the paper would be published "when conditions warrant and the head sawyer [editor Morrison] feels like working . . . A little more steam. Let 'er go, boys. Zip, zip, zip, rip, rip, zip, zip, zip. See the sawdust fly!"

When Morrison migrated to Duluth in 1893, he found a burgeoning city crowded with speculators and prospectors who had contracted mining fever, investing their savings in all kinds of wild schemes and scams, making and breaking fortunes in a matter of minutes. "There was no holding Duluth, thinking in millions, dealing in futures, depending on prospects, building on expectations," as one historian put it. "The zenith city of the unsalted seas," its early tycoons called it.

Mark Twain is reported to have remarked that the "coldest winter I ever spent was a summer in Duluth." With winters of 40 degrees below, Duluth might have remained the sleepy little town which gold prospectors and fur trappers passed by. But Mother Nature had bestowed on it more than arctic cold. The city was a by-product of the vast deposits of iron ore that lay to the north in the Mesabi Range, whose riches lured robber barons, railroad laborers and red-light ladies.

The Mesabi Range ("Sleeping Giant," the Chippewa Indians called it) was a solid wall of minerals when Leonidas Merritt first discovered the red powdery substance on November 16, 1880, at a site that became known as Mountain Iron Mine. "We are going to build a railway with easy grades for transportation from the mines of the Mesabi to the smokestacks of the Zenith," Merritt prophesied. Before he could make his dream come true, he and his brothers ran out of cash. After John D. Rockefeller came to their rescue, it was only a matter of time before the Merritts were out and the Mesabi Range was Rockefeller territory. Eventually Oliver Mining Company, with financial support from Andrew Carnegie, formed an alliance with the Rockefellers, and the great ore boom was on. By the turn of the century the Carnegie-Oliver-Rockefeller combination was included in the purchase of the Carnegie equity for a half-billion dollars by a consortium of steel interests, and thus, in 1901, the U.S. Steel empire was born.

Snaking its way for a hundred miles from Grand Rapids in the west to Babbitt in the east and never more than two miles wide, the Mesabi Range gradually became a terraced amphitheater, a series of miniature Grand Canyons hacked out by massive steam shovels as the deep overburden of glacial drift was stripped away. So rich was the iron content in some of the formations that it actually affected the magnetic field on the compass. The statistics are staggering: in its first eighty years, from 1884 to 1964, the Mesabi Range produced almost 2.5 billion tons of ore.

Iron horses were needed to carry the iron ore. Herds of

them transformed St. Louis County into a network of crossing, spiraling, climbing roadbeds. The Duluth, Missabe & Northern, followed by other chugging railroads, turned Duluth and Superior harbors into one of the busiest freight complexes and fresh-water harbors on the continent. Ore trains, 180 cars long, pulled by the Mikado and later by the giant Yellowstone mallet locomotives, rolled day and night as the range fueled the insatiable appetite of a steel-hungry nation.

The Mesabi was a sinuous magnet for an immigrant seeking his fortune. In European cities, steamship-line posters lured peasants to work in the Mesabi mines, where the streets were paved with iron, with the promise of gold. First came the Norwegians and the Swedes, then the Slavs, Croatians, Italians, Finns, Germans, Ukrainians, Irish, and Cornish, or "Cousin Jacks," as they were called. In 1910, more than half of the Mesabi population was foreign-born. Most of the workers were imported from central and southeastern Europe for their brawn and willingness to work in the mines at $2.40 per twelve-hour day.

The immigrants, lonely men without women or a common language, lived in large boarding houses, where they slept in shifts; when the miner on the night shift was working, the worker on the day shift slept. The mines operated twenty-four hours a day, seven days a week. As mining operations expanded, towns or locations sprang up. Eveleth, Buhl, Hibbing, Chisholm, Virginia, Biwabik—it was a Midwestern scene with a Wild West flavor. "The range towns were one long mining camp, the kind you see in the movies. It was a gold-rush town—every detail right down to the gamblers in their striped pants. There wasn't one single thing missing, even down to the pimps." The miners would come into town every Saturday—payday—in search of women, gambling and booze. Prostitution was frowned upon but tacitly tolerated, and the women were medically inspected by municipal health officials.

The more ore the miners dug, the more they found. The yield from the open pits was so lucrative, the method so efficient, that miners' homes, sitting on rich lodes, had to be purchased at inflated prices by the mining companies and literally lifted to new towns built on the overburden, or dump, in order to mine new deposits.

By the turn of the century Duluth had become a company town, made wealthy by the network of railroad lines and the throbbing terminal of hissing locomotives, clanging cars and fleets of deep-bellied whaleback boats that moved the ore across Lake Superior to the belching coke ovens of Pittsburgh, Youngstown and Gary. The city had flowered into its own golden age of elegance. Minnesota's irreverent novelist Sinclair Lewis must have had Duluth in mind when he located that bumptious booster George F. Babbitt in a Midwestern metropolis called Zenith. Even the family name is derived from the town of Babbitt in the Iron Range country. It was a time when rambling Victorian mansions kept vigil over the city from the elegant Heights overlooking Lake Superior. The lucky few, those who had made their fortunes from the toil of many, lived lavishly on the best that Duluth could import.

But the golden age of elegance began to tarnish as the rough-and-ready character of the range crept into the city. Crooked politicians forced immigrants, many of whom could not read the ballots they were told to mark, to "Vote early and often." Bordellos flourished, and alliances sprang up between lawmakers and lawbreakers.

It was not exactly the type of community in which a teetotaling, strait-laced Midwesterner like Morrison would feel comfortable. A newspaperman by trade, Morrison had drifted from his hometown, Tabor, in Iowa, to cities in Nebraska and Missouri plying his journalistic skills, and had eventually come north to work for the Duluth *News-Tribune*. Tall, balding and with a twirled handlebar mustache, Morrison was a puritanical Christian of courtly dress and manners. He had the righteous indignation of such muckrakers as Lincoln Steffens and Ida Tarbell, but was more self-righteous reformer than investigative reporter.

Early issues of the Duluth *Rip-saw* were hard-driving but temperate. The *Rip-saw*'s primary target was John Barleycorn, and all antiprohibitionists were its enemies. The column "Sawdust and Shavings" poked gentle fun at local politicians. Morrison's favorite targets were two-bit political hacks and corrupt policemen. In fact, in its first year of existence, the *Rip-saw* managed to help oust Chief of Police Robert McKercher and "King" Odin Halden, city auditor, both of whom had been unceasingly badgered by the Head Sawyer's pen. Morrison fought for streetcars, public toilets and higher pay for policemen.

The *Rip-saw* was relentless. Once it had a victim in its sights, it didn't stop until its prey was wounded. And all this was done with sharp albeit prudish wit. Fashionable ladies, the daughters of robust pioneers, would be driven down in their carriages, already yielding to Pierce-Arrows and Packards, to pick up the *Rip-saw* in reserved plain brown wrappers while the hoi polloi gobbled them up from newsboys. Morrison was also a heavy-handed circulation pusher. He was enraged when news dealers ran out of copies of the *Rip-saw,* and once scolded his Hibbing agent: "We had the stuff that sells papers, and you did not take full advantage of it. Such failures discourage a publisher from digging up special stuff. Eternal vigilance is the price of getting all the nickels out of newspaper sales."

Although the *Rip-saw*'s masthead indicated a second-class mail rate, Morrison shied away from delivery by the U.S. mails, fearing interference by prim postal inspectors pressured by the proper Duluth establishment. The *Rip-saw* was a hot item; each of the 5,000 copies passed from household to household, and even to the Kitchi Gammi Club, the elite social club on East Superior Street overlooking the harbor. There were few returns to the publisher.

By its first summer, the *Rip-saw* had enjoyed such popular success that Morrison decided to make it "permanent," a state that coincided with voter-instituted prohibition in St. Louis County. In a series of satirical articles Morrison hailed the ousting of John Barleycorn. In 1917 Duluth was finally to be dry—or so it seemed. Prohibition in the Iron Range was an event almost as disastrous as the flu epidemic. It was not long before hooch was available from all kinds of bootleg outlets. The bootleggers and other vice operators required police protection in order to thrive, and the local politicians not only winked at this liaison but joined in the pleasure and payoffs.

The Iron Range was not alone in its "dry state"; in two and a half years the entire nation joined in an "experiment noble in motive and far-reaching in purpose," as Herbert Hoover later characterized Prohibition. "At one minute past twelve tomorrow morning, a new nation will be born," extolled the Anti-Saloon League. The next day, January 16, 1920, the Eighteenth Amendment to the U.S. Constitution turned the rest of America dry, except for medicinal purposes. In so doing, Prohibition gave birth to a vast underworld network which supplied the nation with all the spirits it was willing to pay for at bloated prices.

New York Congressman Fiorello La Guardia mocked the Volstead Act, the enforcing national prohibition legislation sponsored by Minnesota Congressman Andrew Volstead of Yellow Medicine County: "In order to enforce prohibition, it will require a police force of 250,000 men and a force of 250,000 men to police the police." H. L. Mencken, a devout wet like La Guardia who regarded Congress as the "booboisie," predicted: "Congress is made up eternally of petty scoundrels, pusillanimous poltroons, highly vulnerable scoundrels and cowardly men: They will never risk provoking the full fire of the Anti-Saloon League."

Mencken and La Guardia had history on their side. The Volstead Act turned out to be a national debacle, leaving in its wake more lawlessness, boozing and public cynicism than the addiction it was intended to cure. The impact of Prohibition on Chicago, Minneapolis and New York and the other great cities has been well chronicled by historians and novelists, but small communities such as Duluth and the Mesabi Iron Range were corrupted as much as their teeming neighbors. The Range towns with one foot still in the rowdy lawlessness of the nineteenth century suddenly discovered their other foot mired in reformist-made quagmire. To the miners of the Iron Range and their struggling families, used to living with disaster, Prohibition (and all its attendant evils) was just another disaster, even if created by well-intentioned crusaders.

More than anything else, the illegal trafficking was an affront to John Morrison's sense of decency. As time went on, the *Rip-saw* attacked with more vigor; the explosive front-page stories were adorned with juicy headlines that seemed racy for the "family journal," as Morrison liked to call it. Examples: "Old John Barleycorn Makes Buhl Boisterous," "Chief M'Kercher Is Going Blind . . . Duluth's

Police Chief Can See the Ore Docks but Red Light Joints and Tigers' Dens Have Low Visibility."

The issue of December 11, 1920, under the banner head "Gambling Dens Increase in Duluth," ran a four-column cartoon on the front page. Vice was represented by a pimp, a whore and a naked devil playing poker with a Keystone Kop-type Duluth officer under the balloon caption "Easy Money." Beside the policeman was a treasury box loaded with money and the caption "Light Fines." Next to the cartoon was the lead story: "Madame Peltier Runs Retreat Over Tire Shop." The first paragraph quoted Madame Blanche White of the Zenith Hotel: "Believe me . . . I've got a crotch hold here in Duluth. Just give me two more years of the way things are going and I'll have all I need." An infamous *Rip-saw* interview with a madam from a house of ill repute ended with "she crossed her legs, closed up shop and refused to talk."

How accurate or wild the *Rip-saw*'s charges were are matters difficult to determine fifty-five years later, but Duluth's oldtimers offer some clues. With her late husband, Frieda Monger was the editor and publisher of a Duluth weekly for thirty-eight years. Now in her late eighties, she talks of Morrison as "a God-fearing Christian gentleman with a mission in life . . . He thought he was doing the world a great service. He was a crusader. Mission accomplished. Duluth's a clean city." Mrs. Monger adds with conviction, "Of course, most people despised him for running a sheet like that . . . But he never lied about anything he wrote . . . He found that some fine people were doing awful things. He said it was because no one ever told on them . . . We knew him very, very well. He was a Spartan, wouldn't smoke or drink or even play bridge. I think everything he wrote was true."

Burt Pearson, the editor of the Virginia *Daily Enterprise* (later the Mesabi *Daily News*) for half a century, believes that "most of the people Morrison and the *Rip-saw* wrote about deserved it. I'm sure he believed implicitly in what he wrote. He must have also believed that these people had broken the rules of society." Pearson, a political conservative, volunteers that Morrison, with his puritanical ethics, would have been offended by magazines such as *Playboy*.

But not everyone in Duluth and the Mesabi Iron Range had such faith in Morrison's integrity. Many tycoons and local merchants accused him of trying to shake them down, and politicians attacked Morrison for attempting to force them to buy advertising space at an exorbitant rate to soften or eliminate certain gossip items during an election.

The *Rip-saw* had clout. Miss Evelyn Danahy, who still lives in Hibbing, remembers with much bitterness that her mother would not let her go out with Emmett Butler's son, who wanted to marry her, because of constant stories about her prospective in-laws in the *Rip-saw*. The six Butler brothers—Walter, John, William, Pierce, Emmett and Cooley—were independent mining barons and, some claimed, ruthless operators in Buhl and other towns on the Range. "My mother was usually skeptical about what she read in the *Rip-saw* about the Butlers, but she didn't want me to make a mistake." Miss Danahy remembers that her mother didn't reject everything she read in the *Rip-saw*. One of the Butler brothers, Pierce, chose law as a profession, representing the families and other mining and railroad interests in the Northwest. In 1922 he was appointed to the U.S. Supreme Court by President Warren G. Harding; the impact of the *Rip-saw* stayed with him for a lifetime.

The *Rip-saw* made no national stir, won no journalism prizes. Outside the north county of Minnesota and the wide-open town of Superior, Wisconsin, its neighbor at the head of the lake, Morrison's publication had no impact except for an occasional foray into the twin cities of St. Paul-Minneapolis, where it was dismissed as an obscene scandal sheet published by some Duluth religious nut. The saga of John L. Morrison would have remained an insignificant, localized skirmish in Minnesota history had it not been for the October 25, 1924, issue of the *Rip-saw* and several Mesabi politicians who reacted to its sting.

Chapter 2
The Issue of October 25

His works were hawked in every street,
But seldom rose above a sheet:
Of late, indeed, the paper stamp
Did very much his genius cramp;
And since he could not spend his fire
He now intended to retire.

—JONATHAN SWIFT
August 7, 1712

THE October 25 edition of the *Rip-saw* was typical: fiery headlines exposing sin and corruption, reports of political battles brewing, satirical quips, and never-ending assaults on the evil John Barleycorn. That week's principal targets were State Senator Mike Boylan, Cass County Probate Judge Bert Jamison and Victor L. Power, a former mayor of Hibbing. Front-page stories revealed that Boylan had threatened Morrison with mayhem and death and that Judge Jamison had practically been emasculated from the ravages of syphilis. The lead editorial accused Power of corrupt legal practices and of a weakness for women and whiskey.

Perhaps it was the tension of the upcoming election, perhaps Morrison's invective contained more venom that day, or perhaps he happened to have focused on three politicians who had had enough. Whatever the reasons, Jamison, Power and Boylan decided to fight back; for the next two years, the Head Sawyer and his paper would be in a state of siege.

Judge Jamison, probably the hardest hit, was the first to seek revenge. Morrison had charged that Jamison was "unsafe, unfit and unsatisfactory in deciding cases of juvenile truancy, incorrigibility and immorality." The story reported that twenty-seven years earlier Jamison had visited a brothel in the company of fellow lumberjacks and "picked out a girl with a sad, anemic cough. They retired from the maddening [*sic*] throng and when young Jamison came back, he proudly boasted of his licentious act with the poor creature." *The Rip-saw* claimed that the future judge became "so badly swollen with the effects of venereal poison" that one of his legs had to be amputated and "it became imperative to, at least partially, emasculate the victim of sexual indiscretions." Morrison told his readers. "That, dear fathers and mothers of Cass County, explains why Bert Jamison seems to especially dislike young girls" and why it makes him "a very undesirable judge."

Morrison went on to tell the sad story of Ruth Lambert, a girl of fifteen, who became pregnant, having "fallen the victim" of a nineteen-year-old. She had been committed to a state school by Judge Jamison, but the judge had allegedly promised Ruth's father, Al, that she would be released three months after the baby's birth. Each time he went before the judge, there were additional delays. More than a year later Lambert had come to Morrison. Lambert claimed to have witnessed Jamison's escapades in the bordello and related the whole sordid tale to the editor. He also charged that Jamison had offered to release Ruth if Lambert would support the judge politically. Lambert did not, and his daughter remained at the school. Now, Lambert wanted Morrison to save other children from such a fate.

Jamison fought back. He bought advertisements containing numerous affidavits from hospitals and physicians showing that his operations, twelve in all, were for "glandular troubles caused by tuberculosis, not syphilis, the cause alleged by Morrison." However, he never denied the incident at the bordello or mentioned the Lambert girl in his advertisements.

Within five days a sheriff was sent from Walker, the county seat of Cass County, to arrest Morrison on charges of criminal libel. The editor was swiftly tried and sentenced to ninety days in the workhouse. Within a week Alfred Lambert, the distraught father and informer, was also arrested, tried for slander and criminal libel and sentenced to thirty days in the county jail.

In a news column the Cass County *Pioneer* editorialized: "The laws are entirely too lenient on those who would blacken the characters of others by stating things that are not true." The Walker *Pilot* applauded the conviction. After considerable difficulty in hostile Cass County, Morrison was able to raise the $500 bail and return to Duluth pending appeal.

Despite Morrison's conviction and Jamison's detailed denials, Judge Jamison lost that November's bitter election by 461 votes out of 5,300. He futilely contested the results, charging that his opponent had used unethical methods to win.

Morrison's appeal efforts were more successful. In June of 1925 the *Rip-saw*'s publisher did plead guilty to charges of criminal libel, but he never served time. When Judge W. S. McClennehan reduced his jail sentence to a $100 fine,

Morrison was so visibly relieved that he attempted to make a speech expressing his gratitude to the court. The judge would have none of it. Banging his fist on his desk, he squelched the defendant by shouting at Morrison, "I don't think any more of you, sir, than I do this damn desk."

Victor Power was the second to seek revenge.

A bucolic blend of Mayor James Curley of Boston and Boss Hague of Jersey City, Power was the political power broker and "ward heeler" at its best and worst. Aware of the unique character of his constituency—those who toiled in the mines and worked on the railroads and freighters—Power permitted just enough "blind pigs" (the soft-drink fronts for saloons, brothels and gambling parlors) to satisfy the needs of a male-dominated, wide-open community, while keeping the lid on sufficiently to restrain the few reformers from becoming a serious nuisance. Power had his loyal supporters. "If Vic Power got a ham, you got a ham sandwich . . . Vic Power was the one who paved the streets and put up the lights, as many as forty bulbs on the corner."

Morrison had scolded former Mayor Power in an eight-hundred-word lead editorial for taking money from undesirable clients and then abandoning them. The *Rip-saw* editorial also accused Power of trying "to make the sucker public think that the Little Giant [Power] is dry [a prohibitionist] . . . when he is sopping wet in practice . . . Victor L. Power's adventure with whiskey and women would not be permitted through the mails narrated." The *Rip-saw* quoted Mesabi Hotel employees who had revealed that one night the mayor "crawled into bed so beastly drunk . . . that he used his couch as a privy or puking place entirely without the help of cathartic or emetic."

What angered Power most was a report in the *Rip-saw* that an employee of the St. Louis Hotel had awakened the former mayor when he found him intoxicated in the old rose garden, and that, jarred from his alleged drunken stupor, Power had blurted out, "I—I—I Victor L. Power, the man of the hour." Morrison went on to urge citizens not to support a man such as Power with their votes. Power lost the congressional election and sued John L. Morrison for criminal libel.

The trial began on December 3, 1924. One of the first to take the witness stand was blond, handsome and dapperly dressed George Lommen. He was eager to testify for his friend Vic Power because the *Rip-saw* had also accused Lommen of collecting bribes from the operators of slot machines and of being a "political chameleon," doing flip-flops from being a Republican to a Farm-Laborite. The paper had predicted that chameleon Lommen would end up a Communist. The courtroom was crowded with Hibbingites who wanted to hear what Lommen had to say. He was known as a lady's man, a dandy who wore raccoon coats and beaver hats and a corset to give him a svelte figure. A show-off in his flashy pink Lincoln or Marmon touring car, State Representative Lommen was the talk of Biwabik, Eveleth, Gilbert and the other bustling Range towns, and Morrison despised him for his womanizing and his lack of political ethics.

Lommen bragged that his father was the first white child born in Minnesota Territory. Educated at St. Paul Law School, he prided himself on being a shrewd cross-examiner. He bitterly opposed a proposed law to tax the tonnage on ore, the revenue from which was to be used for the building of roads throughout Minnesota rather than remain in the Iron Range. Lommen always claimed he tried desperately to enlist in the Army during World War I but was turned down after thirteen medical examinations. A former mayor of Biwabik, he had been elected to the state legislature for the first time in 1924—the youngest man to serve in the house. He was admired as an orator, but he had a reputation for temper tantrums. Thus, his court appearance was promising entertainment.

"I'll have them all down to see me about political advertising," said Lommen, who was quoting Morrison. Lommen alleged that the libelous attacks against Power and himself came because they had not bought enough political advertising in Morrison's paper. Lommen said he had purchased a small amount of space, but that Morrison was demanding more, and added, "The paper then made numerous derogatory remarks concerning me, all of which were absolutely untrue."

Shrugging off the charges that he was "so fond of the opposite sex as to incapacitate him for public service," Lommen explained that he had "visited with the girls as much as the average young man." He denied that he had ever taken actual bribes from the slot-machine operators.

Victor L. Power himself also testified in this week-long trial—at that time the longest in Hibbing history—and he made no effort to hide his hostility toward Morrison. He vehemently denied all of the *Rip-saw*'s charges. Power said that he had placed advertisements with Morrison several times in the past, but that the editor had tried to strong-arm more ads by saying it was customary to treat candidates "tough" who didn't come across.

The jury must have been persuaded by the accuracy of the ward-heeler's story because after five hours of deliberating they found Morrison guilty of criminal libel. He was sentenced to ninety days in the county workhouse, but he immediately filed for appeal. Six months later, on June 1, 1925, Morrison was ordered by the judge to make a public apology to Power. The *Rip-saw*'s publisher was forced to admit that the information which he had accepted in good faith turned out to be "malicious and false." Morrison told the court and Power that he was sorry if the *Rip-saw* "had cost Mayor Power the congressional election." Accordingly, the county prosecutor recommended that the criminal libel charges be dropped, and the district court judge in Hibbing consented to rescind the sentence.

State Senator Boylan didn't take his case to court, despite earlier rumblings. Boylan, an Irish political hack, was accused by the *Rip-saw* of bulldozing the people of Virginia, Minnesota. The front-page banner headline said the senator had "threatened to turn from lawmaker to lawbreaker by murdering John L. Morrison." The editor quoted a telephone call in which Boylan screamed, "I'll kill you if you ever mention my name in your dirty, damnable sheet." Perhaps he was discouraged by the Pyrrhic victories of Jamison and Power. He had more potent means of contending with Morrison.

Lommen and Boylan, flushed with revenge, anger and frustration, wished to ensure that no such reporting (if that's what it was) and no libel (if that's what it was) would ever again be permitted in St. Louis County. "There ought to be a law," Lommen and Boylan contended, and proceeded to draft several that would make it possible to stop, to enjoin those publications from "regularly or customarily producing . . . malicious, scandalous and defamatory" matter. Libel laws, said Lommen, were not enough to protect politicians from sensational and lewd scandal sheets in Minnesota.

The charges had been dropped, Morrison was still a free man, and the *Rip-saw* was still on the streets of Duluth every Saturday. It was even picking up some respectable advertising.

The legislation Boylan and Lommen drafted to get the *Rip-saw* and Morrison was the lynchpin for one of those explosive, obscure squabbles that was to provide new meaning to the Bill of Rights. Yet the harsh truth was that it was not just politicians such as Lommen and Boylan who vowed to punish and destroy the *Rip-saw* but also some of the state's major newspapers and newspaper associations.

Boylan and Lommen's bill was to become known as the Public Nuisance Bill of 1925—popularly referred to as the "gag law." Lommen later boasted that drafting assistance was contributed by the Minnesota Editorial Association, including such respectable publications as the Mankato *Free Press,* with the support of the Minneapolis *Morning Tribune* and the Minneapolis *Journal.* * C. L. Butler (no relation to Pierce), publisher of the *Free Press,* wrote later with pride that he was "one of a number of Minnesota publishers who worked painstakingly with an equally conscientious legislative committee to frame this law which attempted to reach the blackmailing type of publication then prevalent in Minnesota." Butler also acknowledged that the publishers' real reason "at the same time was to protect the rights of responsible newspapers."

Mike Boylan drafted six different bills dealing with the suppression of scandalous and libelous newspapers. Representative Lommen introduced the bills in the house; Sen-

---

*The Minneapolis newspapers involved in drafting the 1925 Public Nuisance Law either changed ownership or ceased to exist. The surviving newspapers, the Minneapolis *Star* and the Minneapolis *Tribune,* were purchased in 1935 and 1941, respectively, by John Cowles, who has consistently supported press freedoms.

ator Freyling Stevens, a member of one of Minneapolis' prestigious law firms and renowned for his legislative drafting skills, was the officially credited author, and introduced the senate version of the gag law. The essence of the final joint senate-house bill read:

> **Any person who . . . shall be engaged in the business of regularly or customarily producing, publishing or circulating, having in possession, selling or giving away, (a) an obscene, lewd and lascivious newspaper, magazine, or other periodical, or (b) a malicious, scandalous and defamatory newspaper . . . is guilty of nuisance, and all persons guilty of such nuisance may be enjoined, as hereinafter provided . . . In actions brought under above, there shall be available the defense that the truth was published with good motives and for justifiable ends.**

This law, which permitted a single judge, without jury, to enjoin a newspaper or magazine from publication forever because he considered it to be "obscene, lewd and lascivious . . . or malicious, scandalous and defamatory" was approved by the Minnesota Senate by a vote of 41 to 0. In the House, there were 22 quiet nays, 87 enthusiastic yeas. No newspaper in Duluth, Minneapolis or St. Paul editorialized against the bill. In fact, its passage went without mention except for one tiny paragraph in the St. Paul *Pioneer Press*. Only a five-line squib at the end of another story reported that "the House also passed the Newspaper Libel Bill which is expected to curb the activities of so-called scandal sheets. It has already passed the Senate and now goes to the governor for signature." The news story incorrectly referred to the legislation as a "libel bill" and did not even warrant a headline. There is no evidence of any other newspaper or radio station mentioning the passage of the Public Nuisance Law.

In summarizing highlights of the 1925 legislative session, the gag law was not listed, but the Cass County *Pioneer* noted a new law prohibiting dancing any place in the state between Saturday midnight and Sunday noon.

Governor Theodore Christianson signed the Public Nuisance Law routinely. As for the press's lack of opposition to the law, former newspaper editor Burt Pearson explains its advocacy with embarrassment: "It was just a measure to settle a quarrel between a small group of people . . . newspapermen, unlike today, didn't bother too much about such freedom of the press issues." And Pearson adds, "There wasn't much real investigative reporting. Most of the news stories came in handouts from the mayor's office or the district attorney in those days."

Everyone who was aware of the bill, and this included few citizens other than the 150 legislators who cast their ballots, clearly understood that the intended target of Lommen, Boylan and the lobbyists who worked with them was John L. Morrison. Their avowed goal was to close down the *Rip-saw,* although they usually added "and obscene scandal sheets like it."

Within a year Morrison, as intended, provided the juicy ingredient for a test case. In the spring of 1926 the *Rip-saw* took aim at the mayor of Minneapolis, George Emerson Leach, who was running for governor in the Republican primary, and W. Harlow Tischer, Duluth's Commissioner of Public Utilities. The April 6 issue of the *Rip-saw* proclaimed in huge type: "Minnesotians Do Not Want Loose-Love Governor." One week later, almost as if to celebrate the first anniversary of the Minnesota gag law, the *Rip-saw* attacked the water commissioner: "Tischer and His Gang Fail to Establish Graft Plan." Two weeks later Morrison boasted in the *Rip-saw* that Tischer's alleged graft could not flourish while the *Rip-saw* thrived.

The actions against the *Rip-saw* came fast—on two consecutive days in May 1926 Morrison was served with a warrant for his arrest based on a complaint from Mayor George Leach under an obscene-literature ordinance recently rushed through the Minneapolis City Council. "I'm not going to stand for having such things printed about me," explained the mayor. "The story [of his extramarital adventures] is a vicious attack, entirely unfounded, and absolutely untrue, and I'm serving notice that such things can't be said with impunity about the mayor of Minneapolis." The arrest warrant was sworn out by Mayor Leach, who was also the complainant. The mayor could not bring himself to repeat the alleged obscenity in the complaint, merely claiming that Morrison "had an article unfit to print." The Associated Press reported that a deputy sheriff was sent from Hennepin County to arrest Morrison but returned to Minneapolis when he was told that the *Rip-saw*'s publisher was suddenly stricken ill and could not be served.

But more serious than Mayor Leach's warrant for Morrison's arrest was the action in Duluth for an injunction to suppress the *Rip-saw* permanently with the aid of the pervasive and potent Public Nuisance Law. Commissioner Tischer claimed that the charges of graft were untrue, that they "had injured his character and reputation," and demanded that Morrison be prosecuted and the *Rip-saw* be closed down. Signed by State District Judge H. J. Grannis of Duluth on the complaint of Tischer, it marked the first application of the Public Nuisance Law of 1925. The temporary restraining order against the *Rip-saw* ordered publisher John L. Morrison to appear in Judge Grannis' court the next Saturday. Also named in the injunction were the owners of the Finnish Publishing Company, which had contracted to print the *Rip-saw*. It also barred all news dealers and newsboys from distributing or peddling the paper, warning them that they would be guilty of committing a public nuisance if they did so. The penalty for violating the injunction against the *Rip-saw,* warned the judge, would be "a thousand dollar fine or one year's imprisonment." Morrison, who had scheduled a publication of the *Rip-saw* on May 15, was ordered to desist publication and to be in Judge Grannis' court at nine-thirty that same morning.

The *Rip-saw* did not appear on the streets of Duluth that Saturday, nor did John L. Morrison make it to court. The *Rip-saw*'s publisher had been suddenly stricken with what the local dailies skeptically referred to as "an unidentified illness." The Duluth *News-Tribune*'s skeptical front-page headline read: "Mystery Clouds Morrison's 'Ride' into Wisconsin." The subhead stated: "Superior City Ambulance Carries Duluth Publisher, Facing Arrest, Over State Line."

Morrison had been living in the St. Louis Hotel in Duluth, and the clear implication in the newspaper accounts was that the Head Sawyer was feigning illness to avoid being served. "The circumstances under which Morrison was taken from his room in the St. Louis Hotel early this morning were veiled in mystery," reported the Duluth paper. "Sheriff Magie's forces in whose hands is the warrant for Morrison's arrest could shed no light on the case, and apparently no effort was made to intercept the ambulance and interfere with the transfer of the wanted man across the state line." There was a strong suggestion that there had been a conspiracy to permit Morrison to escape Minnesota authority.

According to the toll collector on the interstate bridge which connected Duluth and Superior, at approximately five minutes past one, early Tuesday morning, an ambulance (some rumors at the time said it was a hearse) crossed the old steel bridge, carrying a large person completely covered by a sheet. The collector observed that when the toll was paid, the sheet was lifted, exposing a man resembling Morrison, bald and with a large black mustache. At one-thirty, attendants at St. Francis Hospital in Superior observed that "a big man with a big, black moustache was admitted to St. Francis," and hospital records indicate that at two o'clock, such a patient was registered under the name of Morrison. The ambulance driver was questioned by a *News-Tribune* reporter after the ambulance had returned to Duluth. According to the newspaper, the driver "denied . . . that their patient was Morrison . . . He told the reporter his patient was a woman."

Sheriff Magie's deputy hot-footed it from Duluth to Superior in an attempt to serve Morrison with the arrest warrant, but the publisher's physician refused to let him enter his patient's room. The Hennepin County prosecutor was denied permission to place a guard at Morrison's door.

On May 18, 1926, nine hours after his admission to the hospital, John L. Morrison died of a brain clot. He was fifty-seven years old, and the *Rip-saw* was in its tenth year. "Death Defeats Warrant for Duluth Editor" was the way the Minneapolis *Tribune* played the story.

But even after Morrison's death, Commissioner Tischer insisted that the injunction against the *Rip-saw*'s publication be maintained. Lawyers on behalf of the deceased John L. Morrison and the Finnish Publishing Company of Superior filed a demurrer against the motion for a permanent injunction. The motion admitted that the facts in the complaints might be true but they contended on behalf of the dead defendant that the the 1925 Public Nuisance Law was in itself unconstitutional.

Within a week of Morrison's death, another county judge, E. J. Kenney, ruled that the *Rip-saw* could be published again, but "without sting." What the court would allow was a continuation of the *Rip-saw* "only without the articles objected to by Commissioner Tischer." Although there were brief efforts to revive the crusading, if flamboyant, publication, the *Rip-saw* died with its Head Sawyer.

There was something sentimental and bizarre about the funeral the city of Duluth provided its "scandalmongering" publisher. A substantial, representative crowd of leading citizens turned out. The pastor of the Central Avenue Methodist Church presided, and Mayor S. F. Snively and City Commissioner W. S. McCormick eulogized Morrison as a good man and the city's booster-turned-crusader. A stranger present at Bell Brothers Mortuary in West Duluth could only have believed that the city had lost a distinguished son. Morrison's body was sent back to Tabor, Iowa, where his newspaper career had begun and where his wife and two children had lived during his final ordeal.

Scandalmonger or crusading muckraker, one epitaph for the Head Sawyer provides perspective to this comical and tragic career. As a slow train was carrying Morrison's body back to Iowa, Harriette Wilbur Porter, one of Duluth's most respected ladies, sent this letter to the *Herald:*

> Unlike the current magazines and books, the *Rip-saw* made evil unattractive, even disgusting . . . Many diseases are now treated with air and sunshine, which was also Mr. Morrison's working principle. Impropriety in any line enjoys secrecy and flourishes best in silence; Mr. Morrison's courageous methods destroyed such protection for those anxious to use it . . . There are many men in Duluth who could be better spared.

Mrs. Porter's tribute to the passing of a "gentleman and a useful citizen" must be weighed against the reputation of a scandalmonger who doubtless invaded some innocent people's privacy and published allegations of wrongdoing which could not be documented. But in her aphorism concerning sunshine vs. secrecy, this unassuming lady from Victorian Duluth was identifying an issue that would move next to the troubled twin cities of Minneapolis and St. Paul.

Chapter 3
The Birth of Another Rag

IN the 1920s throughout America there were literally hundreds of weekly rags, scandal sheets filled with the lurid and the profane, some of them scions of the Hearst brand of yellow journalism. Some survived for years; others vanished as quickly as they had appeared, surviving only long enough for the editors to fleece some well-heeled sucker and then skip town.

When Lincoln Steffens wrote *The Shame of the Cities* in 1904, Minneapolis was one of his classic examples of "a boodle town" where the people were "sober, satisfied, busy with their own affairs" and left law enforcement and the running of the city to corrupt politicians and strong-armed gangsters. "The people who were left to govern the city hated, above all things, strict laws. They were the loafers, saloon keepers, gamblers, criminals and the thriftless poor of all nationalities."

Between the shame of Minneapolis in 1904 and the corruption of the 1920s, little changed except the players. As Steffens told it, it was "a New England town on the upper Mississippi. The people worked hard. They cut lumber by forests or they go out in the prairies and raise wheat and mill it into fleet-cargoes of flour . . . There isn't much time for public business."

As in Duluth, Prohibition had complicated the task of governing. Minneapolis was a crossroads in the Canadian-whiskey trade. In order to get to a liquid market, the hooch had to come through Minneapolis. From there it could be shipped to Chicago and St. Louis and be distributed throughout the rest of the country.

The city's strategic location provided gangsters with a bonanza. "Everybody was in on the take," wrote Nate Bomberg, a veteran reporter for the St. Paul *Pioneer Press.* "You can't have an underworld without an overworld, if you know what I mean. You can't have rackets unless you have the mayor, the chief of police, and the county attorney in your corner."

Frank McCormick was the kingpin of the payoff activity in Minneapolis. McCormick had a restaurant, McCormick's Café, on Fifth Street between Hennepin and Nicollet, and it was the hot spot of the city. In fact, cynics joked that city hall had been moved to McCormick's. All the gambling rackets paid tribute to its proprietor, who then split up the proceeds with the mayor and the chief of police.

Ed Ryan, who was a cop on the beat in the 1920s and who as chief of police under Mayor Hubert H. Humphrey was later credited with cleaning up Minneapolis, recently described the city as a "wide open town with gambling joints, slot machines, houses of prostitution . . . You name it, we had it . . . If you can't buy off the mayor, if you can't buy off the chief, then you can't operate a racket . . . no matter what community you're in . . . When you see slot machines and gambling all over the place, there has to be a pay-off."

But the lawlessness did not stop with gambling and illegal booze. Ryan recalls that the city was also plagued by gang killings. "You could get anyone killed in the Twin Cities for five hundred dollars," a former Minneapolis law enforcement official remembers. Some say a hit could be purchased for as little as $200.

The respectable newspapers permitted themselves to squint at the link between those who broke the law and those charged with its enforcement in exchange for municipal tranquillity, or order without law. Their journalistic ailment was not stories of commission but omission. Many reporters were also on the take. The big-city newspapers' failure to fight city hall created a void in which scandal sheets flourished. In such a climate, the Twin Cities provided a happy hunting ground for Jay M. Near, who had come east from Fort Atkinson, Iowa, and Howard A. Guilford, who had come west from Northampton, Massachusetts. Together they practiced a brand of journalism that teetered on the edge of legality and often toppled over the limits of propriety.

Howard Guilford always had one foot in jail. All 200 pounds of him managed to offend a lot of people, many of them law enforcement officials. In his checkered Minneapolis career he was indicted nineteen times but never convicted of anything—with the possible exception of a parking violation, for which he was fined $1. In his memoirs Guilford tells of diabolical plots cooked up by corrupt politicians and bribe-taking policemen whose purpose was to arrest him. He claimed his only crime was trying to expose the corruption "with its tentacles in pulpit, brothels and public life," but today many remember him as a shrewd con man who was not above blackmail and extortion.

Guilford's bludgeon was *The Reporter,* a St. Paul weekly that he had founded in 1913, which became the *Twin City Reporter* in 1914 when it moved to Minneapolis. It was a sensationalist paper with scant socially redeeming value. To Guilford, a journalist was "a reporter out of a job." The grist for the *Reporter* was gambling, prostitution and the sexual adventures of the Twin Cities' upper crust. A vice president of one of the largest wholesale grocery chains and a member of the exclusive Minneapolis Club was branded as "leaning toward children of ten to twelve years of age rather than the mature old hens of fifteen and sixteen." This was the paper's staple kind of story and tone.

In 1916 Guilford hired Jay M. Near, a reporter of equal reputation but with a different flair. Without an ounce of flab on his tall, gaunt frame, Near dressed beyond his means in slick, showy suits and elevator shoes. He had the look of a handsome leading man in a traveling stock company. Anti-Catholic, anti-Semitic, antiblack and antilabor, Near's pen and typewriter were occasionally weapons for hire, a means of scratching out his living as a sort of scavenger of the sins and political vulnerability of others. He had basic writing skills and a quick-on-the-draw sense of outrage. Unlike John L. Morrison in Duluth, Near and Guilford were not God-fearing, churchgoing men, and did not consider themselves Christian reformers.

The headlines of the *Twin City Reporter* provided a steady diet of gossip. Typical banners read: "Smooth Minneapolis Doctor With Woman in St. Paul Hotel" and "White Slavery Trade: Well-Known Local Man is Ruining Women and Living Off Their Earnings." Their labeling of minority groups was usually pejorative—yids, bohunks, spades, etc.—and they showed a deep-seated hostility for most institutions, from the Salvation Army right down to the "Communist" labor unions.

"It was a shakedown completely," remembers Orlin Folwick, a long-time reporter for the Minneapolis *Morning Tribune*. "Guilford was hanging around the police department all the time, and for a five or ten spot, a cop would give him a tip-off about some prominent citizen who had been found in the back seat of a car in a procreative position. Near and Guilford had access to more adjectives than you and I would ever want to use in a lifetime, and they used them. This is what sold the sheets."

The political corruption in Minneapolis and St. Paul and the truce between bootleggers, gamblers and prostitution merchants and the police and city fathers provided endless material for Near and Guilford. The negative image that the paper gave the Twin Cities was matched by the bad name it gave to all reporters, yet much that the two men published was true or at least more true than false.

Mingled with the exposés of the exploits of Minneapolis' well-to-do were reports of crime and of the corruption of elected officials. One of Guilford's favorite targets was Hennepin County Prosecutor William M. Nash, who retaliated by trying to throw the newsman in the slammer. But finally Guilford won; in 1920 Nash was ousted for being party to the "whisky conspiracy," and for allowing his brother to organize a disorderly house on Second Avenue. Guilford claimed credit for the exposé and scoffed at the editorial in the Minneapolis *Morning Tribune* which labeled the charges against Nash as the work of a "professional blackmailer and a shyster lawyer." Nash's unexpired term was filled by Floyd B. Olson, a name the publishers would soon recognize.

Near and Guilford later conceded that their reputation had been "sullied with the taint of blackmail" but denied that they themselves were guilty of any type of extortion. Guilford had realized that one of their associates, Jack Bevans, had been shaking down some "pigeons" and that Bevans was a sleazy character "who could hurt the paper's reputation."

Guilford did admit in his apologia that he had participated in one blackmail shakedown that involved the *Twin City Reporter* after he had sold out to Near and Bevans. The anecdote is so typical of the flavor of Minneapolis in the 1920s that it is reproduced here *in toto:*

> Speaking of reputations, there has been so much talk of blackmail in connection with my name that I am going to relate an instance of blackmail in which I played a part. To begin with, the wreath of blackmail was hung around my neck by Martin Flanagan, bribe-taking chief of police of St. Paul. The aroma of blackmail was sprayed all over my person by William M. Nash, the bribe-taker, just before he became former County Attorney of Hennepin County. Now I will take up the story of blackmail.
>
> Late in the summer of 1922 my presence was requested at a certain place of business in Minneapolis. Upon my arrival at the place in question I saw about the most depressed crowd of fellows I ever gazed on. They had rented a Minnetonka cottage and "thrown a party." A lot of boys came out to visit them. Some of the boys brought girls, and some of the girls brought out some more girls. Quite a party was thrown.
>
> In the middle of all this one of the ladies set up a howl — she had been robbed of a seven hundred and fifty dollar diamond ring. She had not been seen wearing any sort of a diamond ring. But the boys were in a bad way. Several of them couldn't boast about the party—at home, at least. There was nothing to do but take up a collection and give the lady fair what she claimed.

Upon giving the lady the money the boys ordered her to leave the cottage quick, before she was thrown out. "Hell hath no fury," etc. She went directly to the *Reporter* office and handed in the story of the party, together with as much of the social register as she could remember. The *Reporter* staff became industrious. Telephones rang. Several business men were warned by a "friend" who couldn't give his name, that the *Reporter* had a big story about that cottage party.

The boys gathered. They were steered into the office of William M. Nash, and were there told that the story could be "fixed" for one thousand dollars. On top of what they had donated for the alleged ring, this was considered too much. One of the men sent for me and asked for my help. I refused to mix in the affair at first, as I didn't wish my name connected with it. The one thing that caused me to change my stand was the fact that William M. Nash was doing the "shaking."

I went to the *Reporter* office and told the staff that Nash was out of the deal and the thousand dollar talk was all piffle. The staff was surprised to hear of the thousand. Five hundred was the amount the staff had heard about and was ready to cut 50-50 with William M. Nash. So I shaved fifty off the *Reporter*'s cut, saved the boys a little cash and cheated William M. Nash out of a very fat "fee."

There were also instances in Guilford's career when the *Twin City Reporter* accepted cash from one politician to write malicious items about a rival. The agreement included Guilford's distributing free a few thousand copies in the contested election wards.

In 1917 Guilford, "weary of turning down thousands of dollars" to act as a go-between and split the money with corrupt officials, had decided to sell out his interests in the *Twin City Reporter* to Near and Jack Bevans for $30,000. None of the parties had any cash, so there was no down payment; they simply agreed to apply 40 percent of the net profits against the purchase price.

Later Guilford claimed that he warned Near about taking Bevans in as a partner because "he was a mighty uncertain individual and dangerous to trust," and one whose blackmail habits were so low as to merit even Guilford's contempt. "It was Near's funeral and not mine," Guilford wrote in his memoirs. Bevans may have been the only newspaperman who, according to Guilford, ever operated a brothel on the side.

Near quickly discovered that Bevans had been blackmailing choice victims without his knowledge. He also learned that the paper wasn't really profitable, and he suddenly sold his interests to Bevans and migrated to California for occupations unknown.

Except for an occasional trip back to western Massachusetts, Guilford stayed around Minneapolis, ran for mayor in 1918 and was badly beaten. He had all kinds of odd jobs; he even edited the *Minnesota Police Bulletin,* the house organ of his avowed nemesis, William Nash. During this period Guilford's wife divorced him on seamy charges of infidelity, using the same type of sensational material on which his newspaper had feasted.

About that time the delicate balance of power among the gambling syndicates was slightly upset when Jack Bevans, Near's former partner, and Mose Barnett, a local hood, set up their own game. Rumor had it that Barnett had promised Chief of Police Frank Brunskill that there would be no bank robberies as long as the game was kept out of Frank McCormick's domain. In addition, Bevans and Barnett agreed to split the kitty with Chief Brunskill. It was an ideal relationship: the gambling house got police protection, the chief of police got a moratorium on bank robberies, and they all got rich.

In August 1927 Guilford, down on his luck, was "at liberty and looking for a new opportunity" when he ran into Jay M. Near, his old sidekick who had returned from California. According to Guilford, Near suggested that "we enter the weekly newspaper game together again." Guilford said he was wary because of the kind of extortionist rag Near had permitted the *Twin City Reporter* to become, but finally he consented. He told Near he "would join him with one understanding—that never a word of a sex nature appear in the columns of our paper." The *Twin City Reporter* was still in existence, now owned by Edward J. Morgan and Bevans, but Near and Guilford's avowed primary goal was to run that paper out of business forever because, they charged, it was owned and operated by hoods exclusively for blackmailing and extortion purposes. Indeed, the first issue of the *Saturday Press,* their new venture, was to report on the alliances which allowed the Bevans-Barnett gambling establishment to exist.

The *Saturday Press*'s announced crusade against Near and Guilford's own alma mater, the *Twin City Reporter,* sounded like a case of the pot calling the kettle black. There were rumors that Guilford had demanded a split from Barnett, and that when he had been refused, he threatened to destroy their little racket with an exposé. Guilford later denied this, admitting that he had demanded money but claiming that he was working undercover for the county sheriff.

Word traveled fast. Before the newly born *Saturday Press* even hit the street, Chief of Police Brunskill had sent out his men with an unofficial but clear message: Get the *Saturday Press* off the newsstands. His authority for this was the sheer power of his office. The ill-fated *Saturday Press* had become the only paper on record ever banned in the United States before a single issue had been published. But

Brunskill's actions didn't stop Howard Guilford and Jay M. Near.

The first issue of the *Saturday Press* didn't mention Brunskill's unofficial ban but did report a threat from the underworld to bump off Near and Guilford if they persisted in their exposé of conditions in the city. The editors warned: "Just a moment, boys, before you start something you won't be able to finish."

The next Monday afternoon, September 26, 1927, Howard Guilford and his sister-in-law, Esther Seide, were driving from his home in nearby Robbinsdale to his office in Minneapolis. At the corner of West Broadway and Lowry Avenue a touring car overtook him, and before Guilford could pull his own gun, two assailants pumped four bullets into his car. The last one struck him in the abdomen as his car careened to a stop. Guilford was rushed to the hospital in critical condition.

"I headed into the city on September 26, ran across three Jews in a Chevrolet; stopped a lot of lead and won a bed for myself in St. Barnabas Hospital for six weeks," Guilford later reported. "Wherefore, I have withdrawn all allegiance to anything with a hook nose that eats herring."

Guilford always insisted that "Big Mose" had ordered the shooting. Word had been leaked to Barnett about the first issue of the *Saturday Press,* which told of Barnett's gambling racket on Hennepin Avenue, and Guilford assumed that Barnett was trying to settle the score.

The three-column head in the Minneapolis *Morning Tribune* the next day reported: "Gunner at Large After Shooting Down Guilford in Street Attack . . . Editor Reported Recovering—Was Warned of Shooting." Beside the news story was a front-page editorial entitled "Law and Order or What?" The tone of the editorial was that "gangland [which clearly included characters like Guilford] cannot settle its differences with impunity on our public streets."

The next issue of the *Saturday Press,* the second in its short life, screamed: "Our Defy to Gangland—Guilford's Assailants Indicted by Grand Jury . . . Two Gunmen . . . Positively Identified by both Mr. Guilford and His Sister-in-Law . . . Arrest of 'Higher-Ups' in Gangland Circles Sure to Follow."

The *Saturday Press*'s full front-page news story pounded away at Near's usual implication of links between gambling syndicates and the police. The article also included the comment "You can't have commercialized VICE without having wholesale CRIME." Near warned the mob and the police: "If the ochre-hearted rodents who fired those shots into the defenseless body of my buddy thought for a moment that they were ending the fight against gang rule in this city, they were mistaken."

Chapter 4

Gagging "A Malicious, Scandalous and Defamatory Newspaper"

I T became one of Jay M. Near and the *Saturday Press*'s biggest scoops. One morning in July 1927, young Irving Shapiro stood behind the partition separating the front of his father's dry-cleaning store on East Franklin Avenue from the work area. His father had stationed him there when he realized that Big Mose Barnett was paying them a not-so-social visit.

Barnett, six feet tall and 240 pounds, swaggered into Sam Shapiro's shop. A fancy dresser sporting a small dark mustache, Barnett looked the part of a strong-arm hoodlum. He made his money from gambling—he ran a blackjack and poker joint in the old Elks Building on Fourth Avenue and Eighth Street—bootlegging, and on this occasion, as an enforcer for the Twin Cities Cleaners and Dyers Association, a syndicate whose purpose it was to fix prices and to control the market by keeping small entrepreneurs like Sam Shapiro from doing their own dry cleaning. Shapiro and his partner, Yale Morvitz, had recently added a dry-cleaning plant at the rear of their shop, despite the threats of Philip Moses, head of the local dry-cleaners protection association. For three years the two men had sent out their cleaning to a member of the association; now they were determined to do their own. A tough, stubborn Lithuanian who had started in the business as a pants presser, Shapiro believed he had the right to his American dream.

Shapiro, terrified, stood behind his counter as Mose made his demands: "Sam, cut out your dry-cleaning plant or else there'll be trouble!" But Sam was adamant, and in his blunt way told Mose Barnett that the dry-cleaning operation would continue. Earlier that month, thugs had broken in, ripped the locks off the naphtha tanks and poured sulfuric acid into Shapiro's cleaning fluid. After the incident the police had stationed a man there, but after a short time the guard had been pulled off.

On August 19 Barnett telephoned Shapiro, advising him to "stop operating the dry-cleaning plant or else . . ." But Shapiro, the self-schooled immigrant who kept a shelf of constitutional law books, knew his rights and refused to be shaken down.

The next morning the mob, acting for the dry-cleaning association, struck again. Four men, three of whom Sam Shapiro later identified, entered his shop, "lined me and three employees up against the wall and began to spray my customers' clothing with sulfuric acid."

Shapiro told the police, "When I turned my head, I was struck on it with the butt end of a pistol and I was injured so badly that I was under a doctor's care." At least $8,000 worth of his customers' clothing was destroyed. The assault was reported in the newspapers, without a mention of Barnett or his boys.

That afternoon when young Irving came home from school, he found his father with his head swathed in bandages, the shop in disarray and his mother, Freda, who did alterations in the shop, hysterical. For two years afterward, Shapiro and Morvitz took turns sleeping in the store with a loaded pistol beside them—though, as Irving recounts, "neither of them really knew how to fire a gun."

Sam Shapiro gave up seeking help from the police because of their links with Barnett and organized crime. He went to the county attorney and the grand jury, but still no action was taken. In desperation, Shapiro told his story to Jay Near, who had heard about the incident from a mutual acquaintance, and Near then began writing the story for the *Saturday Press.* Although Near was no doubt an anti-Semite, he and Shapiro eventually became friendly. Irving remembers that his father had a soft spot in his heart for Near, and "occasionally would give him a bag of groceries or a ten-dollar bill to keep him going . . . Near was a smooth-talking operator who had my father coming on pretty good."

The third issue of the *Saturday Press,* published on October 8, carried the Shapiro story, as well as an attack on Chief of Police Brunskill and the Minneapolis daily newspapers, under the banner "A Few of the 'Unsolved' Minneapolis Mysteries." The lead story, with a seven-line, two-column head, was "Police 'Baffled' in Their Attempts to Identify Acid-Throwing Thugs Who Assaulted Sam Shapiro AFTER He Had Been Threatened by Mose Barnett. Guilford Shot Down in Cold Blood by Gangsters AFTER He Had Been Threatened by Mose Barnett. Will the Present Grand Jury Act?"

Near depicted Shapiro as a martyr: "And right here I ask

you as man to man IF SAM SHAPIRO HAD NOT THE RIGHT
UNDER OUR CONSTITUTION TO LAUNCH HIS TINY SHIP ON OUR
COMMERCIAL SEA?" The editor's account of the threats on
the Shapiro dry-cleaning shop, though spiked with his own
brand of bias, had most of the facts straight. He chided the
major dailies for their lack of courage and veracity. "Journalism today isn't prostituted so much as it is disgustingly
flabby," Near wrote and added, revealing his true character, "I'd rather be a louse in the cotton shirt of a nigger
than be a journalistic prostitute." His constant theme was
that the Minneapolis *Tribune* and the other papers were
"afraid to mention the name of Mose Barnett, gambler,
gangster, gunman."

Since Guilford was in the hospital, Near had total control
of the writing, reporting, editing and circulation of the
paper. With each issue his broadsides became more vehe-
ment. He accused Mayor George Leach, Charles G. Davis,
head of the Law Enforcement League, and County Attorney Floyd Olson of being either blind or party to the illegal
gambling joints run by Mose Barnett and Jack Bevans. But
harshest of all were his comments about Chief of Police
Brunskill. In the third issue he accused the policeman of
being the "weak sister" in the Barnett gambling establishment on Hennepin Avenue.

> It is this type, this Moe Barnett, Ed Morgan . . . ilk that
> was mentioned in our last two issues—no law-respecting
> citizens, but blackmailers, gamblers, GANGSTERS, and yet
> we find Chief of Police Frank Brunskill barring this paper
> from the newsstands and business places of Minneapolis.
> Did Mose Barnett, gambler, gangster, TELL THE TRUTH
> when he said that "City Hall" was the fourth beneficiary of
> the gambling den? Was he lying when he bluntly stated that
> Chief Brunskill was the "weak sister" of the combination?

If he was, THEN WHY DID BRUNSKILL FORBID THE
SALE OF THIS ONE PAPER IN THE TWIN CITIES
THAT DARED EXPOSE THE GAMBLING SYNDICATE
AND GANGSTERS?

Although from the start Brunskill had instructed his men
to enforce an unofficial ban of the paper from all newsstands in Minneapolis, the chief officially banned the *Saturday Press* on October 8. His authority was a little-used city
ordinance prohibiting obscene material that would "corrupt the morals of children or any publication devoted
principally or solely to stories of crime, bloodshed or tales
of lust."

Near questioned Brunskill's authority to suppress the
paper, arguing that even the most puritanical would agree
that the paper was not obscene. "The *Saturday Press* will not
submit to suppression even by the Chief of Police Frank
Brunskill."

The paper continued to harp on the connection between
Barnett and Brunskill, and while he was at it, Near also kept
hounding the grand jury, the other Minneapolis newspapers and most public officials. In between the exposés,
Near would desperately plead for subscription money or
"donations" to help him in his fight to rid the city of gang
rule. Sometimes he could only count on Sam Shapiro.

Then the *Saturday Press* launched another offensive: "The
Saturday Press is through playing choo-choo with Frank
Brunskill." An article in the sixth issue threatened that the
next officer who interfered with the sale of the paper would
"find himself the defendant in a damage action . . . This
paper goes on sale on the Minneapolis newsstands or every
paper in the city goes off." On November 5 Near placed an
ad in the paper for "a taxpayer in this city to sell the *Satur-*

day Press on the streets." He warned that the men would be arrested by Brunskill, but that bail and an attorney would be waiting. "Once in court and we shall soon find out if Minneapolis shall hereafter be known as Brunskillville."

Apparently there were no immediate takers, for on November 19 Near was still asking the question. In a box above the front-page flag of that issue, the editors tried to stiffen the backs of their intimidated distributors:

> TO ALL NEWS DEALERS! Our hour of "passive resistance" has passed. Display *Saturday Press* exactly as you do other papers or magazines in your place of business. If you are molested in their sale by the police, refuse to move them from your display stands and we will furnish the legal talent necessary for a "showdown" in the courts. In brief, we will stand back of your *Saturday Press* sales and will carry your case to the court at our expense. If Brunskill still wants a fight, we'll give it to him. Let's force him into court.
>
> —THE EDITORS.

It was also in that November 19 issue that Near and the partially recovered Guilford summoned every ounce of their anger, bitterness and hate. Now the *Saturday Press*'s attacks did not end with the likes of Brunskill and Barnett, but maligned all Jews despite the fact that one of the gang's prime victims was Shapiro. It was an attack that would reverberate beyond the newsstands in Minneapolis:

FACTS NOT THEORIES

> "I am a bosom friend of Mr. Olson," snorted a gentleman of Yiddish blood, "and I want to protest against your article," and blah, blah, blah, ad infinitum, ad nauseam.
>
> I am not taking orders from men of Barnett faith, at least right now. There have been too many men in this city and

especially those in official life, who HAVE been taking orders and suggestions from JEW GANGSTERS, therefore we HAVE Jew Gangsters, practically ruling Minneapolis.

It was buzzards of the Barnett stripe who shot down my buddy. It was Barnett gunmen who staged the assault on Samuel Shapiro. It is Jew thugs who have "pulled" practically every robbery in this city. It was a member of the Barnett gang who shot down George Rubenstein (Ruby) while he stood in the shelter of Mose Barnett's ham-cavern on Hennepin avenue. It was Mose Barnett himself who shot down Roy Rogers on Hennepin avenue. It was at Mose Barnett's place of "business" that the "13 dollar Jew" found a refuge while the police of New York were combing the country for him. It was a gang of Jew gunmen who boasted that for five hundred dollars they would kill any man in the city. It was Mose Barnett, a Jew, who boasted that he held the chief of police of Minneapolis in his hand—had bought and paid for him.

It is Jewish men and women—pliant tools of the Jew gangster, Mose Barnett, who stand charged with having falsified the election records and returns in the Third ward. And it is Mose Barnett himself, who, indicted for his part in the Shapiro assault, is a fugitive from justice today.

Practically every vendor of vile hooch, every owner of a moonshine still, every snake-faced gangster and embryonic yegg in the Twin Cities is a JEW.

Having these examples before me, I feel that I am justified in my refusal to take orders from a Jew who boasts that he is a "bosom friend" of Mr. Olson.

I find in the mail at least twice per week, letters from gentlemen of Jewish faith who advise me against "launching an attack on the Jewish people." These gentlemen have the cart before the horse. I am launching, nor is Mr. Guilford, no attack against any race, BUT:

When I find men of a certain race banding themselves together for the purpose of preying upon Gentile or Jew; gunmen, KILLERS, roaming our streets shooting down men against whom they have no personal grudge (or happen to have); defying OUR laws; corrupting OUR officials; assaulting business men; beating up unarmed citizens; spreading a reign of terror through every walk of life, then I say to you in all sincerity, that I refuse to back up a single step from that "issue"—if they choose to make it so.

If the people of Jewish faith in Minneapolis wish to avoid criticism of these vermin whom I rightfully call "Jews" they can easily do so BY THEMSELVES CLEANING HOUSE.

I'm not out to cleanse Israel of the filth that clings to Israel's skirts. I'm out to "hew to the line, let the chips fly where they may."

I simply state a fact when I say that ninety per cent of the crimes committed against society in this city are committed by Jew gangsters.

It was a Jew who employed JEWS to shoot down Mr. Guilford. It was a Jew who employed a Jew to intimidate Mr. Shapiro and a Jew who employed JEWS to assault that gentleman when he refused to yield to their threats. It was a JEW who wheedled or employed Jews to manipulate the election records and returns in the Third ward in flagrant violation of law. It was a Jew who left two hundred dollars with another Jew to pay to our chief of police just before the last municipal election, and:

It is Jew, Jew, Jew, as long as one cares to comb over the records.

I am launching no attack against the Jewish people AS A RACE. I am merely calling attention to a FACT. And if the people of that race and faith wish to rid themselves of the odium and stigma THE RODENTS OF THEIR OWN RACE HAVE BROUGHT UPON THEM, they need only to step to the front and help the decent citizens of Minneapolis rid the city of these criminal Jews.

Either Mr. Guilford or myself stand ready to do battle for a MAN, regardless of his race, color or creed, but neither of us will step one inch out of our chosen path to avoid a fight IF the Jews want to battle.

Both of us have some mighty loyal friends among the Jewish people but not one of them comes whining to ask that we 'lay off' criticism of Jewish gangsters and none of them who comes carping to us of their "bosom friendship" for any public official now under our journalistic guns.

From his hospital bed, Guilford had written his weekly column charging "Jew lover" County Attorney Floyd Olson with dragging his feet in the investigation of the shooting and of the Shapiro Assault.

GIL'S CHATTERBOX

I headed into the city on September 26th, ran across three Jews in a Chevrolet; stopped a lot of lead and won a bed for myself in St. Barnabas Hospital for six weeks. . . .

Whereupon I have withdrawn all allegiance to anything with a hook nose that eats herring. I have adopted the sparrow as my national bird until Davis' law enforcement league or the K.K.K. hammers the eagle's beak out straight. So if I seem to act crazy as I ankle down the street, bear in mind that I am merely saluting MY national emblem.

All of which has nothing to do with the present whereabouts of Big Mose Barnett. Methinks he headed the local delegation to the new Palestine-for-Jews-only. He went ahead of the boys so he could do a little fixing with the Yiddish chief of police and get his twenty-five per cent of the gambling rake-off. Boys will be boys and "ganefs" will be ganefs.

GRAND JURIES AND DITTO

There are grand juries, and there are grand juries. The last one was a real grand jury. It acted. The present one is like the scion who is labelled "Junior." That means not so good. There are a few mighty good folks on it—there are some who smell bad. One petty peanut politician whose graft was almost pitiful in its size when he was a public official, has already shot his mouth off in several places. He is establishing his alibi in advance for what he intends to keep from taking place.

But George, we won't bother you. [Meaning a grand juror.] We are aware that the gambling syndicate was waiting for your body to convene before the big crap game opened again. The Yids had your dimensions, apparently, and we always go by the judgment of a dog in appraising people.

We will call for a special grand jury and a special prosecutor within a short time, as soon as half of the staff can navigate to advantage, and then we'll show you what a real grand jury can do. Up to the present we have been merely tapping on the window. Very soon we shall start smashing glass.

Olson, the golden boy of Minnesota politics who was to build the Farmer-Labor Party into a vital force of political reform in Minnesota, and who was destined to become the state's three-term governor, was a rising star on the national political scene. Near and Guilford were thorns in his side. "Now go ahead and run for Governor again, Floyd, and you'll find what you took to be a chip on my shoulder is really a tomahawk," threatened Guilford.

A Viking-like figure, with wavy reddish-brown hair accenting his sharp Scandinavian features and penetrating blue eyes, Floyd Olson stood more than six feet tall. He had grown up in the poor, predominantly Jewish north side of Minneapolis. Near and Guilford used Olson's affinity for his Jewish friends as a club against him. His father was a laborer who drank too much; his mother was a dominating personality who wanted her son to be a white-collar worker. This heritage, combined with his exposure to Jewish families with a Talmudic obsession for learning, had produced an ambitious leader who would work his way from selling newspapers on the street corner to the governor's office. His ten years in his first political job had tested the young prosecutor because Minneapolis was known as a "chronically corrupt" city. "Rackets of various sorts flourished," Olson's biographer, George Mayer, observed, "and cheap, ephemeral scandal sheets like the *Saturday Press* maintained a precarious existence by alternately blackmailing petty crooks and condemning county officials for laxity."

Olson understood that every thief was not a criminal, that every gambler was not a gangster, and showed leniency and sympathy to petty offenders who were merely trying to eke out a living. "If they ran honest games and played square with him," Mayer wrote, "Olson was inclined to wink at their minor infractions of the law." To his biographer, Olson seemed like a "kind of modern Robin Hood."

Two days later Near and Guilford were on their way to their day in court, but it wasn't Chief Brunskill who had taken up the challenge but County Attorney Floyd Olson, who promised to wage war on the yellow press and "put out of business forever the *Saturday Press* and other sensational weeklies." His legal justification was George Lommen and Mike Boylan's Public Nuisance Law pushed through the Minnesota Legislature in 1925.

On that day, November 21, 1927, County Attorney Olson filed a complaint with Hennepin County District Judge Mathias Baldwin alleging that the *Saturday Press,* in its short life span, had managed to defame Charles Davis, Chief Brunskill, Mayor Leach, the Minneapolis *Tribune,* the Minneapolis *Journal,* the Hennepin County Grand Jury, Olson himself and the entire Jewish community. Olson described the *Saturday Press* as "a malicious, scandalous, and defamatory publication" and asked that "said nuisance be abated." He wanted the court to issue a restraining order barring Near and Guilford or anyone else from "conducting or maintaining said nuisance under the name of the

Saturday Press, or any other name." Aware that the court would not act until there had been a hearing, he asked that a temporary restraining order be issued until the matter could be settled.

Judge Baldwin did not hesitate to issue a temporary restraining order under the Public Nuisance Law which prohibited Near, Guilford and anyone else "from producing, publishing, editing, circulating, having in their possession, selling and giving away" a publication known as the *Saturday Press.* This applied to issues already printed as well as future issues. But Baldwin went even further by forbidding them "to produce, edit, publish, circulate, have in their possession, see, give away any publication known by any other name whatsoever containing matter of the kind alleged in the plaintiff's complaint."

In response, Near and Guilford demurred to the temporary restraining order six days after it was issued, arguing that the statute was unconstitutional, whatever the truth of factual assertions in the complaint. This was a procedural tactic—a legal way of saying "So what?"—recommended by Thomas Latimer, a prominent Minneapolis attorney who was no rooter of the *Saturday Press,* but who agreed to defend the almost destitute defendants because he believed in their cause. Latimer was a kind of self-appointed Legal Aid Society. In a twenty-three-word answer to the county district court, Latimer wrote, on November 28: "The defendants demur to the complaint herein on the ground that it does not state facts sufficient to constitute a cause of action." Latimer's strategy was to advise his clients to obey the temporary injunction while challenging the constitutionality of the Public Nuisance Law.

When Near and Guilford got their day in court on December 1, Latimer argued that the law was "a subterfuge voted by the 1925 Legislature to get away from the state's constitution and libel laws in an effort to silence the *Rip-saw.*" Latimer added, "There are only two countries in the world today with a statute similar to the one at issue. They are Italy and Russia." There was irony in this reference, for in the same week that the *Saturday Press* was gagged, the Minneapolis *Journal* had published a lofty editorial on press freedom. The subject was not what was happening in Judge Baldwin's case, but the abuses in Benito Mussolini's fascist Italy. "To be truly free, [newspapers] should be able to have opinions and print them; and not only that, but circulated unrestrained," wrote the *Journal.* It was a timely and pointed editorial for the autumn of 1927, but the newspaper's voice of conscience ignored what was happening in its own front yard.

Olson's attempt to close down the *Saturday Press* marked the first serious effort to use the law drafted to silence John L. Morrison, now dead for over a year. Near, who had never come to the *Rip-saw*'s defense, recalled what had happened in Duluth: "Morrison sighed and passed on before the law could be invoked against his sheet." Near promised his few supporters: "I have no intention of being so accommodating."

Judge Baldwin had little sympathy for Near, Guilford or Latimer's tactic. Less than two weeks later, he rejected the demurrer. The judge seemed to regard the injunction against the *Saturday Press* as he would an order against a garbage dump or a burlesque show that was harmful to the public welfare. "The protection of newspapers by the Constitution is strongly stressed by the defendants. . . . But the 1925 law in question seems to have something else in mind than the prevention of personal libels. The designation of such publications as 'nuisances' immediately puts them into that class of things that are harmful to the community at large . . . What is sought is protection of the public." He pointed out that the fact that individuals were libeled was merely incidental and that the law protected classes of people—"as where a creed, a nationality or a class is attacked."

Yet the words of the Minnesota constitution produced some small doubt in the judges' minds: "The liberty of the press shall forever remain inviolate, and all persons may freely speak, write and publish their sentiments on all subjects." This nagging doubt may have led Judge Baldwin to certify the case to the Minnesota Supreme Court, leaving to it the question of the law's constitutionality. Unlike the rule in some other states, if the lower-court judge in Minnesota does not so certify a case involving an injunction, there is no way the case can be appealed. However, the tactic of demurrer made an appeal possible. State law stipulated that if a demurrer to a temporary restraining order was overruled and if the question was certified by a judge, the order could be appealed to the Minnesota Supreme Court. By demurring, Latimer had opened the door for appeal, and by certifying the case, Judge Baldwin had kept the litigation alive and prevented the temporary restraining order from becoming permanent. Of course, by extending the temporary restraining order, the court also kept the *Saturday Press* off the streets of Minneapolis indefinitely.

Few citizens of the Twin Cities mourned the gag on the *Saturday Press*. The technical difference between a temporary restraining order and a permanent injunction was hardly understood, and the suppression of the newspaper was heralded as another feather in Floyd Olson's hat. The action by Judge Baldwin seemed proper too, and was certainly popular.

Gratuitously the Hennepin County Grand Jury, then investigating Near and Guilford's slurs on the Minneapolis municipal government, including the Shapiro attack, announced that "citizens of Minneapolis will suffer no loss and the community will be improved if the *Saturday Press* and the *Twin City Reporter* are put out of business." The grand jury publicly supported the suppression order because "the columns of this paper [the *Saturday Press*] have carried many articles dealing in personalities, questions," and in organizations under investigation by the grand jury. The secret panel of twenty-one citizens felt that if Near and Guilford had any hard evidence of wrongdoing, they should have come forward with it voluntarily.

If the old adage "Justice delayed is justice denied" has merit, it has uniquely punitive meaning for an indefinite temporary restraining order. This "temporary" injunction had a life span of more than a year, while Near and Guilford became frustrated defendants attempting to obtain relief from the gag order that had stopped their presses. It was a slow track for what seemed to be a lost and unpopular cause.

Chapter 5
Rogues and Prophets under Siege

G UILFORD and Near remained pariahs in the communities of Minneapolis and St. Paul regardless of how prophetic some of their muckraking turned out to be. With the *Saturday Press* padlocked, the crimes it had spotlighted and for which indictments had been drawn began to move slowly through the criminal justice system.

Less than two months after Judge Baldwin had issued his ruling, Chief Brunskill himself was the subject of a grand jury probe; according to the local papers, the charges of misconduct had first been lodged against the chief in the *Saturday Press.* County Attorney Floyd Olson called seventeen witnesses in two days, including Howard Guilford, as the grand jury listened to testimony ranging from charges of political impropriety to allegations of crime being protected.

The investigation came to a halt after a young law student, Arthur Kasherman, employed by the *Twin City Reporter* and reportedly moonlighting as a bribe courier for the mob, took the Fifth Amendment when three questions were put to him. Chief Brunskill and Mose Barnett were the targets, but Kasherman would not talk. He later gave the excuse that he did not testify because he was a "newspaperman." Eventually the young man served two jail sentences for contempt, and his appeals were rejected by the United States Supreme Court.

At the time, the questions he refused to answer were not available to the public, but a search of the court record reveals that Kasherman was asked: "1. About two years ago . . . did you see one Mose Barnett give a roll of paper money to Chief of Police Brunskill? 2. Did Chief of Police Brunskill immediately afterwards arrest and imprison you without charge? 3. While [you were] imprisoned did a police officer . . . say to you in the city jail . . . 'Mum is the word'?" Though the grand jury returned a "no bill" in February, Chief Brunskill resigned in May under pressure from Mayor Leach, who then assumed the duties of running the police department. The mayor never commented on the firing other than to say that Brunskill had been "disloyal."

Word on the street offered a more elaborate version: while Mayor Leach was out of town, Brunskill had accepted Leach's weekly envelope. "Leach didn't get his cut that week, and he put the burn on Brunskill to pony up," one reporter remembered. The mayor was so mad that he fired Brunskill.

The charges against those accused of shooting Guilford were suddenly dropped when the victim changed his mind about his ability to identify the gunmen. A hit man from

Chicago with links to Barnett was later arrested "as a dead ringer" for one of the original defendants, but no conviction ever resulted. Guilford's son Warren recalls that his father dropped the charges because the mob paid his hospital bills and apologized.

In the Sam Shapiro case, seventy-five members of the Twin Cities Cleaners and Dyers Association were charged with illegal restraint of trade in attempting to fix prices in the St. Paul and Minneapolis area. Although many of the defendants bargained for nominal fines in exchange for a guilty plea, the Minnesota Supreme Court later disbarred the association's leader, Attorney Philip Moses, for his criminal activity.

Mose Barnett was one of four mobsters indicted on November 4, 1927, for the attack on Sam Shapiro and for the $8,000 worth of damage he had caused. Barnett fled the jurisdiction; two months later he was arrested in Tacoma, Washington, for attempting to rob a department store on Christmas night. Barnett told the police that his name was Charles Mack, jumped bail and disappeared from Tacoma before they realized who he was. After turning himself in to the Minneapolis authorities in 1933, Barnett was convicted of the Shapiro assault and spent four years in Stillwater State Prison.

One of the key witnesses in Mose Barnett's trial was the dry cleaner's son, eleven years old when he hid behind the partition as the hoodlum tried to shake down his father, eighteen at the time of the trial. Irving Shapiro seemed to remember every detail of the incident on East Franklin Avenue and gave a very graphic account of how his father looked after the beating. When his testimony and the intense cross-examination were over, an elderly spectator congratulated him. "Young man," she said, "you were an excellent witness. Someday you may be governor of Minnesota."*

Sam Shapiro continued to befriend Near. Finally running his own dry-cleaning plant, Shapiro knew of Near's deserved reputation as an anti-Semite, but as his son Irving recalls, "There was so much of this kind of prejudice at that time in the Midwest that all that mattered to my father was that Near was fighting to have Barnett and the dry-cleaning association tried and convicted."

Another link between police and mobsters was exposed in a criminal libel trial Olson and Brunskill brought against Near in 1930. While his lawyer was attempting to get the gag order against the *Saturday Press* reversed, Near had several articles published in the *Beacon,* a newspaper used by Harold Birkeland to avenge the alleged murder of his father, the Reverend K. B. Birkeland, a Lutheran minister sometimes linked to shady oil-field sales who had been found dead in 1925 from an apparent heart attack in a Minneapolis brothel. An eyewitness reported that his trousers were open and his genitals exposed when the police found the body. Harold Birkeland was convinced that his father had been kidnapped by Floyd Olson and Frank Brunskill, starved and frozen, and that his body had later been transported to the brothel. In an earlier edition of the *Saturday Press,* Near had jumped at the opportunity to strike a blow at the county attorney and the police chief and rushed to support Birkeland in his crusade. Despite the court's prohibition against writing or printing matter of the

---

*Irving Shapiro never made it to the governor's mansion in Minnesota, but in 1974 he did become chairman of the board and chief executive officer of E. I. du Pont de Nemours & Company. Of Sam Shapiro's two other sons, Jonas is the proprietor of the family dry-cleaning store across the street from its original location on East Franklin Avenue; and Leonard owns the Prestige Carpet Company, just down the block from his father's original store.

kind included in the *Saturday Press,* Near had continued writing about the episode in the *Beacon,* an apparent violation of Judge Baldwin's order. Both Near and Birkeland were eventually acquitted of criminal libel by a jury after a sensational trial, the longest in the history of Hennepin County at that time. According to Near, the jury's verdict meant that the truth of his charges against Olson and Brunskill had been proved. Olson, by then a candidate for governor, contended that the absence of a jury conviction did not mean that the allegations of his participation in the Birkeland death had been verified. Birkeland's son, obsessed by his father's "frame up," later published a small book, "Floyd B. Olson in the First Kidnapping–Murder in Gangster-Ridden Minnesota."

The true circumstances of Reverend Birkeland's death remain clouded in the mists of Minneapolis gang lore, and there is no evidence that Olson was involved. Yet some interesting facts emerged from the trial. A pre-trial deposition given by Chief Brunskill's former secretary Philip De Lage reported that Mose Barnett had free access to the chief and never had to wait in the outer office. In fact, he testified that when Barnett was serving time at Leavenworth in the early twenties, long before the Shapiro incident, Brunskill had written to the warden requesting lenient treatment for Barnett, a friend who was "a victim of circumstance."

The criminal trials of the underworld pouring out of the municipal governments so dominated the news that no one was interested in the constitutional issues growing out of the *Saturday Press* case.

Guilford and Near begged the state supreme court for an early hearing. A January 9, 1928, petition drawn up by attorney Thomas Latimer stated that the two publishers derived their whole livelihood from the *Saturday Press,* and "have invested all of their savings in said *The Saturday Press* . . . that unless it is permitted to issue within the near future . . . [Near and Guilford's] investment will be wholly lost." The petition also asked the court to understand that since the temporary restraining order of last November 22, 1927, the defendants "have been forced to return subscription money and refuse advertising."

One hundred days after the request for an expedited hearing, the state's high court convened to hear oral arguments. Because it was an appeal of Judge Baldwin's order that overruled the demurrer, the supreme court could only decide whether the state legislature had violated the Minnesota constitution when it voted so overwhelmingly for the Public Nuisance Bill. If the 1925 law, which permitted a county prosecutor to appear before a lone district court judge and obtain a temporary restraining order without a trial by jury, was judged to be constitutional, then the case would be sent back to Judge Baldwin's court for him to decide whether the *Saturday Press* did violate the Public Nuisance Law, and whether the temporary restraining order against Near and Guilford should be made permanent.

The full name of the case at this time was *State ex rel. Floyd B. Olson* v. *Howard A. Guilford and another,* but it was Jay M. Near whose will to fight the Public Nuisance Law kept the issue alive. Guilford's interest was waning. He was becoming bored with the glacial pace of the litigation. More interested in nursing his gunshot wounds, Guilford always credited or blamed Near for keeping the case in the courts.

On April 16, 1928, Near sat in the half-empty supreme court in the state capitol in St. Paul as his counsel, Thomas Latimer (who in 1935 would become mayor of Minneapolis), argued before the justices that the Public Nuisance Law was a violation of the Minnesota state constitution and was "null, void and invalid, being in contravention of the Fourteenth Amendment to the Constitution of the United States."

In his argument, Latimer stressed that the *Saturday Press* and its publishers had been denied a trial by jury under the Sixth Amendment and that the entire concept of freedom of the press guaranteed by the First Amendment had been breached. He argued that the due process clause of the Fifth Amendment, which had been made applicable to the states with the passage of the Fourteenth Amendment, had been violated.

Five weeks later, on May 25, Chief Justice Samuel Bailey Wilson, speaking for a unanimous court, upheld the 1925 Public Nuisance Law as constitutional. Wilson likened Near and Guilford's nuisance to that of houses of prostitution or noxious weeds and asserted that it was well within the police powers of the legislature to resort to drastic measures to eliminate such nuisances. In a sweeping affirmation of the gag law, Chief Justice Wilson wrote:

> In Minnesota no agency can hush the sincere and honest voice of the press; but our constitution was never intended to protect malice, scandal and defamation when untrue or published with bad motives or without justifiable ends. It is a shield for the honest, careful and conscientious press. Liberty of the press does not mean that an evil-minded person may publish just anything any more than the constitutional right of assembly authorizes and legalizes unlawful assemblies and riots.

The chief justice went on to speak of the obligation of the press to remain within the bounds of propriety. "It is the liberty of the press that is guaranteed—not the licentiousness. . . . Liberty of the press and freedom of speech under the constitution do not mean the unrestrained privilege to write and say what one pleases at all times and under all circumstances." Further: "There is no constitutional right to publish a fact merely because it is true."

As for the jury trial, the court dismissed Latimer's claim that Near and Guilford deserved to be judged by their peers. The justices concluded that the statute inflicted "no personal penalties as punishment for the evils involved," and that therefore Near and Guilford were not entitled to a jury trial.

The Minnesota Supreme Court justices hammered away at the point that this was not a libel case. "This law is not for the protection of the person attacked, nor to punish the wrongdoer. It is for the protection of the public welfare." But in a sense Near and Guilford had been punished because the temporary restraining order had denied them an opportunity to ply their trade. The court's opinion was handed down in May, nine months after the issuance of the original temporary restraining order. Now the tactic of the demurrer no longer stood in the path of Olson's request to Baldwin to make the injunction permanent. With this smashing defeat of the *Saturday Press,* the way was clear for Judge Baldwin to close the *Saturday Press* forever. But it would take another four and a half months before the judge had both sides back in his courtroom.

In the land of the "Sleeping Giant," the Guilford-Near case remained a dormant irritant to the proper people of Minnesota and the daily press, but in distant New York and Chicago, the term "Minnesota gag order" was beginning to stir a few souls who had never heard of Hennepin County and had little idea who Near and Guilford were.

Then a man in Minneapolis told Near about some new

organization in New York that often championed lost causes and suggested he write its founder, Roger Baldwin. It was June of 1928 when Near's desperate appeal touched a responsive chord at the American Civil Liberties Union in New York. Baldwin sensed the potential impact of the Minnesota decision and committed $150 for Near's legal defense, a lot of money at the time for a struggling new organization.

If the term "strange bedfellows" was ever fitting, this was the case. Near, the anti-Semite, anti-Catholic, antiblack, antilabor, anti-Communist, was allied with Roger Baldwin, a brotherhood-of-man evangelist, a conscientious objector during World War I who had been sentenced to a year in federal prison for refusing military service. The ACLU, whose board included such national figures as Clarence Darrow, Felix Frankfurter and Norman Thomas, had been called an agent of the Soviet Union and had been attacked by the Chicago *Tribune* for "taking Bolshevick gold" as it won a few (but lost more) civil rights cases in the wake of the postwar Red scare.

Although disgusted with much of the content of the *Saturday Press,* in July of 1928 the ACLU announced that it would appeal the Minnesota gag law to the United States Supreme Court. Calling the Public Nuisance Law "a menace to the freedom of the country," the ACLU focused on the phrase that would become central to a series of landmark decisions: "prior restraint." Eleven hundred miles away, the ACLU declared: "Heretofore the only control of the press has been by prosecution for criminal or libelous matter after the offense. We see in this new device for previous restraint of publication a menace to the whole principle of the freedom of the press." The ACLU attorneys perceived the Public Nuisance Law as reaching far beyond a single state: "If the Minnesota law is constitutional, then the 14th Amendment and inferentially, the 1st Amendment, no longer protects the press against previous restraints."

The New York law firm of Shorr, Brodsky and King was hired to prepare the briefs for Near's appeal. They stressed the connection that the complaint had been filed by Olson, who was one of the people whom the *Saturday Press* had attacked. This meant that if the case was sustained, it would make it possible for anyone subjected to newspaper attack to have the paper enjoined if just one judge could be found to issue an order.

Not surprisingly, Floyd Olson's office scoffed at the action of the ACLU, saying that "the decision of the state court is an able one and we do not look for the federal tribunal to overrule it." Prosecutor Olson's spokesman promised: "This office will defend the [public nuisance] law to the last ditch."

Olson's response to the ACLU was predictable, but the immediate reaction of the Minnesota newspapers was a shock to Roger Baldwin and his lawyers. In an editorial that might well have been called "Mind Your Own Business," the Minneapolis *Evening Tribune* accused the ACLU of seeing "a menace, whichever way it looks." Worrying more about the "blackmailer and the scandal monger and the damage they will do" than the possibility of some "judge who would stretch the Minnesota law to impose his will on a legitimate newspaper in legitimate conflict with his views," one of the most powerful newspapers in the state scoffed at the fears of the ACLU and at the specter of an imagined menace from a hypothetical judge. "The Civil Liberties Union will no doubt make a great pother about the freedom of the press, but the legitimate newspapers will be rather bored than excited about it."

Most of the newspapers that agreed with the *Evening Tribune* were either uninterested in or silent about the plight of Jay M. Near, who had not been able to publish or earn a living for ten costly months. Certainly Roger Baldwin and the ACLU understood the massive constitutional issues of the Near case, but there were doubts about whether they had the funds to take the case to the highest court in the land.

Chapter 6

The Daddy Warbucks of the First Amendment

SUDDENLY a giant entered the battle, and not necessarily a benign one. Six feet four inches tall, Robert Rutherford "Bertie" McCormick was a scrappy, swashbuckling, right-wing isolationist, and the publisher of the Chicago *Tribune.* Also known as the "Colonel" for his commission (which originated in the Illinois militia), he was reported to appear occasionally in the city room of the *Tribune* in the military attire of his beloved 1st Division, flourishing a polo mallet in one hand and reining in his German shepherd guard dogs with the other. He had waged pitched battles against mayors, Presidents and giants of industry. His many detractors described him as the most dangerous newspaper publisher in the world and as "one of the finest minds of the fourteenth century." But a veteran *Tribune* reporter was more temperate in his assessment: "He had his megaloma-

niac side, but that only made his reign one of grandeur."
"The *Tribune* was never the 'world's greatest newspaper'*
as it claimed," recalls John S. Knight, who later competed
with McCormick, "but it was run by the world's most obsessed publisher." Knight, who admired the "grim, forbod-
ing colonel," says McCormick carried his "gutsiness to a
fault." The jingoist publisher lived by Admiral Decatur's
toast "Our country, right or wrong" (it was on the *Tribune*'s
masthead for many years), and despite his own English-
Groton accent, despised Great Britain. (For example, he
wanted all Rhodes scholars fingerprinted because he was
sure that after they returned to the United States, they
formed a British spy network.)

But more than anything, the Colonel treasured the First
Amendment, and it was his incorrigible zeal for freedom of
the press—something most Americans had never thought
of—that kept him from tossing Jay M. Near's appeal for
help in the trash basket. Indeed, McCormick read his appeal with a sense of empathy and rage. Near recounted the
events which had led to his unenviable predicament, ex-
plaining that Judge Baldwin's restraining order was keeping his small paper closed, and that the vicious campaign
of misrepresentation and vilification by the Minnesota dailies had ruined his credit and made it virtually impossible
for him to get a job in the state of Minnesota. Near's request was simple: he needed financial and legal aid; would
the Colonel help? Whatever Near's reasons, whatever his
apprehensions about the ACLU, his S O S turned out to

*Although McCormick is usually credited with that brazen slogan, it was James
Keeley, the *Tribune*'s British-born editor, who put the phrase on page one, where
it remained until 1977 when a new generation of publishers and editors thought
the *Tribune*'s claim of greatness was a promotional message no longer appropriate
for a newspaper which had, in fact, established itself as one of the nation's ten
greatest newspapers.

have been sent to the right person at the right time.

The penniless publisher from Minneapolis and the millionaire publisher from Chicago had much in common. Like Near, Colonel McCormick had a reputation as a bigot, and words like "kike" and "nigger" were part of his vocabulary. "If the Ku Klux Klan had a brief life in Illinois, it undoubtedly prospered while it lived because of the *Tribune*'s aid," wrote Oswald Garrison Villard, editor and publisher of the *Nation*. The Colonel had been known to make fun of Jews in public. "In one instance he went so far as to mock the accent and forms of speech of an earlier speaker at the same luncheon table," reporter Frank Waldrop wrote in his biography of McCormick. A 1930 poll of Washington correspondents, reported in *Time* magazine, characterized McCormick's *Tribune* as among the "least fair and reliable" newspapers in America and as a "ceaseless drip of poison." McCormick and Near were both anti-Communist, and convinced that the "Red menace" was more than a scare. William L. Shirer, a foreign correspondent for the Chicago *Tribune* from 1925 to 1933, remembers Colonel McCormick's extreme positions. Once when Shirer filed a study on socialist housing developments in Vienna, McCormick scolded him, "You've been spending too much time with New York newspapermen. All New York newspapermen are parlor Bolsheviks."

Of course, the circumstances of each man becoming a publisher were different. Near had simply gone into the "newspaper game" with his old cohort Guilford, whereas McCormick had been made publisher by a series of bizarre family machinations. The third grandson of former *Tribune* publisher Joseph Medill, Robert McCormick did not have promising prospects at the family paper. He had enrolled at Northwestern Law School after Groton and Yale "because there seemed nothing else to do." Rivalries and jealousies kept the two sides of the family warring and had put day-to-day control of the paper in the hands of its editor, James Keeley, a legend in his own right. First in line was Joseph Medill Patterson, son of the editor in chief, Robert Patterson, and second eldest grandson of Medill. The next logical choice would have been Medill McCormick, Bertie's elder brother. But much to the family's horror, Joe abandoned the family's progressive Republicanism for socialism and in so doing lost his place. Joe's departure led to Medill McCormick's being made a vice president, but the newspaper business was too much of an emotional challenge for him; after running the *Tribune* briefly in Keeley's absence, he checked into a Swiss sanatorium.

Young Robert, by then a lawyer, became more interested in the family businesses, especially the newspaper, offering occasional managerial suggestions and eventually becoming its treasurer. When his Uncle Robert died, he barely convinced the directors that the *Tribune* should not be sold. Mending family wounds, he made a pact with his cousin Joe, who had since retired to farming and playwriting, to run the *Tribune* jointly. In 1911 Joe became chairman of the Tribune Company, principally responsible for the editorial side of the paper, and Robert became president and chief executive officer responsible for the business end of the paper. The one responsibility they shared was the editorial page, rotating the job so that one month the socialist Patterson was in control, the next month the conservative McCormick. As New Dealer Harold Ickes, who jousted with McCormick for decades, wrote: "Thus as to policy, the paper was consistently inconsistent." One could always tell when the paper was "rolling in the trough under Bertie." It was a lifelong partnership, which continued through newspaper wars and World War I. After the war, Robert took over the day-to-day operation of the *Tribune* when Joe left for New York to start the New York *Daily News* for the family company. By 1924, the *News* had become America's largest circulation daily. The Patterson-McCormick partnership boosted the *Tribune*'s circulation as well, from 430,-000 in 1920 to 835,000 in 1930.

McCormick felt that Near's charges were true and assessed the articles in the *Saturday Press* as "fairly temperate and possessed of some literary merit." The Colonel was sensitive to the implications of what he dubbed "the Minnesota gag case." As he ruminated over Near's plight, McCormick was still smarting from the wounds inflicted in two previous First Amendment battles. He couldn't help but think of his legal tussles with Henry Ford and William Hale "Big Bill" Thompson, Chicago's erratic three-time mayor—libel suits that had subjected the *Tribune,* the "world's greatest newspaper," to costs estimated as high as half a million dollars. Whether for personal reasons or because of lofty ideals, the Colonel was a man with a mission far ahead of his times and his peers. He had become a kind of one-man brigade fighting for the First Amendment.

Henry Ford, whose Model T, affectionately called the Flivver, had revolutionized America's transportation and industry, aspired to a role in international diplomacy as well. Although Ford's pacifist activities are best remembered for his ill-fated Peace Ship foolishness to end World War I, his initial involvement in foreign policy erupted in 1916 after President Wilson called up the National Guard for duty along the Mexican border. The Chicago *Tribune* had supported Wilson's action and in a burst of patriotism blasted the motorcar magnate for not giving the guardsmen their old jobs back when they returned from the border. "Flivver Patriotism" was the flaming headline. The next day an editorial inspired by the Colonel screamed: "Ford is an anarchist" who should expiate his "ignominy by moving his flivver factories to Mexico." The *Tribune* concluded by calling Ford an "ignorant idealist and unpatriotic American." The editorial was sloppy with some minor facts, and Ford brought a million-dollar libel suit against McCormick's *Tribune* on September 7, 1916.

The trial became a circus of venue motions and media hype. It was tycoon vs. tycoon, as the most prestigious law firms in Chicago and Detroit jockeyed for home-court advantage. Ford's Detroit attorneys pleaded that he could not get a fair trial in northern Illinois, the primary circulation area served by the *Tribune*, and asked for a change of venue to Wayne County, Michigan, where the *Tribune* was circulated by three newspaper distributors, who could be charged as defendants in the libel action. McCormick was represented by the law firm which he had helped found, Kirkland, Fleming, Green and Martin. His lawyers objected to Wayne County, Michigan, as a trial site because it was Ford territory, where jurors would be hostile to the Chicago publisher.

Eventually a compromise was reached. Cook and Wayne counties were eliminated and Mount Clemens, the county seat of Macomb County in southeastern Michigan, was selected. Early in May 1919, two and a half years after the suit had been filed, hundreds of reporters, photographers and Western Union operators flooded the tiny town of Mount Clemens. The trial lasted three months. When Henry Ford took the witness stand to prove that he was neither ignorant nor anarchistic, as claimed by the *Tribune*, it was a media event that would be surpassed only by the Scopes "monkey trial" six years later.

Ford testified that he opposed overpreparedness, not preparedness, and that "war is murder." One witness for the *Tribune* called Ford a "rotten American" and quoted Ford as reciting Dr. Johnson's phrase as if he had coined it: "Patriotism is the last refuge of a scoundrel." During a stinging cross-examination, the auto pioneer stumbled: he was unable to tell the packed chamber when the United States had become a nation. In response to a question about his quotation in the Chicago *Tribune* in 1916 that "history is more or less bunk," Ford explained that he meant "it was bunk to me." His most humiliating blunder, and one which was carried in newspapers from coast to coast, occurred during interrogation intended to prove his ignorance:

ATTORNEY: Did you ever hear of Benedict Arnold?
FORD: I have heard the name.
ATTORNEY: Who was he?
FORD: I have forgotten who he is; he is a writer, I think.

Ninety-four days later Judge James G. Tucker gave the case to the jury of twelve Michigan farmers. After ten hours of deliberation, they found the Chicago *Tribune* guilty of libel. Ford was awarded six cents in damages, six cents in costs in a trial that had cost Colonel McCormick half a million dollars. McCormick refused to pay, and Ford's lawyers never demanded payment because it would have opened the door to an appeal.

Lawyers on both sides hastened to declare victory, but historians Allan Nevins and Frank E. Hill, in their biography of Henry Ford, accurately characterized the conflict:

"Although the *Tribune* trumpeted its confidence that it had been exonerated in the forum of public opinion, it had really been convicted of reckless and spiteful utterance, and the huge sums it had to pay in fighting the suit offered a needless lesson in decorum and reasonableness."

Both sides were severely wounded by the case. Ford's reputation seemed to have been transformed from world genius to simple garage mechanic; McCormick had been taught a lesson about what lawyers can do to the "world's greatest newspaper."

One year after the Ford judgment, the Colonel and his truculent *Tribune* experienced other ordeals. Mayor Big Bill Thompson despised the Colonel and his powerful newspaper. The common bond between Thompson and the Colonel, once staunch friends, was their Anglophobia. "Down with King George" was the mayor's battle cry. At times "Hizzoner" seemed willing to declare war on Great Britain. But after he took office, his real enemies became McCormick and the *Tribune.* He had once raged to his cronies, "Bob McCormick represents the trust press that would crush the life out of Chicago. He will smear any man that gets in his way . . . He's a . . . pip-squeak and a tool of the public utilities. I'm gonna smash Bob McCormick." By 1918 the mayor had filed four libel suits against the *Tribune* for personal damages totaling $1,350,000 because the paper's editorials had called him pro-German during the war. Nevertheless, the paper continued its attack. The *Tribune*'s investigative reports and hard-hitting editorials charged that the city government under Thompson had looted the public coffers for his own greedy purposes. The administration was characterized as "the Tammany government, which has bankrupted the treasury of the city of Chicago." The mayor was accused of impairing the city's ability to meet its credit obligations. Big Bill was furious, convinced that the *Tribune's* irresponsible coverage would create a self-fulfilling prophecy that would severely injure Chicago's credit rating. Aiming Chicago's heaviest artillery at the paper, Big Bill and the city government brought suit for $10 million, claiming that it had been libeled by McCormick's newspaper.

The Colonel roared his defiance, claiming that he was the victim of a well-orchestrated plot. As he saw it, "The political power of the city, the county and the state was in the hands of the same organization: the judges were dependent on this organization for nomination as were the jury commissioners for their appointment." McCormick was convinced that the state's supreme court judges were being threatened "if they failed to obey the state organization." He was outraged that any government could sue for libel: "I thought all that went out with John Peter Zenger," a reference to the pre-Revolutionary trial of a small New York printer who was acquitted by a jury "in spite of the machinations of corrupt and overbearing judges," as the Colonel put it.

The *Tribune's* defense against the libel action took both an offensive and a defensive tack. First, the newspaper filed two suits demanding the return of almost $3 million which, it alleged, had been paid in graft in connection with major construction projects. In its defense the *Tribune* demurred, pointing out that a municipality could not be libeled. Weymouth Kirkland argued that any payments of damages to the city would violate the First Amendment of the U.S. Constitution and the free-press provisions of the Illinois constitution. The Colonel was still wounded by the Ford verdict, and remained convinced that some crooked political judge would do him in.

He was wrong. The city of Chicago lost in the Cook County Circuit Court, and the case re-established the principle that governments cannot sue for libel. In an eloquent opinion Judge Harry M. Fisher wrote: "The press has become the eyes and ears of the world, and to a great extent, its voice. It is the substance which puts humanity in contact with all its parts . . . It holds up for review the acts of our officials . . . It is the force which mirrors public sentiment."

McCormick then won another surprising judgment in the appeal by the city to the state's highest court. Like a schoolboy who has memorized the Gettysburg Address or Spartacus' charge to the gladiators, in later years McCormick would stand his full six feet four inches and quote Chief Justice E. Thompson: " 'Prosecution for libel on government is unknown to American courts. A prosecution, civil or criminal, for libel on the government has no place in the American system of jurisprudence, as the people have a right to discuss their government without fear of being called for their expression of opinion.' "

While *Henry Ford* v. *The Chicago Tribune* only proved that two of the nation's most powerful moguls could behave like children, *The City of Chicago* v. *The Chicago Tribune* was a First Amendment milestone, reaffirming the principle that every citizen has a right to criticize government without fear of prosecution.

With these legal battles behind him, McCormick was not about to jump into Near's campaign—at least not until he had given the matter some serious thought and consulted a few advisers like Weymouth Kirkland, his old law partner and one of his few lifelong friends. Now Kirkland was his chief strategist in the fight for the First Amendment. (At McCormick's seventieth birthday party, Kirkland would comment, "People ask me how in the world I have gotten along with McCormick all these years. It is really very simple. I find out what he wants and I give it to him.")

While Kirkland and his young associates were searching through files for legal precedents, an article in the June 1928 *Journalism Quarterly* by a twenty-seven-year-old assistant professor of journalism at the University of Illinois piqued the Colonel's interest. He invited Frederick Siebert, the author of "Contempt of the Press," to lunch in his private dining room in the Chicago *Tribune*'s Gothic tower on North Michigan Avenue.

The Colonel's office on the twenty-fourth floor was almost a Hollywood caricature. It was huge—thirty-five feet long with a fifteen-foot ceiling—and richly paneled in English walnut. A visitor about to leave would often remain, embarrassed and confused, because there was no visible means of egress. From behind the seven-foot slab of marble which he used for a desk (with one of his German shepherds usually at his feet), McCormick would mutter in his monotone, "Kick the brass door plate at the bottom." After the visitor complied, a wide chestnut panel would swing open and a secretary would appear to escort him out. The ornate, chandeliered office was dominated by a huge marble fireplace; on the mantel was a bust of Lincoln, and beneath it, the *Tribune*'s 1924 credo: "The Newspaper is an Institution developed by Modern Civilization to present the News of the day, to foster Commerce and Industry, to inform and lead Public Opinion, and to furnish that check upon Government which no Constitution has ever been able to provide." Below the inscription was the occupant's full name, "Colonel Robert R. McCormick."

"The Colonel was an imposing figure . . . in the best military tradition," Siebert remembers. "He was reserved, but affable and an accomplished listener." Coincidentally,

Siebert had grown up on the Mesabi Range in the small town of Eveleth and later had been a reporter there, but he had never heard of the Public Nuisance Law or the *Saturday Press* case. In his article he had written: "It is only recently that the courts have abandoned the Blackstonian theory regarding the meaning of the First Amendment . . . and have adopted the rule that . . . it means relative freedom to publish anything as long as such publication does not degenerate into abuse and license." McCormick was attracted by a quotation from Senator James Reed of Missouri, who had told a meeting of newspaper editors a year and a half earlier, "Liberty of the press is not the right to expose and defend the right; it is the right to advocate the wrong."

Siebert, obviously flattered that McCormick was soliciting his advice, was asked to prepare a paper on the history of press freedom from British common law down to the current changes in the American courts, especially concerning the views of Justices Oliver Wendell Holmes, Jr., and Louis D. Brandeis, whose groundbreaking opinions on First Amendment issues were still usually on the minority side.

For both McCormick and Siebert, the constitutional questions were abstract and philosophical. For Near, the only question was, "When can I get my paper back on the streets?" In a case involving a "temporary" restraining order, the time lapse between May 25, 1928, when the Minnesota Supreme Court upheld the gag law, and October 10, 1928, when Judge Baldwin convened another hearing, seemed unconscionably long. But it was in this span that the American Civil Liberties Union and the Chicago *Tribune* were making their decisions to escalate the battle to the Supreme Court in Washington. New York liberal Roger Baldwin and Chicago conservative Colonel McCormick were not in touch with each other, but obviously neither expected any relief from the Minnesota courts.

By September of 1928 the Colonel had not yet decided to commit the funds and prestige of the *Tribune* to Near's defense, but he was inclined to help. "Minnesota was dominated by lumber and iron exploiters," he said later. "These grafters would not oppose police grafters."

As for Weymouth Kirkland, the Chicago lawyer could not wait to get his hands on the case. After studying the files of the *Saturday Press,* Kirkland wrote McCormick: "Bert, the mere statement of the case makes my blood boil. Whether the articles are true or not, for a judge without jury, to suppress a newspaper by writ of injunction, is unthinkable." He urged the Colonel to act; for "if this decision stands, any newspaper in Minnesota which starts a crusade against gambling, vice or other evils, may be closed down . . . without a trial by jury." Kirkland concluded by warning: "If this decision is sustained in the Supreme Court, how easy it would be for a 'small' administration, through control of the legislature, to pass a like statute in Illinois or some other state." This was the Colonel's fear as well; he remembered Thompson's suit and shuddered. As he was to write later: "It was feared that a method of curbing the press having been found in one state would be copied in other states whenever the corruption and effrontery of the politicians in power reached a sufficient debasement."

Correspondence reveals that it was Kirkland's driving interest in the case that provided the final shove which caused McCormick to commit the *Tribune*'s full resources. Even before he knew there was a man called Near, Kirkland was suggesting that the American Civil Liberties Union might be over its head in escalating this appeal to the U.S. Supreme Court. "I wonder if there is some way we could get in touch with the people appealing to see that their briefs are properly prepared," Kirkland wrote. It was not long before the ACLU was nudged out of the case.

Kirkland's zeal level was now backed by the Colonel, who decided to enter the case by having Kirkland's law firm represent Near. A few days later, on September 21, McCormick wrote the directors of the American Newspaper Publishers Association (ANPA): "The owners of this paper, by reason of the suppression thereof, are wrecked financially, and there is but little chance of there being a reversal of the case unless the ANPA or some other similar public-spirited association takes over the litigation." As chairman of the Committee on Freedom of the Press, McCormick wanted the publishers association to agree to pay for the case. Though he would eventually drag them into the action, his initial plea for help stimulated little support for Near.

In his first letter to the directors of the publishers association in the fall of 1928, McCormick cited the Shapiro dry-cleaning-store episode and wrote that Near and Guilford were being punished by the mayor and police chief of Minneapolis "for [their] failure . . . to proceed against a Jewish gangster named Mose or 'Sheeny' Barnett," who was trying to "organize" the dry-cleaning establishment.

In conversations and in writing, the Colonel later explained his concern. "Our interest was aroused because the *Tribune* had recently been victims of an attempt to suppress by a similar piece of sophistry invoked by an equally guilty city government which was dismissed by the Illinois Supreme Court." In the Colonel's view, the highest court in Minnesota was executing the same kind of infamous gag that Mayor Thompson had tried to use to silence the *Tribune*.

On October 10, 1928, when Judge Baldwin called his

court in Minneapolis to order, Latimer was not the only attorney seated at Near's table; the Chicago *Tribune*'s lawyers William H. Symes and Charles Rathbun sat beside him. One person conspicuously absent was Howard Guilford. As Prosecutor Olson rose to ask that the temporary restraining order be made permanent, he knew from the new faces that Colonel McCormick's law firm was in the case, and that Judge Baldwin's court was to be just another detour on the way to the Supreme Court.

The arguments delivered by Olson and Latimer were almost perfunctory. Prosecutor Olson asked to enter in evidence the verified complaint with the nine copies of the *Saturday Press*. For the defendants, Latimer objected to the exhibits "on the ground that the [Public Nuisance] law, under which the evidence is offered, is null and void and invalid, being in contravention of the Fourteenth Amendment to the Constitution of the United States." Latimer also told Judge Baldwin that "The Supreme Court of Minnesota . . . has so construed the constitution of Minnesota, as to render it . . . a violation of the Fourteenth Amendment to the Constitution of the United States."

Latimer, in his conclusion, stressed again that no state shall "deprive any person of life, liberty, or property, without due process of law; nor deny to any person within its jurisdiction the equal protection of the laws."

Judge Baldwin hesitated not a second: "Objection overruled."

LATIMER: Exception by defendant.

OLSON: Plaintiff rests.

LATIMER: Defendant rests.

OLSON: The plaintiff [the county and state] moves that the court direct the issuance of a permanent injunction, upon the ground that the exhibits as they are made a part of the complaint in question, contain matter which is *per se* malicious, defamatory and scandalous.

BALDWIN: Inasmuch as the Supreme Court of this State has passed upon it, I presume it is a mere formality. You may prepare an order.

The county judge did not put pen to paper on that October day; it would be another three months until the permanent injunction was issued by Judge Baldwin. But when the judge told Olson and Latimer that the Minnesota Supreme Court "had passed upon it," he had made it clear that as a lower-court judge he had no choice but to adhere to the state supreme court's conclusion that the Public Nuisance Law was constitutional.

So after twenty-six months the temporary order against the *Saturday Press* became a permanent, "perpetual injunction." To use the judge's final order: "Let said nuisance be abated."

Chapter 7
Grumbling in the Ranks

... if I am going to be made an ass of by Mr. Ellis and the laughing stock of this city because of his actions while here—I'm not and I don't believe you expect me to.

—JAY M. NEAR,
in a letter to Colonel R. R. McCormick

L IKE any nuisance, the *Saturday Press* had few friends, and as the copies of the once avidly read paper grew yellow with time, it had even fewer. Among the lost allies were Howard Guilford, Near's old partner, and Roger Baldwin's ACLU, though their reasons were as different as their basic philosophies. Guilford had grown impatient with the tedious litigation. No longer interested in tilting at constitutional windmills, he sold his interest in the paper to Near for an unknown sum of money (some say no cash changed hands). Since Near and McCormick had no objections, the state supreme court complied with Guilford's request to be severed from the case, which would eventually become *Near* v. *Minnesota.*

The ACLU, Near's first national ally, had been crowded out by McCormick and his powerful *Tribune,* putting the

ACLU's nose slightly out of joint. Instead of turning over to the new champions what legal work had been prepared, the forsaken ACLU asked the richer *amicus* to reimburse the organization for its out-of-pocket expenses. In a letter to the *Tribune* the ACLU pointed out that Near himself would be liable for the expenses "if we were to resort to a suit," while also making it clear that the ACLU was pleased to have the *Tribune* "rendering this high public service." In this spirit, the *Tribune* was reminded that the ACLU relied solely on contributions, and was asked whether the newspaper might be willing "out of consideration for Mr. Near and fairness to us to meet the $150 expense."

McCormick was unsympathetic. The response to the ACLU was signed by E. S. Beck, the *Tribune*'s long-time managing editor, but it obviously had been composed by the legal department: "I am advised by our attorney, who has handled the case for us, that he entered into no agreement to pay for any work done by your organization."

Meanwhile, the legal battles continued in Minnesota. Although McCormick was anxious to escalate the case to the U.S. Supreme Court, there was still one more round to be played out before it could consider the case. County Judge Baldwin's second opinion that Near and Guilford had violated the Public Nuisance Law had to be appealed. So, once again, Jay Near and his lawyer Tom Latimer climbed the steps to the state's highest court.

Obviously impressed with the attention he was getting from the Chicago *Tribune*'s reporters, Near sat in the courtroom waiting for the arguments, more self-assured and cocky now that he was represented by McCormick's high-priced legal corps and its 377-page brief. But on that December 2 in 1929, the oral arguments in Chief Justice Wilson's court more resembled a procedural ceremony than a legitimate clash of arguments. The Minnesota high court had already declared the Public Nuisance Law constitutional, and there was virtually no chance that the court would overturn Judge Baldwin's ruling that the *Saturday Press* was in fact a public nuisance. The decision to demur had virtually guaranteed that.

Near listened to his high-powered litigators lecture the court with quotations from John Milton's *Areopagitica,* from John Stuart Mill and from Justice Oliver Wendell Holmes. The Chicago lawyers reminded the court of the past governments which had sought to usurp the right to speak: the Athenians who had put Socrates to death on charges of blasphemy and corruption of the youth; the Jewish government (the high priests) who, according to the *Tribune*'s brief, had put Christ to death "because He was opposed to the Jewish laws . . . [and] He was crucified for criticizing Mosaic Law—a libel on government."

Perhaps there were a few new lofty locutions, but basically the arguments Near heard from Kirkland's law firm were the same ones he had been hearing for almost two years. Floyd Olson, who was about to launch his successful race for the governorship, seemed more occupied with politics than interested in squelching a half-dead nuisance. As it became more and more apparent that McCormick's law firm had no serious intentions of winning in the Minnesota courts but was aiming for the U.S. Supreme Court, Near began to fume. Much more anxious to earn a living and make some Minneapolitans eat crow than become a landmark case for the Colonel and his legal dandies, Near felt he had been betrayed and was not impressed with either the arguments or the courtroom style of Howard Ellis, a partner of Kirkland's, who was in charge at this step of the proceedings. Near, who had boasted about his new legal stars to his Minneapolis detractors, was humiliated by their limp showing in court. It was their first real test, and they were an embarrassing disappointment to him. During the oral arguments Near sat in the courtroom and mentally began drafting a bitter letter to the Colonel in Chicago. When it was received, marked "Strictly confidential," his tirade stunned even the thick-skinned McCormick.

The case as you know was argued in the Minnesota Supreme Court on December 2nd, inst. Two attorneys of the firm, Caldwell and Ellis came to Minneapolis on either Thursday night or early Friday morning, Nov. 28 or 29, ostensibly to "prepare for the argument." Mr. Kirkland came up on the morning of the Supreme Court hearing.

The argument was made by Mr. Ellis. It had better not been made at all. I concede that Mr. Ellis might be a Daniel Webster, but Daniel never sampled our Minnesota brand of moonshine. Mr. Caldwell, I have no criticism to offer of.

The point is this:

I was given to understand more than a year ago that the case would be pushed forward as rapidly as possible. When it was set for hearing on May 23, last, Mr. Kirkland, so I am informed, protested that he could not make the argument because of other business and refused to permit the argument to be made by another member of the firm. As a result the case went over to the Fall term, being set for hearing on October 1st.

At the request of, I presume, Mr. Kirkland (at any rate the firm), it was postponed until December 2nd and THEN Mr. Kirkland, unprepared to make the argument, sent Mr. Ellis, not withstanding the Latter's condition, in to argue the case.

If, as I have since been told, it was never the intention to make a real fight in the Minnesota court, then why the delay last Spring and a further delay (postponement) from October 1st to December 2nd?

If, on the other hand, it was the intention from the first

to get the case into the U.S. Supreme Court at the earliest possible date, then why the procrastination and the post-ponements from the start?

This case means everything to me. It is I who am deprived of a chance to make a living, of my property. True, I am defying court orders and inviting a jail sentence for writing for the *Beacon,* but I have got to live and Mr. McCormick, if I'm going to be made an ass of by Mr. Ellis and the laughing stock of the city because of his actions while here —I'm not and I don't believe you expect me to.

If, when the case gets to the U.S. Supreme Court, it is to be handled by Mr. Ellis in the same manner as before the State Supreme Court, there isn't one bit of use spending your money or tapping my slim stock of patience going higher, to a higher court.

Near was enraged, but his impulsive letter, an echo of the style and content of the *Saturday Press,* was understandable, given the circumstances and Ellis' occasional drinking problem. It was now clear to Near that he and McCormick had different goals. The Colonel and his lawyers were striving for a great constitutional test in the nation's highest tribunal; the fact that Near couldn't get his shoddy weekly out on the streets of Minneapolis and St. Paul was second-ary. To Near, down on his luck and dependent on occa-sional odd jobs and handouts from the likes of Sam Shapiro, McCormick's preoccupation with a national hear-ing was a bore. Whether it happened in the state court or the Supreme Court was of little consequence; he wanted to get back to work.

Near's letter set off a series of dispatches between Min-neapolis, the Chicago law offices and Miami Beach, where McCormick was in winter residence. After reading one of Near's bombasts (which also included a pitch for funds to expand and promote a new *Saturday Press,* if and when it

won its right to survive), McCormick sent a one-line response to Kirkland: "I take it that this Johnny's trying to
shake us down."

Kirkland replied: "I think you draw the right conclusion . . ." He also referred to an earlier instance when Near
had asked for money to start a national magazine which he
felt would do well because of the publicity associated with
the case. "You will remember," the lawyer wrote, "that
some time last fall I told you we had a request from him for
money which you very properly refused to grant. Ellis
transmitted this information to him and since then he has
had no use for Ellis."

Yet despite his disdain for Near's character and the
shakedown attempt, Kirkland urged the hot-tempered
McCormick to stay in the fight. "Whether we take up the
case or not, Near will have someone do it and with his lack
of means, it will probably be very poorly briefed." Kirkland
also felt that no one in the United States could argue the
case as well before the United States Supreme Court as he
could.

The Minnesota Supreme Court was no more impressed
with the rhetoric and reasoning of Howard Ellis than Jay M.
Near was with his courtroom acumen. This time it took the
court only eighteen days to issue a single-page rejection of
Near's final appeal. To no one's surprise, the court affirmed
the charge that the *Saturday Press* was a public nuisance. The
justices did make one clarification: "We see no reason however for defendants to construe the judgment as restraining
them from operating a newspaper in harmony with the
public welfare. . . . The case has now been tried. The allegations of the complaint have been found to be true . . .
defendants have in no way indicated any desire to conduct
their business in the usual and legitimate manner . . . judg-

ment herein is affirmed." As a result, Near was as enraged with the members of McCormick's law firm as he was with the Minnesota judges. To him, the latter were corrupt and the former inept stuffed shirts from Chicago.

McCormick and lawyers Kirkland and Ellis had expected, indeed almost hoped, to lose this second appeal to the Minnesota Supreme Court. They were finally eligible to appeal to the U.S. Supreme Court now that the ultimate judgment had been rendered in the state of Minnesota. There was little question that the Supreme Court would take the case because under federal law, the Court is required to consider cases which uphold state laws while possibly denying federal rights.

Before making the final appeal, McCormick needed one more ally, the support of the American Newspaper Publishers Association. Gently needling ANPA president Harry Chandler, McCormick wrote: "You will have seen in that excellent medium, the Los Angeles *Times* [Chandler's own paper], that the Supreme Court of Minnesota reaffirmed its opinion in the injunction case. If we don't do something, free press in this country would disappear." But Chandler was reluctant to escalate the Minnesota case to the Supreme Court of the United States, at least until other states attempted to enact similar gag laws. Let "sleeping dogs lie," he wrote back to McCormick. "If we go to the Supreme Court now and that tribunal upholds the Minnesota court, we will have stirred up the matter to a point strongly conducive to similar legislation in other states."

Eastern newspapers had mixed reactions to the *Tribune*'s crusade. The *Christian Science Monitor,* one of the nation's most enlightened newspapers, belittled the fuss the Colonel was making, stating in an editorial that whatever menace exists to freedom of the press, "it is a menace which comes from the unscrupulous within the ranks of the profession"; if "responsible journalism" were to preserve its rights and good name, it "must repudiate activities of the sensation-seeking newspaper." The unethical standards which produced the Minnesota gag law are the menace, concluded the *Monitor*.

The New York *Herald Tribune* and the Houston *Post-Dispatch* supported Near and McCormick, but the weekly magazine the *Literary Digest* blamed the Minnesota law on "the most flagrant and offensive violations of public decency and journalistic ethics," warning American editors that attacking the law would not prevent more dangerous statutes and more censorship.

Accustomed to having his own way, Colonel McCormick had to cope with a reluctant ANPA. Chandler hoped that ignoring the problem would make it go away, most Minnesota newspaper publishers wanted to let the litigation exhaust itself in the state courts, and all parties were concerned about the high cost of litigation. Weymouth Kirkland told the Colonel, who informed the ANPA board, that the appeal might amount to $24,000 (the final figure was higher). McCormick kept applying the pressure until the newspaper association finally advised the Colonel that "they would like to see the Freedom of the Press case prosecuted [*sic*] through the Supreme Court, but they can't afford the cost of it at this point."*

McCormick clearly wanted the association's name even more than its money. He asked that each and every member of the ANPA be polled; he was afraid that unless all

---

*Note that defense cannot prosecute. At most ANPA could have contributed to the cost of the suit.

publishers acted together, "the politicians will begin knocking them off state by state until they have shown they can get away with it and then vote injunctive laws throughout the Union." The Colonel wanted a referendum. "If they won't commit money, I want them behind us," he told his staff.

So the 259 members of the ANPA cast their ballots, and to McCormick's satisfaction and surprise, 254 of them voted to support the appeal to the Supreme Court as long as the Chicago *Tribune* would assume most of the financial responsibility. It was generally believed that several of the five nays came from Minnesota publishers. The resolution voted by the publishers association on April 24, 1930, read:

> Now therefore be it resolved . . . that the statute is one of the gravest assaults upon the liberties of the people that has been attempted since the adoption of the Constitution and is inherently dangerous to the republican form of government; and be it further resolved that the members of this association cooperate in all respects to secure a repeal of said statute and of any statute directed against the right of free utterance.

The next day the New York *Times,* goaded by Colonel McCormick's crusade and by the ANPA resolution, published an editorial calling the Minnesota statute "a vicious law." Harry Chandler, who had originally opposed McCormick's course of action, was also impressed by the ANPA's action. He agreed that the membership ballot was commendable, but in a generous gesture he wrote the Colonel: "We will all be beneficiaries or suffer equally with you . . . The fair thing would be for the membership to share the expense pro rata with the Chicago *Tribune.*"

On April 26, 1930, in a three-line letter, the clerk of the U.S. Supreme Court notified the Minnesota Supreme Court that *Near* v. *Minnesota* had been docketed. This marked the first time in U.S. history that a freedom-of-the-press case involving prior restraints had reached the Supreme Court.

Chapter 8

Death Holds Two Wild-Card Seats on the Supreme Court

As they did each Saturday, on March 8, 1930, the Justices of the Supreme Court of the United States began their weekly conference. It was to be a festive day, marking the eighty-ninth birthday of Oliver Wendell Holmes, who had been an Associate Justice since President Theodore Roosevelt appointed him in 1902. Painfully stooped, his thick, snowy hair glittering, his blue-gray eyes flashing, Holmes arrived slightly late because of an earlier celebration at the Senate. There the Great Dissenter had been praised as "The grand old man of the judiciary."

That afternoon the Court, after an informal ceremony honoring Holmes, was just getting down to cases when a page interrupted to announce that Associate Justice Edward T. Sanford had died suddenly. They later learned that the sixty-five-year-old Justice from Tennessee had collapsed in his dentist's office while having a tooth extracted. (The coroner's report stated, "Cause of death: unknown," but it noted that Sanford suffered from kidney disease.) The Justices adjourned immediately, only to be jolted again five hours later by the news that William Howard Taft, the only former President in history to serve as Chief Justice of the United States, had also died. Having resigned a month earlier, the seventy-two-year-old Taft, broken in health and spirit by a stroke and arteriosclerosis, had slipped into a coma and died at his home on Wyoming Avenue. Three days later the funeral services were broadcast on NBC and CBS, making it the first time such an event had been carried coast to coast on radio.

So the frail Holmes lived on, and Taft and Sanford were borne to their graves. The impact of Sanford's death and Taft's resignation and death on the Court that would decide Jay M. Near's fate was not yet clear to anyone, but this was hardly the scenario that Chief Justice Taft had envisioned. Even after his death, Taft's imprint on the tribunal that would hear *Near* was a factor. By his own numerous appointments to the Court while he was President, and his acknowledged influence on other Presidents, Taft had tried to mold the court in his own image. When he left the White House in 1913 he told his five appointees, "Damn you, if any of you die, I'll disown you."

During his nine years as Chief Justice, William Howard Taft had made the stature and stability of the Supreme Court his primary concern. Appointed by fellow Republican Warren G. Harding, Taft had been an accomplished administrator, whittling away at the Supreme Court's backlog of cases. His vision of an efficient and effective Court was one that would issue few minority opinions and uphold strict constructionist, constitutional principles. "I love judges, and I love courts," he said. "They are my ideals that typify on earth what we shall meet hereafter in heaven under a just God." To Taft, the Court had a presumption of infallibility, with a declared conservative tilt. He preferred to have a constitutional issue settled some way other than to force the nine judges to reverse themselves. In 1911 he had told an interviewer that he wished the question of an income tax to be submitted to the state legislatures and ratified as an amendment to the Constitution rather than have its constitutionality decided by the Supreme Court. An earlier version of an income-tax proposal had been struck down in 1895 by the tribunal; for the Court to change its mind in such a short time would, he felt, result in a loss of dignity.

Rocking the stability of the Court was also unacceptable. "I would not think of opposing the view of my brethren if there was a majority against my own," Taft averred, and in his nine years on the job, he only participated in some twenty dissenting opinions. "A good fellow, in the mind of Chief Justice Taft," wrote his biographer, Henry F. Pringle, "was an associate who did not come forward with embarrassing dissenting views, who added to the unanimity of the court and who was, all in all, a fairly strict constructionist on matters pertaining to the Constitution of the United States."

Five of the Associate Justices had, indeed, been good fellows and stalwart supporters: Pierce Butler, Willis Van Devanter, James C. McReynolds, George Sutherland and Edward T. Sanford. With Taft's vote, they provided a consistent conservative majority of six to three, with Justices Louis Brandeis, Oliver Wendell Holmes and, often, Harlan Fiske Stone dissenting. Although he had at one time been concerned that conservative Justice Van Devanter might not recover from a "near breakdown" after his wife's death, the Chief Justice anticipated the retirement of the legendary and now ancient Oliver Wendell Holmes, who occasionally napped during oral arguments and whom Taft affectionately characterized as being too old to be handing down opinions. What he really objected to was Holmes's growing dependence on Justice Brandeis. Taft commented ruefully that "he is so completely under the control of Brother Brandeis that it gives to Brandeis two votes instead of one." Taft was frequently irked by the three dissenters. "I think we can hold our six to steady the Court. Brandeis is of course hopeless, as Holmes is, and Stone is . . . The only hope we have at keeping a consistent declaration of constitutional law is for us to live as long as we can . . ."

As Taft's health failed, the death watch began and rumors abounded about possible successors. Justice Stone's name was most often mentioned, and Taft became more concerned about his six-to-three balance. In a letter written during the fall of 1929 to Justice Pierce Butler, sensing his own imminent retirement, Taft wrote:

> What you say with reference to Stone's promotion to succeed me, I have no doubt has a good deal of truth in it, and it can hardly be called news. All that we can hope for is continued life of enough of the present membership of the court to prevent disastrous reversals of our present attitude. With Van and Mac and Sutherland and you and Sanford, there will be five to steady the boat, and while the appointment of Stone to be Chief Justice would give a great advantage to the minority, there would be a good deal of difficulty in working through reversals of present positions, even if I either had to retire or were gathered to my fathers, so that we must not give up at once.

Of course, what Taft could not foresee was Sanford's sudden death. The voting of this Associate Justice had been so in tandem with Taft's that it had been eclipsed by the Chief Justice's 340-pound shadow; now even his demise had been obscured by obituaries about Taft. Only history would recall that Sanford had written the majority opinion in 1925 upholding the conviction of Benjamin Gitlow, an avowed radical socialist, for publishing a socialist paper. In that seven-to-two decision, the majority had upheld the constitutionality of New York State's Criminal Anarchy Law, which sent Gitlow to prison for five to ten years for advocating the dictatorship of the proletariat. "A single revolutionary spark may kindle a fire that, smouldering for a time, may burst into a sweeping and destructive conflagration," wrote Sanford. Holmes and Brandeis scoffed at such fear of revolutionary rhetoric. "Every idea is an incitement," wrote Holmes. ". . . The only difference between the expression of an opinion and an incitement . . . is the speaker's enthusiasm for the result."

But nestled in Sanford's sweeping denunciation of inflammatory language by a dangerous socialist was one sentence that even the dissenters Holmes and Brandeis treasured. For the first time a majority opinion of the Supreme Court hinted that the First Amendment could be applied to the states:

> For the present purposes we may and do assume that freedom of speech and of the press which are protected by the First Amendment by the Congress—are among the fundamental personal rights and "liberties" protected by the due process clause of the Fourteenth Amendment from impairment by the States. We do not regard . . . [our prior statement] that the Fourteenth Amendment imposes no restrictions on the States concerning freedom of speech, as determinitive of this question.

Justice Sanford's dictum in this had of course no impact on the prison sentence of Gitlow (who was eventually pardoned by Governor Alfred E. Smith of New York), but it was not the Court's last word on free-speech cases. Indeed, it was the first word in a new concept of First Amendment protections. The Court was suggesting that First Amendment rights are so fundamental that they must apply to the states just as they do to the federal government. Constitutional scholars refer to that expansion as the incorporation of the First Amendment into the Fourteenth.

Thus, in the spring of 1930, there was not only the question of which new Justices might hear Near's case, but also the undeveloped territory of the relationship between the First Amendment and the due process clause of the Fourteenth Amendment. Jay Near was bored with the legal niceties that made the First Amendment apply to the states, but on this fulcrum much of his fate would pivot.

Enacted after the Civil War as one of three amendments to protect the civil rights of former slaves, the Fourteenth Amendment makes every person born in the United States a citizen and guarantees everyone the equal protection of the law. Further, the amendment prohibits the states from depriving "any person of life, liberty, or property without due process of law . . ." However, by the late nineteenth century the due process clause, still serving as a guarantee of procedural fairness, was being used as a reactionary economic tool. A series of state court rulings, followed by Supreme Court decisions, first accepted, then reinforced and entrenched the concept that the due process clause of the Fourteenth Amendment prohibited state legislatures from meddling with certain economic relationships such as contracts, employment and trade. This interpretation came to be known as "substantive due process."

The concept was first concocted by shrewd corporate lawyers who extended, some say perverted, the original purpose of the Fourteenth Amendment in order to prevent states from enacting reform legislation. These high-powered lawyers argued that state legislatures were taking away property without due process by passing laws that set minimum wages or maximum work hours. On behalf of their corporate clients, they maintained that the Fourteenth Amendment guaranteed an unlimitable "liberty of contract." That liberty soon became a license to exploit. Sanctifying and extending that concept, the Supreme Court overturned many state reform laws.

By the 1920s the proliferation of sweatshops and child-labor abuse and the specter of the Great Depression had challenged the dogmas of substantive due process. In angry dissents, Holmes and Brandeis maintained a steadfast and pervasive pressure against the concept as a subversion of the original purpose of the Fourteenth Amendment by the very institution charged with its preservation, the Supreme Court. For Holmes especially, the due process clause was merely designed to ensure that no person was denied the opportunity of a fair hearing.

Yet the same progressive Justices who objected to the use of the due process clause of the Fourteenth Amendment to strike down economic-reform legislation were willing to use the amendment as a vehicle for nullifying state laws which they believed fettered essential individual rights of political expression. Conversely, the conservatives were cool to the use of the due process clause for the preservation of individual liberties. The sweatshop was beyond governmental control; the soapbox was not.

What divided the Court factions was their method of interpreting the term "liberty" as set forth in the Fourteenth Amendment. Holmes, Brandeis and Stone looked to the Bill of Rights for guidance in defining the concept. The result was that they would incorporate the fundamental principles guaranteed in the Bill of Rights into the Fourteenth Amendment and make them applicable to the states. But to the majority, substantive due process was a means of preserving a way of life, a way of organizing society by which the establishment retained control of the institutions of business and government. Thus, they defined "liberty" to mean "liberty of contract," a term not expressly stated in the Constitution.

So the sordid little fight, begun seven years earlier, which shut down the *Rip-saw* and the *Saturday Press* and caused Colonel McCormick to rally the newspapers of the nation, had set the scene for a constitutional dispute whose resolution would give new meaning to the Fourteenth as well as the First amendments. *Rip-saw* against Lommen and Boylan, replaced by Near and Guilford against Brunskill and Olson, had metamorphosed into Holmes and Brandeis against the four conservatives of the old guard.

Had *Near* v. *Minnesota* been argued and decided in 1930 as was anticipated or had Taft and Sanford lived one more year, the two Justices' interpretations of substantive due process and of the interrelationship of the First and Fourteenth amendments would have decided not only *Near,* but conceivably, press-freedom cases for the next half-century. The cornerstone of Taft's carefully laid conservative foundation was gone, but it was expected that President Hoover would appoint two more conservatives to replace the "Big Chief" and his legal shadow.

Hoover, the thirty-first President of the United States, would appoint the eleventh Chief Justice. The holder of that office is the chief administrative officer not only of the Supreme Court but of the entire federal judiciary. The office is not mentioned in the judicial article of the Constitution, but its power has been formidable ever since John Marshall, by sheer will, virtually invented the post. In fact, the only mention of the office is that the Chief Justice shall preside at the impeachment of the President. It was also Marshall's Court which, in *Marbury* v. *Madison*, in 1803, established the power of judicial review, the Supreme Court's responsibility to decide the constitutionality of laws enacted by Congress.*

---

*Article III of the Constitution describes the judicial branch of the federal government in cryptic terms. Compared with the comprehensive provisions of Articles I and II, relating to Congress and the President, Article III is unspecific as to the structure of the federal court system, the size of the one Court it does create (the Supreme Court), and the qualifications of Supreme Court Justices. Most important, the Constitution is silent as to the power of the federal courts to review acts of Congress in order to determine their constitutionality.

Although some accounts of the Constitutional Convention, and contemporaneous writings such as *The Federalist*, suggest that the framers expected judicial review to be a normal part of the judicial function, no mention of the subject appears in the Constitution. *Marbury* v. *Madison* established the power of the federal courts to engage in judicial review. It held that the Supreme Court has the last word as to the constitutionality of actions taken by its coequal branches of government. The tribunal "without the sword or the purse" thus sits as the ultimate judge of whether congressional or presidential acts are committed in excess of the powers delegated to those branches of the federal government under the Constitution.

As for the capacity of the Supreme Court to overturn state laws, the Constitution is somewhat more specific. Article VI declares:

> This Constitution, and the Laws of the United States which shall be made in Pursuance thereof . . . shall be the supreme Law of the Land; and the Judges in every State shall be bound thereby, any Thing in the Constitution or Laws of any State to the Contrary notwithstanding.

The first time the Supreme Court established that its Justices, on an appeal from a state court, could authoritatively decide whether a state law contravened federal law was in *Martin* v. *Hunter's Lessee* (1816), a case that ranks with *Marbury* as establishing a fundamental principle of federal power. This time it was Justice Joseph Story, another architect of federal supremacy, who wrote that "it is a mistake [to believe] that the Constitution was not designed to operate upon the states in their corporate capacities. It is crowded with provisions that restrain or annul the power of the states in some of the highest branches of their preroga-

During much of 1930, Hoover was overwhelmed by the realities of the Depression. Three million workers were unemployed and the numbers increased daily; the panic on Wall Street and Prohibition's gang wars had wasted the American spirit. The President knew that the person whose name he was about to send to the Senate for confirmation as Chief Justice would have an impact not only on the next two years of his Administration but for decades to come. Taft's fragile health had prompted the President and many of his advisers to consider a successor even before Taft's resignation. Hoover's first choice was his fellow Republican and long-time friend from New York, Associate Justice Harlan Fiske Stone, who had been rumored for nearly all major posts since Hoover took office and who had been given clear signals to expect the elevation to Chief. But equally clear signals were being sent out by Taft that he did not consider Stone a suitable successor; as early as September 1929 Taft, with the aid of Associate Justices Willis Van Devanter and Pierce Butler and Attorney General William D. Mitchell, began searching for an alternate. Letters discussing possible candidates and proper tactics were circulated among the members of this self-appointed nominating committee. Soon it was apparent that Taft's first choice was either former Associate Justice Charles Evans Hughes or Attorney General Mitchell.

By December of 1929 Taft was slipping fast. The final blow to his health came when he traveled in January to Ohio to attend his brother's funeral. He returned to Wash-

---

tive." Story did not mean that the Bill of Rights should apply to the states. Nor did Thomas Jefferson believe that the Bill of Rights was intended to limit state power. "While we deny that Congress has a right to control the freedom of the press," he wrote in 1804, "we have ever asserted the right of the states and their exclusive right to do so."

ington incoherent at times and gravely ill. Justice Van Devanter convinced the Taft family that the Chief Justice should leave Washington until the question of a successor had been settled, and Taft was moved to Asheville, North Carolina.

What happened thereafter is not so clear. The truth has been tangled in Washington gossip and cocktail-party folklore for fifty years and may never be completely settled. The first story to emerge was that when the President shared his intention to nominate Stone with his confidant, Joseph P. Cotton, Undersecretary of State and a former Wall Street lawyer, Cotton pointed out that Hoover might have a slight diplomatic and political problem if he did not first offer the post to another New York Republican, Charles Evans Hughes, reminding the President that he owed a considerable political debt to Hughes for his support in the 1928 election. Hughes, Cotton predicted, was certain to turn down the job; after all, he had already served on the Court as an Associate Justice from 1910 to 1916, had then resigned to run against President Wilson, and had narrowly lost in one of the longest election nights in American political history. Hughes had also been Secretary of State under Harding, and was, in 1930, a justice on the World Court. Now a prestigious and wealthy New York corporate lawyer, he would want no part of administering a divided Court. Further, Hoover was reminded, Hughes's son was Solicitor General and would be compelled to resign if his father presided over a Court before which Charles Evans Hughes, Jr., argued his cases. In short, after Hughes turned the job down, Cotton suggested, the President could appoint Stone.

Alpheus T. Mason, biographer of Stone and Brandeis as well as historian of the Court, recounts the scene when

President Hoover placed the call to Hughes in New York to make the face-saving political gesture. "As the conversation proceeded, Hoover blanched, his jaw dropped. . . . 'Well, I'll be damned. He accepted.' " This, according to Mason, "seemed the perfect illustration of the old Yankee story of the man who aimed to blow medicine down the horse's throat through a straw, but the horse blew first."

Doubt about this version has grown over the years. Henry F. Pringle was the first to put it in print in a *New Yorker* article on Chief Justice Hughes, yet later, when he wrote Taft's biography, he did not include the anecdote. In addition, letters written between the President and the Chief Justice refute the story.

The less colorful scenario leading to the nomination is more closely tied to the behind-the-scenes work of the conservative cabal pressing for Hughes. With Taft's resignation imminent, Mitchell dispatched Justices Van Devanter and Butler to New York on January 28, 1930, to determine if Hughes would accept the nomination if it was offered. (Hughes had already turned down several posts in the Hoover Administration.) After that supper meeting, which his daughter inadvertently witnessed, Hughes was summoned to the White House and was offered the job over breakfast the next day. Whatever the truth, the much-talked-about legend of Taft's successor never ceased to be a source of embarrassment for all involved.

The sixty-eight-year-old Chief Justice designate, with his Jove-like beard, long, flowing gray-white mustache and luxurious eyebrows, was a sculptured vision of a Chief Justice. "He looked more like God than any man I ever knew," former Solicitor General Erwin Griswold recently observed. Although his physique bore no resemblance to Taft's, Hughes's philosophy was perceived by many as

made in Taft's own image, a corporation-loving conservative. The *Nation* magazine opposed the Hughes appointment: "here is a fixed set, intolerant mentality, closed on
various issues and deadly conservative." Ironically, one of
the Senate's major objections to Hughes was that he had
resigned from the Court in 1916 "to mingle with such truck
as themselves. He had soiled the ermine by abandoning his
post as Associate Justice to accept the Republican nomination for President." Senator Hugo L. Black, who one day
was to wear the robes of the high court, voted against
Hughes.* It was a bitter debate challenging the integrity of
Hughes, and in the process wounding him. As his daughter,
Elizabeth Hughes Gossett, later commented, "He looked at
his defeat for the presidency philosophically, but when his
character was impugned during the confirmation fight, it
hurt him."

The image projected of Hughes was far from accurate,
especially the charges of conservatism and of his being the
benefactor of Wall Street and big business. Back in 1906,
when Brown University awarded him an honorary degree,
several university trustees boycotted the ceremony because
he was considered a "dangerous radical." Actually, of the
fifty-four cases he argued from 1925 to 1930, most were on
behalf of large corporations, but during his legal career he
also fought for the United Mine Workers, socialist legislators in New York, and the Legal Aid Society. Perhaps the

---

*In 1937, when Senator Black of Alabama was sworn in as an Associate Justice
of the Supreme Court, he was somewhat apprehensive about how Chief Justice
Hughes would greet a politician who had participated in the fight against his
confirmation seven years earlier. But Black's fears were unfounded. "When I
viewed his Jovian countenance and heard the warmth of his greeting, I was
overwhelmed. In no way did he ever reveal anything but friendship." When asked
about the spirit of the first meeting, Hughes responded, "Of course, what would
one expect? I was the Chief Justice."

liberal senators who denounced Hughes would have felt easier had they bothered to look at his opinions as an Associate Justice from 1910 to 1916. Far from predictable, Hughes had voted to uphold minimum-wage laws and to restrict working hours for women and children, in the belief that the Constitution does not protect property more than personal liberty. Hughes considered himself less of a conservative than the "four horsemen" of the old guard (Van Devanter, McReynolds, Sutherland and Butler); less the crusading liberal than Holmes and Brandeis were perceived. "It is well to be liberal, but not messy," Hughes was to write of himself.

History teaches that it is pointless to predict how Supreme Court appointments will turn out. Hughes himself liked to mention that President Wilson had appointed fellow Democrat Justice McReynolds in the hope that he was contributing a formidable liberal to the Court, only to have him turn out to be a hard-headed reactionary. Indeed, Hughes's detractors and the President who sent his name to the Senate lived to see the "deadly conservative" turn out to be a Jeffersonian Democrat.

It seems fitting that Hughes should follow Taft to head the Court; he had followed him before. Many historians believe that Hughes could have been President instead of Taft if he had played his cards right. The 1908 Republican nomination was almost surely his if he had been willing to embrace all the views of President Theodore Roosevelt; he wasn't. Taft then elevated Hughes to the Court in 1910, and it was he who convinced Hughes to make his unsuccessful bid for the presidency in 1916. Hughes had inherited Taft's badly divided Republican Party. Now, in 1930, he inherited an equally divided Supreme Court.

With the Minnesota courts out of the way, McCormick began mapping his Supreme Court strategy from his war room in Miami Beach. Memos, wires and communiqués flowed daily to his troops at Kirkland, Fleming, Green and Martin, who were compiling the documents necessary for appeal and writing briefs for the Supreme Court confrontation.

McCormick was anxious to get the appeal to the Court while Brandeis and the aging Holmes, both favorable to individual constitutional rights, were still on the bench. McCormick knew that Justice Brandeis was crucial to his success. He was only one of the nine Justices, but his vote would be pivotal because he possessed one of the most elegant and persuasive intellects on the Court. As the Colonel looked over the briefs from the Minnesota case, he wrote to Kirkland: "Leon Stoltz [the *Tribune*'s chief editorial writer] suggests that Brandeis is in the way of being a fairly orthodox Jew, and it may *not* be wise to greatly emphasize the crucifixion as in the appeal to the Minnesota case."

Although McCormick had a reputation for sometimes being anti-Semitic, the *Tribune* had supported President Woodrow Wilson's controversial nomination of the Jewish lawyer to the Supreme Court in 1916, whereas the New York *Times* opposed it, arguing that if Brandeis wanted to enter political life, he should run for office, not accept an appointment to the Court: "To supplant conservatism by radicalism would be to undo the work of John Marshall and strip the Constitution of its defenses. It would tend to give force and effect to any whim or passion of the hour."

Brandeis had also been opposed by six past presidents of the American Bar Association, including Taft, and by the president of Harvard University. Brandeis' supporters felt he was the victim of anti-Semitism and of powerful financial institutions castigating him for his public-interest law crusades. At the height of the debate the *Tribune* published an essay by Robert Herrick, a noted author and scholar at the University of Chicago. Next to a large, almost heroic sketch of Brandeis in the newspaper, Professor Herrick asked why national men of such presumed principle should so violently oppose the nomination. "Mr. Brandeis' garland of enemies may well be his laurel wreath of character . . . As for the dangers from his radical mind, an entire bench of Brandeises might be a bad thing, but one social radical in that conservative group of elderly gentlemen might serve as a useful irritant, might suggest to the Supreme Court, which has become the real law-creating body of our government, that the world does move these days."

Tall, lean and in some ways resembling a beardless Abraham Lincoln, Brandeis was a strange creature in Washington. Besides being Jewish, he didn't drink, tell jokes or spend more than $10,000 a year, no matter how much he made. For many years he had ridden in a horse and buggy when other high-powered lawyers rode in chauffeur-driven limousines. In Boston, he had donated his legal talents to protect the public interest. No wonder this ascetic maverick seemed out of step in the fast-paced Washington society.

After one hundred and twenty-four days of bitter debate, on June 1, 1916, Brandeis was confirmed in the Senate by a vote of 47 to 22, generally along party lines. Two progressive Republicans, George Norris of Nebraska and Robert La Follette of Wisconsin, broke ranks to cast their votes for Brandeis.

Brandeis was soon to be recognized for his Scripture-like prose and his biting dissents opposing the conservative bloc. But at the very beginning Brandeis had still been an enigma on freedom-of-the-press issues, especially when they were balanced against the right of privacy. In association with his law partner, Samuel D. Warren, in 1890, Brandeis had written a *Harvard Law Review* article on the right of privacy and argued eloquently for the establishment of civil-damages laws that would protect individuals from invasion of privacy. Prompted by reports in a sensational weekly that gave intimate accounts of personal and social life, the *Law Review* article charged: "The press is overstepping in every direction the obvious bounds of propriety and of decency. Gossip is no longer the resource of the idle and of the vicious, but has become a trade, which is pursued with industry as well as effrontery." This accusation was due in part to the increased and extensive use of photographs in newspapers and magazines, which must have seemed to be startling incursions on the individual's privacy.

In cases involving the constitutionality of child-labor laws, Brandeis had been arguing that state legislatures needed the widest latitude to experiment in order to meet the needs of society. "Denial of the right to experiment may be fraught with serious consequences to the Nation," he would write. "It is one of the happy incidents of the federal system that a single courageous State may, if its citizens choose, serve as a laboratory; and try novel social and economic experiments without risk to the rest of the country." The question for McCormick and the lawyers on both sides was whether Brandeis would consider Minnesota's attempt to police the yellow press the experiment of a single courageous state or whether his protective attitudes on speech and press liberties would lead him to vote to invalidate the statute. The Colonel was fairly sure that Brandeis would not consider the Minnesota statute a worthy experiment of a courageous state and would convince Holmes and some of his other colleagues to invalidate the law.

Still, even Holmes could not be counted as a sure vote, for it was and is a mistake to try to fit him into the mold of a liberal. Although his dissents on free-speech cases had endeared him to liberals and newspapers, in an earlier press case he had declined to interfere with a state that had punished a newspaper for what it had published. The case was *Patterson* v. *Colorado,* written during Holmes's fifth year on the court. The Patterson case did not involve a prior-restraint issue but was the first clue as to how Holmes viewed the extent and consequences of editorial discretion. A Denver newspaper, the *Rocky Mountain News,* had published several scorching articles and a cartoon challenging the motives and conduct of the Colorado Supreme Court in certain cases that were still pending, and the angered state judges had held that the publication of such criticisms, which could be read by potential jurors prior to a trial, constituted a contempt of court. Publisher Thomas M. Patterson was fined and in 1907 appealed to the U.S. Supreme Court. In a forward-looking dissent, Justice John Marshall Harlan called the Colorado contempt action a violation of Patterson's First and Fourteenth amendment rights, but Holmes, writing for the Court's majority, which dismissed the case for lack of jurisdiction, hinted that First Amendment provisions against restraints *prior* to publication do not prevent punishment by a state after publication. Holmes disagreed with "my lion-hearted friend," contending that "what constitutes contempt . . . is a matter of local law." Harlan had failed to convince Holmes that his opinion would be a signal to every state legislature that it could "impair or abridge the rights of a free press and of free speech whenever it thinks that the public welfare requires that to be done."

Holmes had also sanctioned curbs on free speech during times of war. In his "clear and present danger" test, he stated that Congress had a right to protect the nation from the utterance of words that may have all the effect of force. "When a nation is at war," Holmes wrote, "many things that might be said in time of peace are such a hindrance to its effort that their utterance will not be endured so long as men fight and that no Court could regard them as protected by any constitutional right." In that same wartime context, Holmes spoke of "falsely shouting fire in a theatre and causing a panic" as words whose speakers could be punished.

But in the quarter century between *Patterson* and *Near,* Holmes had drifted closer to Harlan's view of the First Amendment. After the heated passions of war, Holmes, joining Brandeis or joined by him, began departing from the majority to protect the expression of "the thought that we hate." In *Abrams* v. *United States,* the first in a trilogy of dissents, Holmes rejected all control of political expression except when the words created an imminent danger of overthrow of government or other serious violence. "The ultimate good desired is better reached by free trade in ideas," Holmes declared, ". . . the best test of truth is the power of the thought to get itself accepted in the competition of the market . . . That at any rate is the theory of our Constitution."

In that particular opinion Holmes was disagreeing with his fellow Justices on what was usually referred to as subversive advocacy. In *Near,* the Olympian aristocrat from Boston, who prided himself on not reading newspapers, would have to weigh the competing constitutional theories that he espoused in the 1907 Colorado newspaper case against the 1919 Abrams speech case; and those trying to predict the vote of the various Justices would oversimplify this complicated Yankee if they anticipated that his allegiance to the First Amendment automatically put him on Near's side. Supreme Court watchers could not ignore Holmes's fundamental precept that the states should be free to enact those laws which their legislatures thought necessary. The courts had no business obstructing the will of the majority. Where Brandeis saw progressive activism as the mission of the Court, Holmes saw its role as more passive. "Here lies the supple tool of power," he suggested as his own epitaph.

If McCormick and Near were not completely confident of the Brandeis and Holmes votes, they had even fewer reasons to rely on the other seven members. They could almost certainly count on losing what was left of Taft's conservative block, the "four horsemen" of the old deal: Van Devanter, McReynolds, Sutherland and Butler.

The quarterback and the most engaging, forceful and rigid of the four was Associate Justice Pierce Butler. A lifelong Democrat and a Roman Catholic from Minnesota, he had been appointed in 1922 by President Harding. He had practiced law in the Mesabi Iron Range and the Twin Cities, and had been the attorney for his family, the Butler Brothers who operated eighteen mines in the Mesabi. Butler knew first-hand John L. Morrison's *Rip-saw* and the Public Nuisance Law that was created to stop its publication. Near and Guilford's *Saturday Press* was a publication he openly detested, and he was convinced the publishers were scoundrels and blackmailers. An aggressive debater, Butler was intellectually gifted, possessed of wit and Irish eloquence, and was always ready to take on his liberal adversaries on the Court. With chagrin and affection, Holmes once described the moralist laissez-faire Butler as "a mono-lith": "There are no seams the frost can get through. He is of one piece."

Butler relished jousting with Brandeis, but was capable of rude outbursts. "One might disagree with him, but there was seldom any doubt as to where he stood or that his stand was based on deep conviction," wrote Butler's biographer, David J. Danelski. "A product of his age and environment," Butler highly valued "patriotism, laissez-faire, morality, law, order, justice, tradition and freedom." Yet despite his deep convictions, it was not always clear how he would balance those values when they came into conflict. Butler had become the Court's champion of *procedural* due process. Originally a criminal lawyer, he was angered by unfair police practices and corrupt judges, and by 1930 was becoming a champion of defendants' rights. However, in cases involving *substantive* due process, he was not as consistent. While he firmly supported due process for property rights, he sometimes voted against freedom of speech or conscience, and whenever individual rights clashed with his concept of patriotism, the latter would most certainly win. Thus, in earlier free-speech cases involving Communists or aliens who would not swear an oath of allegiance, Butler had voted against them. So even the "monolith" was a bit of a puzzle: sensitive to unfair police practices, but a limiter of freedom of speech, and most important, a Minnesotan.

Justice James C. McReynolds of Tennessee was the most cantankerous of the four. Even the affable Taft described him as "fuller of prejudice than any man I have ever known, and one who seems to delight in making others uncomfort-able." Once when a persistent Washington lawyer, who happened to be a woman, appeared before the Court,

McReynolds was heard to mutter, "I see the female is here again." On one occasion McReynolds was still sitting in a Senate barber chair when the other eight Justices, fully robed, were waiting to enter the courtroom. When Chief Justice Hughes sent word to him that the others were waiting, McReynolds snapped at the messenger, "You tell the Chief that I don't work for him."

A bitter and bigoted opponent of Brandeis, McReynolds had been President Wilson's first appointment in 1914; Brandeis was the second two years later. "The splenetic Tennessean" was an anti-Semite, and so hostile to Brandeis that the two almost never spoke, and could not be invited to the same parties, even when the host was the Chief Justice. Once a professor of law at Vanderbilt University, McReynolds perceived himself as the mentor for all new Justices appointed to the Court except for Brandeis. McReynolds' overt prejudice was painfully disturbing to his colleagues. Stone recounted the incident in 1932 when Benjamin N. Cardozo, an esteemed judge of the New York Court of Appeals, was appointed by President Hoover to fill Holmes's seat. As the Justices assembled soon after Cardozo's confirmation, which was virtually without opposition, McReynolds turned to Stone and scoffed, "Cardozo! To be a Justice from New York, all you need is to be a Jew and have a father who was a crook." This was a snide reference to Albert Cardozo, who, sixty years earlier, had been a judge reputed to be in Boss Tweed's pocket. Justice Stone was so appalled by the remark that he told his law clerk, "It was the first time in my adult life that I wanted to punch someone in the nose."

McReynolds' opinions reflected support for state laws that denied blacks the right to vote, and he believed that separate but equal schools for Negroes constituted equality. Yet he was willing to strike down any state attempts to place restrictions on business.

McReynolds was not likely to be offended by Near's abuse of the Jews of Minneapolis, but there was little chance that he would break rank with the other members of the four horsemen on a constitutional issue of such importance. Besides, he was no defender of the press; he had once led a successful campaign in Nashville to ban the police gazette from all newsstands.

Willis Van Devanter was the most lucid and least reactionary of the four horsemen. He had become rich representing the Union Pacific Railroad, had been a circuit-riding judge in Wyoming Territory (before it became a state) and was a federal Court of Appeals judge when Taft appointed him to the Court in 1911. But when he became a Justice, Van Devanter developed a major ailment—"pen paralysis," his closest associates called it. In conference, as the nine judges debated issues and established their conflicting positions, Van Devanter spoke with eloquence and clarity and was carefully heard. But he simply could not get his wisdom down on paper, and his procrastinating crippled the four, whose opinions could not emerge from conference with persuasiveness and the poetry of Holmes and Brandeis. The condition was later exacerbated when, according to Taft, Van Devanter nearly suffered a breakdown after his wife's death.

Justice George Sutherland believed passionately that meddlesome legislation was against the American grain. In 1923 he wrote an opinion striking down a law enacted by Congress to protect the rights of women and children working in Washington, D.C., by establishing a minimum wage. A children's hospital in the capital had attacked the law in *Adkins* v. *Children's Hospital*, and Justice Sutherland wrote the majority opinion that struck down the law. Four other Justices agreed with Sutherland that the minimum-wage law for the District of Columbia violated the due process clause of the Fifth Amendment and what he described as "liberty of contract." This was also a major reaffirmation of the substantive due process doctrine that had stalled social reform for the previous forty years. Sutherland stated that since women's suffrage had established the equality of women at the polls, Congress lacked the constitutional right to single them out for special protection in working laws. In a caustic dissent, Holmes countered that "it will need more than the 19th amendment to convince me that there are no differences between men and women." As for Sutherland's dogma of liberty of contract, Holmes called it "windy and poor."

It would be a paradox that the four horsemen, led by Sutherland into second-guessing the legislature in *Adkins* v. *Children's Hospital,* might affirm Minnesota's experiment to curb press abuses, as they were expected to do, but such was the confusion of the interpretations of the First and Fourteenth amendments. Across the ideological spectrum from economics to civil rights, from substantive due process to the Bill of Rights, the conservative Justices were as inconsistent as their opponents.

In the Near case, the votes that could not be counted at all were those of the new Chief Justice, Associate Justice Harlan Fiske Stone and Associate Justice Owen J. Roberts, who had been appointed in 1930 by Hoover to replace Sanford. To win, Near and his sponsors would require all three of these swing votes for even a bare majority.

Stone had been Attorney General of the United States and for thirteen years before that, Dean of Columbia Law School. President Calvin Coolidge had appointed him to the Supreme Court in 1925.

At the time, as Chief Justice, Taft not only approved of

Stone's election but liked to say that "I rather forced the President into his appointment." In those days the sitting Justices, particularly the Chiefs, had much more to say about appointments than they do now when such lobbying would be considered inappropriate. Actually Stone, the fifth Justice appointed by the Republican administrations of Harding and Coolidge, was expected to restore the bulwark of strict constitutional construction that was Taft's vision of what the Court should be. But devout Republican and corporate lawyer though Stone was, he did not fit into anyone's mold. He viewed that part of the legal profession which believed that law existed chiefly to protect big business as "a very sad spectacle." A teacher of trusts, equity and mortgages, Stone made no pretense of being an authority on the U.S. Constitution. At the time of his appointment he considered himself a novitiate. "As a practicing lawyer I have had occasion to advise on constitutional questions and occasionally to argue a case . . . but that is far from making one an expert or one who may speak with authority on a subject of this kind." But one of his Columbia faculty colleagues prophesied that the new Justice might align himself more with "the skepticism of Mr. Justice Holmes and . . . the realism of Mr. Justice Brandeis." Stone, who defined the Supreme Court as "the sober second thought of the community . . . that firm base on which all law must ultimately rest," was to sit on the Court for twenty-one years, five of them as Chief Justice, at the appointment of President Roosevelt in 1941.

But that Harlan Fiske Stone was different from the one President Coolidge thought he had appointed a quarter of a century earlier. After 1925 Chief Justice Taft's pride in the appointment quickly vanished and their relationship cooled when the progressive new Associate Justice aligned

Subscribe For
THE DULUTH RIP-SAW
Only $2.00 Per Year.

Subscribe For
THE DULUTH RIP-SAW
Only $2.00 Per Year.

THE DULUTH RIP-SAW.

VOL. IV, NO. 21.   DULUTH, MINN., SATURDAY, DECEMBER 11, 1920.   PRICE FIVE CENTS.

GAMBLING DENS INCREASE VERY RAPIDLY IN DULUTH

RIP-SAW INSPECTORS FIND LIVELY REDLIGHT RESORTS

Carl Laf Runs Big Resort—Big Joe Frolics at Hotel Esmond The Saratoga Hotel Abounds in Booze and Poker— Madam Peltier Runs Retreat Over Tire Shop.

AN UNHOLY AND UNDESIRABLE ALLIANCE.

MAX MASON IS CONVICTED OF RAPING IRENE TUSKEN

Defendant's Lawyers Ask New Trial—Miller is Acquitted on Similar Charge—Colored Lawyer Scrutchin Discredits Young Sullivan and Defeats County Attorney.

AUTO LEADS AS MAN KILLER

Terrible Gas Wagon Juggernaut Reaps More Than Rightful Percentage of Accidents in United States—Negligence Causes Three-Fourths of Accidental Deaths.

VIC. NEARLY CONVERTS BEN

Little Giant Almost Causes Judge Goldberg to Become a Christian—Hibbing's Mayor Pays War Heroes Bonuses From Fees in Murphy-Bradley-Schaefer Booze Cases.

The Duluth *Rip-saw*, December 11, 1920

John L. Morrison, 1916

The *Saturday Press*, October 15, 1927

The Saturday Press

Vol. 1, No. 4   Minneapolis, Minn., Oct. 15, 1927   Price 5 Cents

A Direct Challenge to Police Chief Brunskill

The Chief, in Banning This Paper from News Stands, Definitely Aligns Himself With Gangland, Violates the Law He Is Sworn to Uphold, When He Tries to Suppress This Publication. The Only Paper in the City That Dares Expose the Gang's Deadly Grip on Minneapolis. A Plain Statement of Facts and a Warning of Legal Action.

Possibly there are moments when "a soft answer turneth away wrath" but as against such short periods there are long hours when the English language becomes woefully deficient in expressive words, and I find that deficiency painfully evident right now.

On September 24th, the first issue of the Saturday Press made its appearance. It launched no attack against the police department nor against Chief of Police Frank Brunskill. Its pages prove the truth of this statement.

We (Mr. Guilford and myself) attacked a gambling syndicate that has operated brazenly in this city for more than four years. We attacked that blackmailing rag, the Twin City Reporter and the men who own and publish it. We minced no words. We knew our own gang!

When it had become a matter of common knowledge that we were to expose these, we were offered a weekly "envelope" if we would "lay off" and when we spurned this bribe we were coolly informed that we would be given a "receipt" (killed) if we persisted. But I am not going to rehash that story. I'm going to rip the seams and see what is inside the rotten garment.

We made no attempt to place that first issue on the news stands FOR WE HAD BEEN TOLD BY THE GAMBLING SYNDICATE THAT CHIEF OF POLICE BRUNSKILL WAS THE "WEAK SISTER" OF THE SYNDICATE. Think of it—the Chief of Police on whom every citizen must rely for protection of life and property, a member, by the gang's admission, of THE GAMBLING SYNDICATE! Do you wonder that we made no attempt to place the Saturday Press on the news stands of Minneapolis where they would be at the mercy of an alleged gang member?

Moe Barnett, "Big Moe," acknowledged gunman, gang leader, the man who has boasted that he intended recruiting an army of gunmen that would rival Chicago's machinegun corps, is the man who declared that Chief Brunskill was the "weak sister" of the gambling syndicate—not "Dame Rumor" but Moe Barnett.

The Saturday Press was first published on September 24 or rather dated as of that date and actually off the press on the 22nd. On Monday, September 26th, Mr. Guilford was shot down by gunmen as he drove from his home in Robbinsdale to the office in Minneapolis. Moe Barnett had threatened Guilford with a "receipt" less than one week

(Continued on page 7)

Respectfully Submitted

There seems to be an impression among gentlemen of peculiar bent that the suppression of our street sales has rendered abortive our attempt to cleanse this city of gang rule. These gents are intellectual single-trackers; twenty - two caliber, saps rattling around in a four hundred thousand city. Lest they become too hilarious, I beg to call their attention to the following letter, the original of which was mailed to the Hennepin County Grand Jury on Wednesday of this week.

Read it carefully, "me brave buckos" and see if you can discern a flutter of a white flag. We've just begun to fight!

Minneapolis, Minnesota, October 12, 1927.
To the Hennepin County Grand Jury—
Gentlemen:

Permit me to call the attention of your honorable body to the October 1st and October 8th issue of the Saturday Press in which issues both Mr. Howard A. Guilford and myself have exposed conditions that actually exist in this city or did at the time (and long prior to) of our expose.

I especially wish to call your attention to the article, written by myself, in the October 8th issue under the caption of: "A Few of the Unsolved Minneapolis Mysteries."

In that article I gave the name of one of the numerous victims of Minneapolis gangsters, Mr. Samuel Shapiro of 2615 East Franklin Avenue, and I am positive that were Mr. Shapiro given a chance to

testify before your body he would be more than glad to give you sufficient evidence upon which to base an indictment of the acknowledged gang-leader, Mose Barnett, the man who threatened Mr. Shapiro just a comparatively few days before the assault upon his person and property was made by four gunmen.

The article as published stands unchallenged by either Mose Barnett or any other gangster in the city. I have not been sued for libel nor has any such action been intimated, therefore it stands that I published the truth.

Gentlemen, gang rule of this city can and only with your approval and by your action. Mose Barnett, gangster, who boasts that he has shot one man (Roy Rogers) and escaped even arrest for that act, today walks the streets of the city a free man, a menace to lives and property.

I trust you will not consider me too presumptuous if I again suggest that you subpoena Mr. Samuel Shapiro and those of that gentlemen the opportunity, heretofore denied him, of telling his own story of HIS experience with Mose Barnett and the latter's hired thugs.

I am, sirs,
Very truly yours,
J. M. NEAR,
Editor, The Saturday Press
240 S. 4th Street
Minneapolis, Minn.

And further, I might add the edification of the "unpinched gang" that I have mailed, each week, two copies of this paper to each member of the Grand Jury. I shall continue

(Continued on page 3)

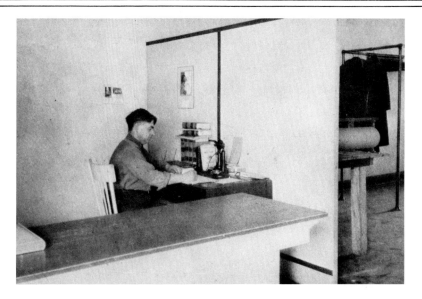

Sam Shapiro in his dry-cleaning shop on East Franklin Street

Floyd B. Olson, circa 1925

The Minneapolis *Tribune*, September 7, 1934

Robert Rutherford McCormick,
waiting to testify before a
U.S. Senate Committee, July 1930

Weymouth Kirkland,
February 1930

Associate Justices Oliver Wendell Holmes, Jr., and Louis D. Brandeis

Charles Evans Hughes leaving
the U.S. Capitol Building prior
to his appointment as Chief Justice

The Old Supreme Court Chamber in the Capitol Building

THE ADMINISTRATION OF GOVERNMENT HAS BECOME MORE COMPLEX,
THE OPPORTUNITIES FOR MALFEASANCE AND CORRUPTION HAVE MULTIPLIED.
CRIME HAS GROWN TO MOST SERIOUS PROPORTIONS.
AND THE DANGER OF ITS PROTECTION BY UNFAITHFUL OFFICIALS AND OF
THE IMPAIRMENT OF THE FUNDAMENTAL SECURITY OF LIFE AND PROPERTY
BY CRIMINAL ALLIANCES AND OFFICIAL NEGLECT,
EMPHASIZE THE PRIMARY NEED OF
A VIGILANT AND COURAGEOUS PRESS, ESPECIALLY IN GREAT CITIES.
THE FACT THAT THE LIBERTY OF THE PRESS
MAY BE ABUSED BY MISCREANT PURVEYORS OF SCANDAL
DOES NOT MAKE ANY THE LESS NECESSARY THE IMMUNITY OF THE PRESS
FROM PREVIOUS RESTRAINT IN DEALING WITH OFFICIAL MISCONDUCT.

CHARLES EVANS HUGHES
CHIEF JUSTICE UNITED STATES

A quote from the decision in *Near* v. *Minnesota*, chiseled in
marble in the Chicago Tribune Building lobby

The only photograph which exists of Jay M. Near, from
his obituary in the Minneapolis *Tribune*

himself more and more with the Holmes-Brandeis opinions, although not always. Taft came to regard Stone as "a learned lawyer . . . but his judgments I do not altogether consider safe." As for the Minnesota Public Nuisance Law, passed the same spring as Stone's appointment, no one could predict where this new Justice, who was just beginning to ponder constitutional issues, could be counted. There was nothing yet in his writings to indicate that he would view the substantive due process issue of the Fourteenth Amendment as Holmes and Brandeis did.

The ninth man, Owen J. Roberts, often referred to as the most powerful member of the Court because he was the roving, swing vote between conservatives and liberals, owed his appointment to a series of coincidences. With Sanford's seat to fill, Hoover first turned to federal District Court Judge John J. Parker of North Carolina. The Senate liberals, frustrated by their inability to stop the Hughes confirmation, blocked Parker because his record revealed that he had once upheld a "yellow dog" contract in a labor dispute in the Fourth Circuit Court, and because of a speech that was interpreted as a slur against blacks. The furor over Parker's qualifications became so heated that for the first time in the twentieth century, a Supreme Court nomination was rejected by the Senate.

Hoover then turned to Owen J. Roberts, whom the Senate approved without examining his clients, who ranged from J. P. Morgan and Company to the Pennsylvania Railroad. As a Philadelphia lawyer, Roberts' annual income was reported to be $150,000. In those days a Supreme Court Justice was paid $20,000. Overlooked was a Roberts speech in which he had castigated "big" government in the 1920s for threatening big business: "Are we to go into a state of socialism, or are you men . . . prepared to go out, take off your coats and root for good old-fashioned Anglo-Saxon individualism?" What impressed the Senate and the press about Roberts was his determined prosecution of the Teapot Dome oil scandals which sent several members of the Harding Administration to prison. Roberts' views on the First Amendment were not known, but he considered that the Fourteenth Amendment had worked revolutionary changes on the U.S. Constitution—greater, he believed, than those embodied in any other amendment before or since its ratification. The equal protection clause, Roberts observed frequently, imposes an additional restriction "on the pristine powers of the states." To those who had known him in Pennsylvania, he was classified as conservative, but not in the style of McReynolds and Butler. Some critics assailed him as a moderate Republican for leaning slightly to the right when America was turning to progressivism.

Never attaining the degree of greatness on the Court that his University of Pennsylvania admirers had prophesied, Roberts was not considered a scholar of the law. Respected as a methodical craftsman, he wrote opinions that proved to be neither innovative nor sparked with new philosophical insights. "I have no illusions about my judicial career," he wrote when he stepped down from the bench after fifteen years. "Who am I to revile the good God that He did not make me a Marshall, a Bradley, a Taney, a Holmes, a Brandeis or a Cardozo?" Those using the *Adkins* v. *Children's Hospital* yardstick to speculate on how Roberts' views of the Fourteenth Amendment would affect his vote on *Near* would be frustrated even if they could have been clairvoyant about the new Justice's future votes on substantive due process, for in successive cases, less than a year apart, Roberts voted, in effect, to uphold the principles of the Adkins case—only to vote to reverse *Adkins* the following year. The latter decision came down during President Franklin Roosevelt's attempt to enlarge and pack the Supreme Court. Roberts was accused, perhaps unfairly, of switching his vote in order to take political pressure off the Court. Roberts' detractors dubbed it "a switch in time to save nine." Roberts' record indicates that he was almost always pivotal in close votes. Hughes and Stone were occasionally on the dissenting side, Roberts almost never, which is another way of saying that in narrow decisions his vote was the one that made the difference for the majority.

Of course, when *Near* began in 1927, no one could have known that Hughes and Roberts would be on the Court when it was argued. One thing seemed certain. If Taft was still Chief Justice and Sanford was still sitting, there would have been at least five votes, perhaps even six, for the Minnesota law.

There exists a brutal critique of the make-up of the Court that was to decide *Near,* spoken contemporaneously by one of its members. In one of his confidential conversations with Professor Felix Frankfurter of Harvard Law School, Brandeis assayed the various Justices, whose average age was sixty-eight. As he often did, Frankfurter then dictated a memorandum of Brandeis' comments on his brethren:

Memorandum—May 30, 1930

If Holmes and a few of us live a little while, the Court ought to come out of the trough of recent years. Hughes is mundane but intelligent and the recent events in the Senate and their aftermath ought to have considerable influence. As a matter of fact the tail feathers of Butler and some of them have been completely plucked. The truth is that Taft for some time had really lost his grip and V.D. and Pierce Butler and McReynolds were running him. In addition to his being with them in their desires, they were with him in some of his own independent foolishness.

Hughes has real energy and intelligence. In the conferences, time is not much wasted. Hughes doesn't read long statements, as did Taft, in regard to certioraris. And certioraris on Federal Employers' Liability have stopped. Time isn't wasted in needlessly stating matters and he uses good judgment in selecting writers for opinions. For instance, Butler when a Corporation is to be curbed and himself taking the Texas and New Orleans Case. It is quite amusing to see how Butler has been soft-pedalled.

Hughes' opinions are like his old opinions on the Court —he has no imagination but he is a good artisan. Of course he has a strong feeling for the reputation of the Court and hasn't been wanting to upset recent decisions of the Court like the Farmers Loan and Trust Co. v. Minnesota, as to the taxing power of the state, because he does not want the Court to appear to be a see-saw. But if Roberts is what we expect him to be, I think we may gradually see a decidedly different temper on the Court.

Stone feels very happy—he feels vindicated by all that has happened and he likes the joy of combat. He really does not know how to work, though he likes to be working.

Oral arguments on *Near* were scheduled for Friday, January 30, 1931. Holmes would be ninety years old that same winter. "I shall not resign or retire," he would answer when asked by the press, "until the Almighty Himself requests it." In fact, however, *Near* v. *Minnesota* was argued and decided during Holmes's last full year on the Court. Publisher McCormick hoped that this would not be the occasion for another of the old man's classic dissents.

Chapter 9
Argument Day in the Supreme Court

In the autumn of 1930, Louis Brandeis' law clerk was H. Thomas Austern, who had a hard time learning to decipher the Justice's handwritten notes, which were endless, and adjusting to his work schedules, which began before dawn. Austern remembers delivering his memoranda and documents at sunrise to the Brandeis apartment. "I could see a light under the door, and as I would push a manila envelope through the crack, I could feel the tug at the other end as Justice Brandeis picked it up." On October 14 and 15, three months before the *Near* oral arguments, the traffic between Brandeis and his twenty-five-year-old clerk, just out of Harvard Law School, was heavy. The Justice wanted to see copies of the *Saturday Press* and also of the coverage that local papers had given to the alleged corruption in Minneapolis and to the gag law. Further, what about the

Nation and the *New Republic?* "1. I note that this American Newspaper Publishers Association and American Society of Newspaper Editors took action on this—look at their organs, if any—at their annual reports and let me see them. 2. Also watch the Law Reviews as they appear from time to time." Austern's notes to Brandeis apologize for "unfamiliarity with your handwriting which caused me to misread some of the directions." He noted that Minneapolis papers of May 22 and 25, 1928, reported the "ousting of Police Chief Brunskill, the official attacked in the suppressed paper," and that indices to the *Nation* and the *New Republic* revealed "no discussions" of the case. Nine pages of Brandeis notes indicate that he had saturated himself with all the available documents and especially the content of the issues of the *Saturday Press.* Damned and beloved for being not just a judge but also a crusader and an investigator, Brandeis would be prepared when the new Chief Justice called *Near* v. *Minnesota* to order.

As the Chief Justice entered the semicircular chamber adjacent to the great rotunda in the Capitol Building, he smiled at his wife, Antoinette Carter Hughes, who was often there when argument day gave promise of being historical or lively. At the stroke of noon on this Friday, January 30, 1931, the old marble clock above the golden eagle summoned the nine Justices in their rustling silk robes. It was the same eagle beneath which Daniel Webster, John C. Calhoun and Henry Clay had dueled in their classic debates, culminating in the Compromise of 1850. But the U.S. Senate, which by 1930 had grown to ninety-six members, moved in 1859 from this mahogany jewel to its more spacious chamber in the new north wing of the Capitol. The focal point of the tiny room—only a few score specta-

tors could be accommodated on its pewlike benches—was
the long mahogany bench, decorated with spooled balus-
trades, from which the nine Justices ruled. Around the arc
of the semicircular chamber were the busts of men who had
served before them—John Jay, John Marshall and Roger
Taney among them. The courtroom's intimate size did not
detract from the majesty of "this unique and hallowed
spot"; its coffered ceilings, marbled Ionic columns and red
wool carpet gave it a quality that caused visitors to whisper
in hushed awe.

Near v. *Minnesota* was to be one of the last landmark cases
argued in the old Senate chamber. Pneumatic drills were
already making test borings on the vacant block across
Capitol Plaza, where the new temple of justice of bone-
white marble would soon rise. "Almost bombastically pretentious," Justice Stone was to call it. Spacious offices for
the Justices, their clerks and secretaries would be part of
the new formal order, whereas at this time, most of the
Justices worked in their homes or apartments. The Chief
Justice kept an office in the Capitol, but it was used only for
formal meetings. The one place where all the Justices'
names appeared together was in the robing room across
the hall from the courtroom; there, a brass hook indicated
where each Justice's robe was hanging until replaced by his
suit jacket just before the Court members' noon entrance.
The names, painted in gold on black plaques, were arranged according to protocol, beginning with the Chief
Justice and going down to the most junior member, who,
at this time, was Owen Roberts.

"The Honorable, the Chief Justice and the Associate
Justices of the Supreme Court," trumpeted the Court crier.
"Oyez! Oyez! Oyez!" The room settled down to respectful
and absorbing silence. "All persons having business before

the Honorable, the Supreme Court of the United States are admonished to draw near and give their attention, for the Court is now sitting." Those with the most pressing business before the Court, Jay M. Near, R. R. McCormick and the people of the state of Minnesota were not in attendance, but their attorneys were. The crier ended his ceremonial chant: "God save the United States and this Honorable Court."

Before each Justice was a blue blotter, on top of which lay a stack of records and briefs from the cases being argued; at each Justice's feet was a china cuspidor. Chief Justice Hughes, seated, looked to his left: Brandeis, Butler, Roberts; then to his right: Holmes, Sutherland, Stone. Justice Van Devanter, who usually sat at Hughes's immediate left, and Justice McReynolds, who sat between Holmes and Sutherland, were absent. As was his practice, Hughes leaned forward and said in his bass voice, "I presume Justices Van Devanter and McReynolds are vouched in," meaning that even though they would miss the oral arguments, they could participate in the decision. No one objected, and the Court proceeded. (The practice has since been changed. Those who don't hear an oral argument don't vote.)

Hughes kept a taut courtroom. As Felix Frankfurter, himself later an Associate Justice, once observed, "To see him preside was like witnessing Toscanini lead an orchestra . . . [He] radiated authority, not through any other quality than the intrinsic moral power which was his. He was master of the business. He could disembowel a brief and a record . . . Everybody was better because of Toscanini Hughes, the leader of the orchestra."

The advocates sat at the green-covered tables in front of the bench, counsel for appellant Jay M. Near on the right, the attorneys for the appellee, the State of Minnesota, on the left. In front of them were old-fashioned quill pens, provided by the Court. As was the tradition, the lawyers were dressed in striped trousers and long swallow-tailed coats. As each session began, the Chief Justice would place on the bench the gold watch his law students at Columbia had presented him a half-century earlier. Each side would be allotted an hour to argue its position. Hughes was known for his timekeeping. The moment an advocate opened his mouth he was being timed, and the Chief Justice was meticulously strict but courteous about informing counsel when his time was up. As a former law clerk recalled, "It has been reported that on one occasion he called time on a leader of the New York bar in the middle of the word 'if,' and once when the same gentlemen asked how much time remained, he replied, with beard bristling, 'Fourteen seconds.'" Any one of the Justices could interrupt an argument to ask questions. Hughes believed that questions from the bench brought out the weak points of arguments which often were also the most important points in a case. He became annoyed when a lawyer would answer a question from the bench with an "I'll-be-getting-to-that-point-in-a-moment." Hughes would then didactically rephrase the same question, not allowing the attorney to get away with his delaying tactic.

Before getting to the Near case, arguments between the United States and the Atlanta, Birmingham & Coast Railroad Company continued from the previous day, and these were concluded at 2:32 P.M.

Weymouth Kirkland, who as appellant's counsel was the first to address the Court, approached the lectern, which was placed directly in front of the Chief Justice. He bowed, arranged his notes and began, "May it please the Court," and then proceeded to summarize the arguments presented in the sixty-seven-page formal brief which had been delivered to the Court months earlier. The arguments were not much different from those presented at the two previous hearings in the Minnesota Supreme Court—that the injunction was a prior restraint violating the First and Fourteenth amendments to the Constitution—but the temple-like setting made them sound more profound.

Kirkland asserted that the Minnesota law violated the United States Constitution because freedom of the press was a fundamental right which no state could take away. Laws such as this "instituted by the Crown under George III were among the grievances against which the colonists fought in wars of revolution," argued Kirkland. The words were delivered by counsel, but the rhetoric was vintage McCormick. "The statute is unconstitutional, I contend, unless the evil sought to be remedied was of such paramount importance as to threaten the destruction of the state politically, morally, industrially or economically. History is evidence that it is better to suffer from such an evil than from the manifold evils which arise when the press is fettered."

Kirkland admitted that the articles published were defamatory, but added, "So long as men do evil, so long will newspapers publish defamation. Boss Tweed would have invoked such a law as this against the newspapers that exposed the corruption of his regime . . . with [Judges] Barnard and McCune on the bench, they could have suppressed the exposures of the New York *Times* had this statute been in force." (Kirkland was using as an illustration the New York City scandals of the infamous William M. "Boss" Tweed, whose Tammany Ring in 1871 had bilked New York City of millions and millions of dollars. The New

York *Times,* then fighting for its own survival and ridiculed by the powerful New York *Sun* and the *World,* resisted all kinds of pressure from "Boss" Tweed, who offered to buy out the *Times* for $5 million. Two of Tweed's cronies—Judges George A. Barnard and John H. McCune—were impeached and removed when the exposés of the *Times,* along with Tom Nast's devastating political cartoons in *Harper's Weekly,* sent Tweed to prison.)

"It is argued that legitimate newspapers need not fear this statute," Kirkland continued. "On the contrary, every legitimate newspaper in the country regularly and customarily publishes defamation, as it has a right to in criticizing government agencies."

But Kirkland's arguments went even further. First citing Blackstone's doctrine against prior restraint, he contended that "Every person does have a constitutional right to publish malicious, scandalous and defamatory matter, though untrue and with bad motives, and for unjustifiable ends." Kirkland added that such a person might be subject to punishment *afterwards,* and he had touched on the central issue of the conflict: Was the injunction a prior restraint against future publication or was it merely a punishment for publishing malicious, scandalous and defamatory stories?

Fifty-four minutes later Kirkland ended his presentation by reminding the Court that his client Near had been deprived of his First Amendment rights without even "the right of a trial by jury" and an opportunity to defend his actions.

"So long as men do evil . . ." The words stuck in Justice Butler's craw; he felt the evil was on the other foot, and he had little sympathy for Kirkland's free-press arguments. Butler had often quoted from the *Saturday Press* and con-

stantly reminded his fellow Justices of the blackmailing record of the *Twin City Reporter*. He liked to point out that the
Saturday Press was a hate sheet which regularly published
defamatory articles and now asked if it wasn't "fanciful" to
prevent a state such as Minnesota from enforcing a decree
to prevent further publication of malicious articles. In his
questioning, Butler also made the point that a judgment
favorable to Near could make it safe for any insolvent publisher to put into effect a scheme for oppression, blackmail
or extortion.

Kirkland answered that blackmailers and extortionists
could be prosecuted but that the proper remedy for persons feeling themselves defamed was to seek indictments
and criminal trials before juries against the editors accused.
The Minnesota gag law, a remedy worse than the evil it
attempted to cure, said Kirkland, amounted to permanent
censorship of the defendant's newspaper, whereas criminal
proceedings on a specific complaint were always available
to the state.

Arguing for the State of Minnesota was Deputy State
Attorney General James E. Markham, along with William C.
Larson and Arthur I. Markve, representing the Hennepin
County prosecutor's office, which had brought the original
injunction against the *Saturday Press* in 1927. Markve
remembers that Markham did most of the talking; in fact,
Markve spoke for only two minutes.

Markham began his arguments at 3:26 P.M. by contending that the law was constitutional and that the injunction
was not a prior restraint. Defending the Public Nuisance
Law as well within the police powers of the state, Markham
drew a few raised eyebrows from the bench when he submitted that it was the responsibility of the state supreme
court to interpret the provisions of the state constitution.

The implication was, of course, that the federal Constitution had not been violated. Markham insisted that the Minnesota law that enjoined Near and Guilford did not violate the guarantees of the Constitution "because it provided for due process of law as commanded by the Fourteenth Amendment."

Chief Justice Hughes interrupted Markham, "You need not argue further whether or not freedom of the press was a privilege or immunity under the Fourteenth Amendment." The Chief Justice made it clear that in his mind "prior decisions of the court so held it." He was referring to Justice Sanford's majority opinion in the Gitlow case, which held: ". . . we may and do assume that freedom of speech and of the press . . . are among the fundamental personal rights and 'liberties' protected . . . from impairment by the States." Hughes then asked that Mr. Markham address himself to the basic question raised by Near's attorney that the Minnesota Public Nuisance Law "was an unconstitutional prior restraint so as to be a deprivation of liberty without due process."

Markham denied that the Minnesota action against Near amounted to a previous restraint* or censorship. He pointed out that no injunction had been issued until after the *Saturday Press* had defamed public officials and become a nuisance. Markham said the injunction was a punishment for an earlier wrong, that the Constitution "was intended to protect the liberties of the individual, and was not intended to apply to the commission of a wrong." He told the Justices that the law was beneficial to newspapers because it would "have the effect of purifying the press."

---

*In 1931, as in Blackstone's day, the term "previous restraint" was used for what is now commonly referred to as "prior restraint."

But again Markham was interrupted. When Justice Brandeis began to speak, his quiet authority created an expectancy which commanded the attention of everyone in the courtroom. Now the first and—at that time—only Jew on the Court was about to deliver his homily. The Justice directed his hard questions not to Near's attorney, who was defending a newspaper which had attacked "the entire Jewish race," but to the lawyer for the State of Minnesota.

"Mr. Markham," the gentle catechism from Brandeis began, "in these articles, [in the *Saturday Press*] the editors state that they seek to expose combinations between criminals and public officials in conducting and profiting from gambling halls. They name the chief of police and other officials." Brandeis glanced alternately at his notes and Markham. "They [Near and Guilford] state that they have been threatened with being, to use their own words, 'bumped off.' They state that shortly after commencing publication, Guilford was set upon by thugs and shot in the abdomen.

"We do not know whether these allegations are true or false," Brandeis went on, "but we do know that just such criminal combinations exist to the shame of some of our cities. What these men did seems like an effort to expose such a combination. Now, is that not a privileged communication if there ever was one? How else can a community secure protection from that sort of thing if people are not allowed to engage in free discussion of such matters?"

Brandeis' voice did not seem to increase by a decibel but his level of intensity rose with his lesson. "Of course, there was defamation; you cannot disclose evil without naming the doers of evil. It is difficult to see how one can have a free press and the protection it affords in the democratic community without the privilege this act seems to limit.

You are dealing here not with a sort of a scandal too often appearing in the press, and which ought not to appear to the interest of anyone, but with a matter of prime interest to every American citizen. What sort of matter could be more privileged?"

"Assuming it to be true," Markham countered. He hoped that Brandeis and his fellow Justices would not accept everything in the *Saturday Press* as gospel.

"No!" Brandeis snapped back, meaning that even if it wasn't true, a malicious and scandalous statement could not be restrained before publication. "A newspaper cannot always wait until it gets the judgment of a court. These men set out on a campaign to rid the city of certain evils."

"So they say," Markham interposed again.

"Yes, of course, so they say," Brandeis echoed, sounding more like an editor than the Boston lawyer who thirty-seven years earlier had lectured the press on privacy. Near and Guilford, he continued, "went forward with a definite program, and certainly they acted with great courage. They invited suit for criminal libel if what they said was not true. Now, if that campaign was not privileged, if that is not one of the things for which the press chiefly exists, then for what does it exist?"

In the dramatic pause that followed, Markham could find no words. Brandeis was being patient, for he understood Minnesota's position even though he found it unacceptable. "As for such defamatory matter being issued regularly or customarily, how can such a campaign be conducted except by persistence and continued iteration?"

Rattled by Brandeis' line of questioning, Markham turned in desperation to Justice Holmes, and reminded him that twenty-four years earlier in one of the Supreme Court's first press cases, *Patterson* v. *Colorado*, he had written the majority opinion. Holmes had stressed that First Amendment protections were intended to prevent "all such *previous restraints* upon publications as had been practiced by other governments," but not, as Markham reminded him, "against subsequent punishment of such as may be deemed contrary to protect the public welfare." Holmes had written: "The preliminary freedom extends as well to the false as to the true; the subsequent punishment may extend as well to the true as to the false." Markham was suggesting that the Holmes decision in the 1907 Colorado judgment was precedent for permitting the Minnesota statute to stand.

Remembering how he had differed with Justice Harlan's lonely dissent, which favored the newspaper, Holmes now permitted a faint smile to appear below his bristling cavalry mustache. "I was much younger when I wrote that opinion than I am now, Mr. Markham. If I did make such a holding, I now have a different view."

Markham now knew that his impromptu maneuver had cost him Holmes's vote—if, in fact, he had ever had it. Brandeis' questions left little doubt as to how he would vote. Chief Justice Hughes made it clear that he felt the First Amendment had been incorporated by the Fourteenth, but had given no indication as to whether he considered the Minnesota law a prior restraint or simply a punishment for past abuses against the public welfare, as the Minnesota courts had held.

There was, in fact, one clue as to how the new Chief Justice might decide, but only a clerk and Brandeis were privileged to see what he had scratched on a piece of note paper during the arguments: *"Adkins* v. *Children's Hospital."*

Butler had said very little during the oral arguments but

there was no doubt how he would vote, and he would probably carry McReynolds, Van Devanter and Sutherland with him. The two Justices at the extreme ends of the bench, Stone and Roberts, revealed nothing of where they stood. So even if Hughes were to join Brandeis and Holmes in supporting Near's position, there were already four votes against such a finding. If Near and his defenders lost either Stone or Roberts, the Minnesota gag law would prevail. Once again, history would turn on a single vote.

Jay M. Near had neither the curiosity nor the money to take the train from Minneapolis to Washington to hear his case argued before the Court. That month he was in a rage at the "shenanigans" of the Minnesota State Legislature. In a strange switch of strategy George Lommen, the architect of the Minnesota gag law who was now a state senator, and Governor Floyd B. Olson, who had once proudly applied its injunctive power against the *Saturday Press,* suddenly moved for its repeal. "I have been gagged for forty months [and] . . . I have some slight right to protest against any attempt to repeal that law," Near fumed. Though he wanted the Minnesota law judged unconstitutional, perversely he wished to punish the legitimate newspapers of Minnesota with the law they had inflicted on themselves "to get me." He wrote to Lommen: "I prefer to remain under the gag law's stern restraint (in the event it is held constitutional by the highest court) rather than witness other members of the fourth estate escape its malignant tools in the next political campaign."

Colonel McCormick, who knew the vote in the Supreme Court would be close, wished no victory by default, and from Chicago he hurled his invective at Olson for being a coward, ready to throw in the towel before the knockout.

McCormick felt that the law had to be tested by the Supreme Court.

Forgetting the fervor with which he had brought the injunction against the yellow press in 1927, Governor Olson claimed that as a prosecutor he could not be concerned with the "wisdom or lack of wisdom" of the suppression law, but that now, as governor, he believed that "the possibilities for abuse" make it an unwise law and that "the freedom of speech and the press should remain inviolate and any law which constitutes an entering wedge into that inviolability is unsafe." Lommen, who begged the Minnesota senators and representatives to repeal the statute that he had conceived, echoed Olson, declaring that with the demise of the *Saturday Press,* his "so-called gag law . . . has served its purpose . . . [and] can be repealed at the next session of the legislature." Senator Lommen admitted that the law had been inspired, "drawn by the very finest lawyers in Minnesota who were hired by the daily press of this state." It was ridiculous, he said, "for such organs as the Chicago *Tribune* and the St. Paul *Pioneer Press* to fear that this law could ever be invoked against any publication other than the vilest purveyor of obscenity."

But the Minnesota lawmakers and many of the newspapers which had drafted the original bill did not want their law mooted before it was tested. Five days after the oral arguments in Washington, the Minnesota House of Representatives decided to repeal the Public Nuisance Law by a vote of 68 to 58. But Lommen's own colleagues in the state senate denied him his wish for repeal. The senator's motion was caught in a log jam that required a two-thirds vote to rescue the bill and it failed by eight votes when twenty-three senators opposed repeal of the law. H. L. Morin, the senator from Duluth, who still shuddered at the memory of

John L. Morrison and the *Rip-saw,* as well as the *Saturday Press,* led the fight to retain the gag law. He told the senate: "The newspapers have a dirty mess at their door, and it's up to them to help clean it up. If this law is repealed, the racketeers who operate the scandal sheets will start up again."

All remedies in Minnesota having been exhausted despite Olson and Lommen's second thoughts, the gag law still stood. Now it was up to the Supreme Court to decide not only whether such a suppression was constitutional in Minnesota but whether such policing of the press was constitutional in forty-seven other states.

Chapter 10
The Barest of Margins

"THE country's business at Washington is conducted in an odor of dead and dying cigars suspended in steam heat," wrote Walter Lippmann. In 1931 the hardest work of the Supreme Court was conducted in a hot, stale room on the ground level of the Capitol, one floor below the Court's chamber, with a view of the Washington Monument. Every Saturday at noon the nine Justices assembled at a stubby mahogany conference table presided over by Hughes. The Chief sat at one end of the table surrounded by stacks of law books and legal briefs, each stuffed with notes and page markers. To his left on one side were Holmes, Stone, Sutherland and Brandeis; to his right were Butler, Roberts, McReynolds and Van Devanter. Unlike the seating arrangement in the courtroom upstairs, the Justices did not sit according to seniority. This was because the late

Associate Justice Rufus W. Peckhan had objected to changing his seat every time one of his brethren retired or died; thereafter a new member would simply take the seat of his predecessor.

Closeted behind two double doors, with the windows bolted to prevent a recurrence of a few recent leaks that had scandalized the Court, the Justices would conduct the vital business of listening to and debating one another's views on cases, and then voting. Robeless and often without jackets in the stuffy room, the Justices argued often without the dignity of the courtroom as majority and dissenting views were hammered out.

It was up to the Chief Justice to set the agenda, and if he was voting with the majority, assign the writing of opinions. When the Chief Justice dissented, the most senior Justice voting with the majority would assign the opinion. It is a "special opportunity for leadership," as Hughes described the chief justiceship after having viewed Saturday conferences as an Associate Justice earlier in the century. "He is the most important judicial officer in the world," Hughes wrote. "The Chief Justice, as the head of the court, has an outstanding position, but in a small body of able men with equal authority in the making of decisions, it is evident that his actual influence will depend upon the strength of his character and the demonstration of his ability in the intimate relations of the judges." Hughes's leadership permeated all parts of the judicial process, from the courtroom to the conference room, but it was the assignment of opinions that he regarded as one of his most serious duties. He tried to use this role to ease pressures both within the Court and within the nation. A former law clerk, Edwin McElwain, wrote of Hughes's leadership: "In making assignments his first consideration naturally was to balance the work load amongst the Justices, to assign each his fair share of important cases, and generally to make the best possible disposition of the legal forces at hand. He considered the previous opinions of each Justice and quite often assigned a single line of cases to a single Justice, but that was by no means his invariable practice . . . Of particular interest was the way he would assign 'liberal' opinions to 'conservative' judges, and vice versa."

As was the practice, on that last Friday in January 1931 Hughes gave his eight associates a list of cases to be discussed the next day. It had been only a few hours since *Near* had been argued; it would require four months of circulating drafts and redrafts to iron out the intricacies and subtleties of the opinions.

It was the beginning of the Hughes Court, still divided, but with some of the testy characteristics of the Taft Court now muted by the imperious, no-nonsense dignity of the new Chief. As usual, McReynolds ignored Brandeis before the beginning of the conference when each Justice shook hands with all the others (a custom that still prevails). Yet Hughes's impeccable gentility left no room for further bad manners, and imposed at least an air of civility and decorum.

Of course, there exists no record of the conference on *Near* v. *Minnesota,* or in any other case. The deliberations of the Supreme Court were, and remain, the only process in all government protected by a cloak of perpetual secrecy, contributing to its own mystique. In 1931 each Justice carried a thick leather-bound docket book to conference. The name of each case was inscribed as a heading in the book, and the Justice would keep notes and record the votes taken in conference. Like diaries, the docket books were locked after each conference, and at the conclusion of each

term, the Justices destroyed most notes. Clerks (they were
called secretaries then) were never permitted inside the
conference room. By tradition, the most recently appointed Justice served as doorkeeper if additional reference books were required.

It is impossible to reconstruct a debate that was known
only to nine men, the last of whom died in 1955. Yet it is
possible to capture some of the tone and substance of what
happened behind those double doors. The Hughes Court,
driven by a Chief obsessed with time, became a creature of
habit and tradition. The names of the cases changed, but
the ritual did not. Letters from some of the Justices, conversations with their families, former clerks and especially the
final drafts of the opinions, provide important clues for
describing and analyzing some of the debate which probably occurred that Saturday afternoon.

At the stroke of noon, the Chief Justice sat down to begin
the conference. As usual, there were many items on the
afternoon's agenda. The regular workload was to discuss
about thirty cases, twenty of which were petitions for certiorari,* and the rest argued cases. That winter day they
would be discussing issues as diverse as double jeopardy in
a tax case and patents for the "false rabbit" at a dog track.

The petitions for certiorari came first. Hughes began the
discussion of each item by giving a brief summary of the
case. In this way he was able to attach a relative importance
to it, and determine how much time would be spent discussing it. He did not like to spend more than three and a
half minutes on each certiorari question. He remembered
the court under Chief Justice Edward D. White, when fail-

---

*A petition for certiorari is a request that the Supreme Court review a decision
of a lower court. The Justices have discretion to accept or reject the petition.

ure to budget precious time often led to neglect of important constitutional issues. That Saturday he raced through the petitions asking the Court to consider such cases as disputes between New York and New Jersey over water from the Delaware and interest claims on taxes; it was a tediously long list. In addition, the fourteen cases which had been argued the previous week had to be discussed and voted on.

Hughes was especially anxious to get through the petitions because one case in particular interested him. He would later speak of his role in the case as a high point in his career. He was acutely aware that the eyes of many state legislatures would be watching the Court's resolution on the constitutionality of the Minnesota gag law to determine whether such a curb on press abuses should be enacted in their own states.

Hughes opened the discussion on *Near;* he was always first to give his views, followed by each Associate Justice in order of seniority. Reaffirming his position during oral arguments, he made it clear how he felt about the jurisdictional question: there was no doubt that the liberty of the press was within the liberty safeguarded by the due process clause of the Fourteenth Amendment. To emphasize his position, he doubtless cited Justice Sanford's opinion in *Gitlow.*

After the sermon delivered in Court, there was little doubt among the judges about Brandeis' position. He believed that the founding principle of freedom of the press was to prohibit all previous restraints. This meant, he argued in conference, that every man has a right to publish what he wishes, and if it be defamatory or libelous, suffer the consequences later. Supported by Holmes, Brandeis emphasized that Near and Guilford were not simply writing scandalous stories in a frivolous yellow sheet, but rather were charging public officials with wrongdoing. "What else could be more privileged?" he had asked.

The Public Nuisance Law, Brandeis and Holmes argued, was not a punishment for printing malicious, defamatory and scandalous matter, but a suppression—and not just of the issues of the offending paper, but of any future publications by the offenders which criticized public officials. They invited suit for criminal libel if what they printed was not true.

The liberals in the *Near* debate were willing to concede that a paper might be enjoined under certain circumstances. Holmes had invented the "clear and present danger" test. Surely, they admitted, when a nation is at war there might be times when a government would need to prevent obstruction of its recruiting service or the publication of the number and location of troops. But those examples, they believed, were the exceptions; in the absence of those critical exigencies, they could not tolerate attempts to impose prior restraints on the press.

Justice Butler found such reasoning outrageous. With clippings from the *Saturday Press* to support his position, he stressed that it was undisputed that Near and Guilford had been in the business of issuing a malicious, defamatory and scandalous publication. He was frustrated to find that the liberals were unwilling to acknowledge that the *Saturday Press* was run by con men with long histories of blackmail and extortion. Pierce Butler III, now a prominent member of the Minnesota bar, remembers vividly his grandfather's sense of outrage that Hughes, Holmes and Brandeis should accord First Amendment protection to such scoundrels. With the amen of his fellow conservatives, Butler insisted that by permitting scandalmongers such as Near and Guilford to destroy the reputation, peace of mind, and even personal safety of other citizens, society not only was encouraging malice and revenge, but could inflict distressing punishments upon the weak, timid and innocent.

To buttress his case against the *Saturday Press* and his defense of the Public Nuisance Law, Butler recalled a shocking incident that had occurred during his six-year tenure as a prosecutor in a Minnesota County attorney's office. It had been his painful duty to prosecute a murderer who had been the victim of a blackmail plot. In desperation, the accused had resorted to killing the extortionist. Now Butler argued that the existence of scandalmongering publications such as the *Saturday Press* led to just such unfortunate situations, and he reminded his brethren, as he later did his grandson, that Guilford had also been the target of a shooting, and had nearly died.

The conservatives' warning was that society could not long endure under such threats of character assassination and blackmail, and that if the courts did not protect them, injured parties would then be obliged to resort to private vengeance to protect their reputation.

Interpreting Blackstone in his own way, Butler maintained that the Public Nuisance Law was not suppression, but punishment for an injustice already committed. He insisted that the law was within what was a necessary police power of the state. This sort of leeway was needed by legislatures, he added, in order to experiment and to control the vicious elements within a frontier society. In short, in this case he felt that the "liberty" guaranteed by the Fourteenth Amendment did not include the right to publish whatever one wished, especially if it was published with bad motives and was scandalous and defamatory.

After each Justice had had his chance to speak, Hughes

called for the vote. Reversing the order of comment, the most junior member voted first, the Chief Justice last. And so, late that Saturday afternoon, the roll call was taken on the fate of the nation's press and reading public. Was the Minnesota statute constitutional? Roberts: No. Stone: No. Butler: Yes. Sutherland: Yes. Brandeis: No. McReynolds: Yes. Van Devanter: Yes. Holmes: No. It was up to the Chief Justice to cast the deciding vote. Hughes: No. By the barest of margins, five to four, previous restraints were declared to be unconstitutional.

No one was more acutely aware of how precarious the issue had been than the Chief Justice himself. At about five-thirty, after the other Justices left for home, Hughes sat down with his law clerk and began working out the assignment of opinions. He realized that the opinion in *Near* v. *Minnesota* would have to include the absolutist views of Brandeis and the far-from-absolute ones of Roberts. It would have to be a temperate opinion that would carry judicial weight; next to *Near* he wrote the name "Hughes."

Hughes approached his own opinions with "meticulous care, turning out innumerable drafts in order to be certain of the most correct and precise language . . . It was the Chief's purpose to secure as great a degree of unanimity as possible without compromising the integrity of a majority opinion." By May of 1931, drafts of both the majority and minority views in *Near* were being circulated among the Justices.

Brandeis was probably dismayed that Hughes had cited three major substantive due process cases with approval in a draft of his opinion. To Brandeis and other members of the *Near* majority, *Adkins* v. *Children's Hospital* was not simply a close call that had come out the wrong way: it was anathema. As he struck a blow for personal liberties in *Near,*

Hughes was legitimizing those instances of misguided judicial energy which exalted property over civil rights. Brandeis brought this concern to the Chief's attention. Hughes hastened to reply. "I cited the Tyson, Ribnik, and Adkins cases to expose the inconsistency of the dissenters," he wrote to Brandeis in an unusual explanatory note.

This was not simply a matter of satisfying Brandeis' doubts: Hughes wanted to signal to Brandeis that he, too, rejected the philosophy of substantive due process and was not above deriving a bit of pleasure out of using the four conservatives' own logic against them. On the logical and principled face of the *Near* opinion, the three cases are cited for the proposition that legislatures cannot alter liberties which the founding fathers carefully identified in the Constitution. As a document of Court politics, however, the letter reveals Charles Evans Hughes in the process of finding his alignment with the Court's progressive wing on the substantive due process question.

"I understand that they will insist that the only question is whether the State regulation was 'reasonable,' and I am pointing out the decisions in which they have held that, as to contract, there are certain indispensable requirements of the liberty guaranteed. So here," Hughes added, "the liberty of the press, by its history and connotation, must be deemed to have certain essential attributes."

Hughes's memo demonstrates the tension that existed over the limits and definitions of "liberty" as guaranteed by the Fourteenth Amendment. In *Near,* the battle lines had been crossed with each faction taking new and unsure ground.

It must have been excruciating for Colonel McCormick, not a patient man, to know that the case had been argued and voted on, and that drafts of the opinions were being passed around among the Justices, and not know the outcome. Each Monday afternoon as the Court handed down a few more of its year-end opinions, McCormick waited for word from Washington. But by May the Court was sending somewhat conflicting signals about its position on the First Amendment. On the eighteenth of that month, *Stromberg* v. *California* was handed down. Yetta Stromberg, the supervisor of a summer camp in the San Bernardino Mountains, had been prosecuted under a California statute which made it a felony to display a red flag in any public assembly "(a) 'as a sign, symbol or emblem of opposition to organized government' or (b) 'as an invitation or stimulator to anarchistic action,' or (c) 'as an aid to propaganda that is of a seditious character.' " Each morning at the camp, a reproduction of the Soviet flag had been raised as the campers saluted and recited in unison a pledge of allegiance "to the worker's red flag, and to the cause for which it stands; one aim throughout our lives, freedom for the working class." A California jury had convicted Yetta Stromberg and she was sentenced to five years' imprisonment. The verdict and sentence might have been based on any one or all three of the statutory clauses. The Court overturned the first clause of the California law and thus found it unnecessary to consider the other two, since the conviction may have rested on the first alone. Chief Justice Hughes wrote the majority opinion, which set aside Stromberg's conviction as depriving her of her "liberty" provided in the due process clause of the Fourteenth Amendment, stating: "The maintenance of the opportunity for free political discussion . . . is a fundamental principle of our constitutional system."

But if McCormick and Near were encouraged by the Stromberg decision, despite their anti-Communism, they were confused by an apparent retrenchment of the Court on the following Monday. Douglas Clyde MacIntosh, a Canadian professor and chaplain at the Yale Divinity School, had been denied naturalization because he would not swear he would take up arms for the United States in any hypothetical future war. A chaplain for the Canadian forces in France during World War I, MacIntosh had later been in charge of a YMCA hut at the front until the armistice. No act of Congress made the oath necessary or barred pacifists from citizenship. Four of the Justices believed that Reverend MacIntosh's reservations were justified under the First Amendment, since they were based on deep religious convictions. But the freshman Roberts and the four conservatives did not. And thus MacIntosh was denied citizenship, as "four of the strongest men ever to sit on the supreme bench—Hughes, Holmes, Brandeis and Stone—stood together and lost," as Hughes's biographer, Merlo S. Pusey wrote of the defeat. Thus, *Stromberg* was a ray of hope for *Near*, but *MacIntosh* was an ominous signal.

So as the days grew longer in Chicago and Minneapolis, a handful of people watched the pile of undecided cases shrink to a critical few, and waited for a bulletin from Washington.

Chapter 11

Judgment Day

When People talk of the Freedom of Writing, Speaking or
Thinking I cannot choose but laugh. No such thing ever
existed. No such thing now exists: but I hope it will exist.
But it must be hundreds of years after you and I shall write
and speak no more.

—LETTER FROM JOHN ADAMS TO
THOMAS JEFFERSON, *July 15, 1817*

J AY M. Near would have to share his final day in court with
two men who were also absent, and who would have had
little sympathy for him. The small Court chamber was
packed; even the standing-room area behind the narrow
benches was overflowing with officials from the White
House, the Justice Department and the Washington bar.

As Chief Justice Hughes and the other Justices entered,
they bowed respectfully to the widows and families of the
late Chief Justice Taft and Justice Sanford. June 1, 1931,
was a special-tribute day, a memorial service by the Court
to its two brethren who had died fifteen months before.
Although the Court never gives advance notice of when
decisions will be handed down, there was little doubt that
Near v. *Minnesota* would be announced that afternoon, the
last day of the 1930 term, which ran from October to June.

Only rarely were argued cases held over until the next term in the fall.

As Attorney General William D. Mitchell and the Chief Justice paid homage to Taft and Sanford, both mentioned Justice Sanford's majority opinion in the Gitlow case, which upheld, in clear terms, "the power of the State as affecting freedom of speech, upholding the necessary authority to punish abuses of that freedom." Hughes also mentioned another opinion of Sanford's which, he said, sustained "the constitutional limitations which safeguard the liberty of the citizen." Had Sanford and Taft lived and been on the bench that day instead of their successors, Hughes and Roberts, the case dealing with those same liberties might have been decided differently. Perhaps Hughes sensed this twist of fate as he concluded the memorial service to his predecessor and friend, Taft: "The figures of today, like those of yesterday, will soon be replaced, and the best endeavors, striking as they may be in their immediate aspect, will soon form but the backdrop of another picture. Without illusion, and with steady will, we continue in our task, heartened by the exemplars of our faith, among whom no one has a more inspiring or abiding influence than that of the late Chief Justice."

The memorial ceremony concluded, Hughes put aside his eulogies and reached for the six opinions and various orders of the Court. He nodded to Justice Brandeis, who read the first two opinions, then to Justice Van Devanter, who read the next three. Opinions were delivered like sermons from the bench. As one clerk remembered it, Hughes saw the practice as an opportunity "to make a public demonstration of the dignity and responsibility of the Court to the bar and to the thousands of visitors" who come to see federal justice at work. Hughes virtually invented the ritual of summarizing opinions and delivering them forcefully, like a stump orator, rather than reading every word in a monotone.

However, straying slightly from his own tradition, Hughes would read the *Near* opinion word for word from beginning to end. On this day of high tributes and landmark decisions, there was a special need for the Court to demonstrate its power and dignity. Hughes's voice had a rich stentorian timbre as he began the sixth and last opinion of the day and of the term: "In the case of *Near* v. *Minnesota* . . . Chapter 285 of the Session Laws of Minnesota for the year 1925 provides for the abatement, as a public nuisance, of a 'malicious, scandalous and defamatory newspaper, magazine or other periodical.' "

After reading the fifteen paragraphs summarizing the facts, Hughes raised his voice and eyes as he recited his opinion, which he appeared to have almost memorized. "It is no longer open to doubt that the liberty of the press and of speech is within the liberty safeguarded by the due process clause of the 14th Amendment from invasion by state action." Until this point, spectators might not have detected any signals of what the judgment was to be, but now it was clear. Hughes's voice echoed across the chamber as he summed up his view of the law:

> If we cut through mere details of procedure, the operation and effect of the statute in substance is that public authorities may bring the owner or publisher of a newspaper or periodical before a judge upon a charge of conducting a business of publishing scandalous and defamatory matter—in particular that the matter consists of charges against public officers of official dereliction—and unless the owner or publisher is able and disposed to bring competent evidence to satisfy the judge that the charges are true and

are published with good motives and for justifiable ends, his newspaper or periodical is suppressed and further publication is made punishable as a contempt. This is the essence of censorship.

"Chief Justice Hughes threw all his ardor" into his delivery, the Chicago *Tribune* correspondent Arthur Sears Henning wrote. "In a loud voice into which he injected considerable feeling at times, the head of the judicial branch of government, who in a long public career has been subjected to a vast amount of bitter denunciation in the press, argued for the liberty of the press to criticize public officials as an outstanding safeguard of the people from the imposition of tyranny."

Hughes's majority opinion had borrowed richly from Blackstone, adamantly insisting that libel laws, not suppression, were the proper solution to false accusations and defamation. Quoting James Madison, who he said was a leading spirit in the preparation of the First Amendment, the Chief Justice stated:

Some degree of abuse is inseparable from the proper use of everything, and in no instance is this more true than in that of the press. It has accordingly been decided by the practice of the states, that it is better to leave a few of its noxious branches to their luxuriant growth, than, by pruning them away, to injure the vigour of those yielding the proper fruits.

Hughes was buttressing the position that the right to criticize public officials was one of the bulwarks of the nation:

The fact that for approximately one hundred and fifty years there has been almost an entire absence of attempts to impose previous restraints upon publications relating to the malfeasance of public officers is significant of the deep-seated conviction that such restraints would violate constitutional right. Public officers, whose character and conduct remain open to debate and free discussion in the press, find their remedies for false accusations in actions under libel laws providing for redress and punishment, and not in proceedings to restrain the publication of newspapers and periodicals. The general principle that the constitutional guaranty of the liberty of the press gives immunity from previous restraints has been approved in many decisions under the provision of state constitutions.

As one reporter wrote, "The Chief Justice fairly thundered as he came to the meat of the coconut," emphasizing that the importance of the immunity had not lessened, and that the problems of abuses of the press had not increased:

> Meanwhile, the administration of government has become more complex, the opportunities for malfeasance and corruption have multiplied, crime has grown to most serious proportions, and the danger of its protection by unfaithful officials and of the impairment of the fundamental security of life and property by criminal alliances and official neglect, emphasizes the primary need of a vigilant and courageous press, especially in great cities. The fact that the liberty of the press may be abused by miscreant purveyors of scandal does not make any the less necessary the immunity of the press from previous restraint in dealing with official misconduct. Subsequent punishment for such abuses as may exist is the appropriate remedy consistent with constitutional privilege.

Yet Hughes's views were not absolute. One carefully drawn paragraph in the majority opinion, which few newspapers highlighted, acknowledged that there could be limitations. Borrowing from Holmes in *Schenck* v. *United States* to make his point, the Chief Justice wrote:

> . . . the protection even as to previous restraint is not absolutely unlimited. . . . "When a nation is at war many things that might be said in time of peace are such a hindrance to its effort that their utterance will not be endured so long as men fight and that no court could regard them as protected by any constitutional right.". . . No one would question but that a government might prevent actual obstruction to its recruiting service or the publication of the sailing dates of transports or the number and location of troops. On similar grounds, the primary requirements of decency may be enforced against obscene publications. The security of the community life may be protected against incitements to acts of violence and the overthrow by force of orderly government.

But, Hughes concluded, "These limitations are not applicable here."

The final paragraph reiterated the Court's view that the Minnesota gag law was "an infringement of the liberty of the press guaranteed by the 14th Amendment." Hughes paused and proclaimed, "Judgment reversed." Then he turned to Butler three chairs to his left, and signaled with a nod that now it was the four dissenters' turn to be heard.

The Court's guards kept the doors closed, and no reporter or spectator was allowed to leave until the minority decision was completed. The wire services (there was no television, and radio networks were not concerned with such news coverage) would have to wait. Even the Colonel back in Chicago would have no word of the result until the entire opinion had been read.

Butler's voice was vibrant and intense. He was speaking for a lost cause, which also flashed a warning signal to other state legislatures that might have been concerned with press abuses and wished to enact laws to protect victims of such abuses.

Butler was shocked by the scope of the Hughes opinion, which, he complained, "declares Minnesota and every other state powerless to restrain by injunction . . . malicious, scandalous and defamatory periodicals . . ." He denounced the Court's judgment: "It gives to freedom of the press a meaning and a scope not heretofore recognized and construes 'liberty' in the due process clause of the 14th Amendment to put upon the states a Federal restriction that is without precedent."

Butler's opinion included a lengthy footnote quoting from the November 19, 1927, edition of the *Saturday Press,* to demonstrate not only that these were "malicious, scandalous and defamatory articles concerning the principal public officers, leading newspapers . . . and the Jewish race," but also that many of the statements were "highly improbable."

As Hughes had quoted Blackstone on previous restraints, Butler and the minority relied on the theories of Joseph Story, who had been an Associate Justice from 1811 to 1845. Story defined freedom of the press guaranteed by the First Amendment to mean that *"every man shall be at liberty to publish what is true, with good motives and for justifiable ends* [Butler's emphasis]." Butler and the minority attacked the veracity and motives of Near and Guilford. Further, they contended that the Minnesota Public Nuisance Law "does not operate as a *previous* restraint on publication within the proper meaning of that phrase." To Butler, a previous restraint was "administrative control in advance such as was formerly exercised by the licencers and censors . . ." In this case the minority of four, including the two who had not heard the oral arguments, argued that there was previous publication—in fact, nine malicious, scandalous and defamatory editions. "The business and publications unquestionably constitute an abuse of the right of free press," Butler wrote. ". . . There is no question of the power of the state to denounce such transgressions." The restraint on publication, Butler continued, "is only in respect of continuing to do what has been duly adjudged to constitute a nuisance."

Though much shorter than Hughes's and virtually ignored by history, Butler's opinion did appear to strike at a vital weakness in the majority's claim that previous restraints are an infringement of essential liberties—but are not absolutely forbidden. Hughes's majority opinion had conceded that obscene publications might be enjoined, and had ignored the section of the Minnesota statutes dealing with obscene publications. However, Hughes had not agreed that a public enterprise could be suppressed *as a nuisance,* but merely that the dissemination of material found to be obscene might be enjoined. As Butler, his voice bristling with irony, phrased it: "The opinion seems to concede that . . . the business of regularly publishing and circulating an obscene periodical may be enjoined as a nuisance." If "lewd publications constitutionally may be enjoined, it is hard to understand why the one resulting from a regular business of malicious defamation may not." To his dying day, Butler could not understand why the government had censorial power against obscenity and not against malicious, false defamation.

Butler ended his dissenting opinion by denying the majority's view that existing laws could effectively eradicate the evils resulting from such publications as the *Saturday Press.* As Butler, Van Devanter, Sutherland and McReynolds put it, in the name of freedom of the press the Supreme Court of the United States "exposes the peace and good order of every community" to "malicious assaults of any insolvent publisher who may have . . . sufficient capacity to contrive and put into effect a scheme or program for oppression, blackmail or extortion.

"The judgment [of the Minnesota Supreme Court] should be affirmed" were the last words of the dissent.

Jay M. Near had lost all four previous battles, but he won the fifth and final one.

Chapter 12
The Forgotten Champion

It is a fair summary of history to say that the safeguards
of liberty have frequently been forged in controversies
involving not very nice people.

—ASSOCIATE JUSTICE FELIX FRANKFURTER,
United States v. *Rabinowitz (1950)*

J AY M. Near was gloatingly triumphant when he heard the
news, but none of the national, state or even local newspapers bothered to report his reaction; indeed, most of the
papers did not even mention his name when they spoke of
the decision, referring to it as "the gag law case." The
Minneapolis *Tribune* falsely reported that Guilford had
been the one to take the case to the Supreme Court. Near,
the unorthodox champion of the First Amendment, was all
but forgotten.

While the local papers might not have been interested in
what Near and Guilford had to say, most of them did print
the reactions of many of the other participants in the Supreme Court fight. Reached at French Lick, Indiana, where
he was attending the National Governors Conference,
Floyd Olson hailed the Supreme Court decision. Forget-

ting the forceful language with which he had launched his campaign against the yellow press, Olson acknowledged that he had, as Hennepin County prosecutor, been "obliged to enforce [the gag law] and suppress several publications, despite my opposition to it as an invasion of the rights of freedom of the press." He told the Associated Press that the Court's reversal "accomplished what the Legislature, which rejected my request for repeal of the law, failed to accomplish."

The two original drafters of the 1927 Minnesota gag law were split in their reaction. State Senator Lommen announced that he was satisfied and that the gag law "has served its original purpose in suppressing newspapers that printed news of a scandalous nature." Mike Boylan, now a former legislator, still supported the law, pointing out that only three blackmailing scandal sheets had ever been suppressed under the law. "In more than six years," said Boylan, "this law was not invoked against a decent newspaper." He added, "These newspapers with their scandal and blackmail have caused families to separate, suicides and divorces. They have made neighbors hostile to each other. Many persons are inclined to think that whatever they see in print must be true, that papers do not publish things that are untrue and the suppression law was the only means of combatting this evil."

Some newspapers quoted Colonel McCormick's statement that the "decision of Chief Justice Hughes will go down in history as one of the greatest triumphs for free thought." Subsequent editions even included reactions of senators from neighboring states; still, there was nothing about Jay M. Near.

Of the three major Minneapolis papers, only the *Star* heralded the decision with any semblance of praise. Under the heading " 'Gag Law' Too Broad," the extremely short editorial said that the law, which had been "enacted with the laudable purpose of putting 'scandal sheets' out of business," put the newspapers at the mercy of a judge. "The court's action need not signalize the return of scandal sheets to Minnesota. There are laws enough to handle the situation if they are used and enforced with nerve and determination."

The Minneapolis *Tribune*'s editorial of June 2 was more cynical. "The decision of the [S]upreme [C]ourt invalidating the Minnesota law . . . will no doubt be hailed with joy by the great majority of newspapers throughout the land. Newspapers for the most part are so sensitively jealous of their freedom of speech that they oppose to the utmost the slightest curtailment." The editorial predicted that the decision would not be as widely celebrated in Minnesota because the state was so "fertile in the production of blackmailing and scandal sheets. The suppression law put an end to them, but no doubt they will be back with us, now that the law has been declared unconstitutional." The *Tribune* also disagreed with Hughes's contention that libel laws would suffice, since, it said, most editors of such sheets lacked the capacity to pay damages. It concluded: "Certainly the *Tribune,* as a newspaper, is not at all anxious to see even the beginnings of a press censorship. At the same time it recognizes the existence of these scandalmongering blackmailing sheets which thrive and prosper under the guarantee of a free press. Thus it is that our satisfaction over the vindication by the [S]upreme [C]ourt of [the] right of the press to a free existence is diluted by the knowledge that the scandal sheets will quickly revive in Minnesota."

The next day, after studying the majority and minority texts, the *Tribune* ran another editorial underscoring the first by calling on "the bar to apply itself to the discovery of a constitutional means whereby these scandal and blackmailing sheets may be put out of existence."

The Minneapolis *Journal* (which no longer exists) regarded the gag law "knock-out" as unfortunate. Its editorial scoffed at the liberals who would hail the five-to-four vote as a great victory while denouncing one-vote majorities that didn't suit them. "Minnesota must now grope for some other remedy for an evil which she thought had been effectively scotched." Later that year at a press convention, the *Journal* called upon major American newspapers "to devise constitutional means of purging the press." It concluded: "Freedom of the press is no more important than the good name of the press."

One suggestion made by the *Journal,* and also in a Minneapolis *Tribune* editorial, was that newspapers be required to register and even post bonds so that those with grievances would know who was responsible for the alleged libel and might have some means of redress. Perhaps the *Journal* and the *Tribune* had not been paying close attention to their own legislature, which had passed such a law on April 21, 1931. It was an attempt to force the publishers of fly-by-night sheets to identify themselves. Well-established papers, those qualified to accept legal advertising, were not required to comply. "Every newspaper printed or published within the state of Minnesota, except legally qualified newspapers, shall register in the office of the register of deeds, a statement of the owners, printers and publishers of said paper, and the residences of each . . ." Failure to file would be a "gross misdemeanor."

In nearby St. Paul, the publisher of the *Pioneer Press* and the *Dispatch* said that his newspapers were pleased with the Supreme Court's decision declaring unconstitutional this "dangerous attempt to place a previous restraint upon the publication of the press."

At the Chicago *Tribune,* the tower shook with Bertie McCormick's jubilation. Not since Charlie Root pitched the Chicago Cubs to a pennant in 1929 had there been such a celebration. The Colonel immediately ordered an editorial, which not only praised the Court's decision but again castigated the entire "political, economic and social history of Minnesota . . . a long struggle for domination by powerful and ruthless private interests over law and government." McCormick often quoted a paragraph that stated: "The *Saturday Press* was not suppressed for the lies it told. It was suppressed for the true stories it printed of official perfidy." McCormick had always believed that the *Saturday Press* was gagged for forcing the dismissal of Chief of Police Brunskill, and the *Tribune*'s editorial damned the lumber and iron barons who had corrupted the Minnesota Legislature and pushed it into enacting laws to throttle the press which demagogues and grafters had used. "The Minneapolis police under the radicals was as vile if not more vile than it had been under the Big Money Rule."

On the same day, McCormick dictated a letter to the Chief Justice of the United States:

June second
1931

Dear Mr. Chief Justice Hughes:-

Never having been concerned before in a case before the Supreme Court, even indirectly, I do not know whether it is customary or is considered bad form to write to a member of the Court about its decisions. However, if I am wrong in doing so it is from lack of experience and not from disrespect.

I think your decision in the Gag Law case will forever remain one of the buttresses of free government. Heaven knows we err constantly and there are those among us who are not guiltless of deliberate misbehavior.

I will welcome well studied measures to protect citizens from the views of arbitrary newspaper men but the method proposed in Minnesota would have destroyed the only check we have upon corrupt government.

Yours very sincerely,
Robert R. McCormick

There exists no indication that the Chief Justice ever acknowledged McCormick's note, but subsequently, when the Colonel wrote again, advising Hughes that he had ordered "a key sentence in your opinion" carved in marble in the *Tribune*'s cathedral-like lobby, the Chief Justice thanked McCormick for "your courtesy." The Hughes scripture adjacent to those of John Milton, Benjamin Franklin, Thomas Jefferson and Euripides is the reference to crime and corrupt cities—affirming "the primary need of a vigilant and courageous press, especially in great cities."

Even one of McCormick's competitors, the Chicago *Times* (now merged with the *Sun*), published an editorial praising the Chicago *Tribune* for performing "a public service of high order when it carried the Minnesota case to the Supreme Court." The Chicago *Daily News* hailed the decision, regretted that it was by so close a margin, but omitted the role of its arch rival, Colonel McCormick. The New York *Times* called the decision "weighty and conclusive" and lauded McCormick, "who has placed the entire newspaper profession in his debt." But the *Times* warned that "freedom of the press, now again happily vindicated and affirmed, is not freedom to be a 'chartered libertine.'" Adolph S. Ochs's *Times* editorial asserted that each "newspaper's own conscience" could not "be violated without incurring automatic penalties graver than any which a hastily devised statute could inflict."

Editor and Publisher, the trade publication which had devoted more space to the story than any other magazine, was alarmed that four Justices had signed the Butler dissent and warned that in some future "acid test issue . . . the Butler dissenting opinion may possibly in time become the majority of the nation's high court." The role of Roger Baldwin's Civil Liberties Union was remembered only by *Editor and Publisher,* which recalled that "a little band of citizens, calling themselves the Civil Liberties Union, has fought scores and hundreds of liberty cases; and for their pains, often have been bullyragged, assaulted, framed and sneered at. Few people seemed to have understood their mission."

The New York *Herald Tribune* supported the decision and added an insightful observation: "The very fact that the exercise of liberty of the press in this momentous case came before the Supreme Court in the least favorable light adds a buttress of steel to the constitutional guaranty."

Not much changed in the Twin Cities, however.

The Supreme Court's decision may have been the law of the land, but it certainly wasn't the rule in Minneapolis. Ragtag four-sheeters kept rolling off the presses, and police chiefs continued to confiscate them. Early in 1931 Arthur Kasherman, the law student who had taken the Fifth Amendment during the grand jury probe on Chief Brunskill and who had been given a jail sentence for contempt, started the *Public Press,* a spiritual cousin to the *Saturday Press.* The first edition of the paper assailed his contempt sentences, and shortly after its appearance, intruders entered his printing plant at night, the type which was already set for the second edition was thrown on the floor, and a linotype machine was broken. A few weeks later Kasherman was hit over the head with an iron pipe only a few blocks from City Hall.

A few more editions of the *Public Press* came out without any incident, but on May 9 an issue criticizing Mayor William F. Kunze was seized by police, who warned Kasherman to stop printing. Both Kasherman and the mayor were running in the May 11 primary election; both lost. The next edition of the *Public Press* was also confiscated by the order of the police chief, who said that the paper, which contained exposés of official corruption, was scandalous. Citing the Supreme Court decision in *Near,* Kasherman asked for a court order restraining the police from confiscating his paper, but his request was denied. Kasherman was convicted of extortion in 1937 and served two and a half years in the state penitentiary.

In October of 1932 the most famous sheet of all hit the streets of Minneapolis. Bearing the caption "The Paper That Refused to Stay Gagged," the *Saturday Press,* edited by Jay M. Near, reappeared. Another slogan under the flag of the paper contained the slightly exaggerated statement "The only paper in the United States with a United States Supreme Court record of being right; the only paper that dared fight for freedom of the press—fought and won."

The character of the paper hadn't changed much, and neither had its editor. He was still broke, was still spreading scandal and was even more bitter. He had managed to eke out an existence in the intervening years by being a "poison pen for hire," resurrecting his career as a propagandist and ghost writer, this time for Ray P. Chase, a notorious, vicious anti-Semite and unsuccessful gubernatorial candidate on the Minnesota Republican ticket. Near's self-styled mission, devised by the candidate's brother, Roe, was to run a smear campaign depicting Governor Floyd Olson as the willing tool of "Jew pigs," "thugs" and "Communists." His correspondence and writings for Chase reveal Near to be an unprincipled bigot, with no aim other than to get rid of Olson and "godless communism." Eventually Near even turned on his dedicated defender Thomas Latimer, when Latimer supported Olson. Finally, after saving a little money, Near began to publish again.

The second anniversary of the *Near* decision was marked by the seizure of another paper, the *Pink Sheet,* edited and published by Howard A. Guilford. The publication, which contained an attack on Mayor William A. Anderson, was seized by Police Chief W. J. Meehan. The police chief had unsuccessfully tried to justify his actions by relying on the newspaper-registry law of 1931. However, later that day Meehan said he would allow the paper to be circulated despite the many complaints that had been lodged against it. "Sheets of this nature will not be tolerated on the streets of Minneapolis in the future," said the police chief. "The playing up of sensational criminal cases and sexual matters in heavy black-faced type before the children of Minneapolis must stop." But it didn't stop—at least not immediately.

Near was also having troubles. His paper was floundering economically. He finally took back his old partner, Guilford. Even so, it was clear that the paper wouldn't survive. By August he was fed up. Writing to Chase on August 30, Near said: "I severed my connection with the *Saturday Press* yesterday morning. For weeks, Guilford has growled and snarled about my writing these . . . articles and in the current issue, he insisted that scandal so vile it stunk should fill the paper. I made him take my name off the masthead and quit, cold. If I can't make a living without turning what little ability I have or may have to no better purpose than smearing sex filth I'll quit and dive off a bridge."

Guilford tried to keep the *Saturday Press* going, but within a year Guilford was out, and Near was back running the paper. Then, during the summer of 1934, Guilford announced that he would run for mayor of Minneapolis and would soon inaugurate a series of radio commentaries in which he would "tell the whole story of Governor Floyd Olson's connection with the Twin Cities underworld." The broadcasts never took place.

On September 6, 1934, while driving his car in the exclusive Pillsbury Avenue district, Guilford was crowded to the curb by a black sedan driven by gangsters, and an instant later a shotgun blast at close range all but blew his head off. When the police arrived they found Guilford's car radio still tuned to the Minneapolis-Milwaukee baseball game. There were no witnesses able to identify the gunmen, and subsequently, no indictments.

Near did not hesitate to state who had killed his old buddy: "Howard was undoubtedly killed by hired assassins, and I think the killers were hired by communists."

Jay M. Near died at Northwestern Hospital, Minneapolis, on April 17, 1936. He was sixty-two years of age, and his death was due to "natural causes." The brief obituary in the Minneapolis *Tribune* made no reference to the landmark case that bears his name. The Chicago *Tribune* ran a much longer story in its news section under the headline "Editor J. Near Dies in Minnesota; Foe of Governor Olson and Crime." Four paragraphs were devoted to *Near* v. *Minnesota* and the Chicago *Tribune*'s role in bringing it to the U.S. Supreme Court. The life that had caused such an uproar in the courts had ended with no more than a whimper.

Colonel McCormick and Floyd Olson continued to slug

it out even after Guilford and Near's deaths. To McCormick, the murder of Guilford and the subsequent killing of another Minnesota muckraking heckler of the Farmer-Labor Party, Walter W. Liggett, was just another chapter in Governor Olson's conspiracy with the underworld. Liggett, editor of the *Mid-West American,* had written McCormick, just after Guilford's death and just before his own assassination, predicting that the same gangster elements that got Guilford were out to get him. He was shot five times in the back as he was entering his apartment building on December 9, 1935. "We can only believe that murder was used by public authorities and the underworld," wrote an enraged McCormick, "to coerce the freedom of the press after unconstitutional law had failed." Ten years later Arthur Kasherman, publisher of the *Public Press* and a convicted extortionist, was also shot down in gangland style. Having had a premonition of his death, Kasherman had told a reporter a few days before that although he had always admitted seeing money pass between Mose Barnett and Police Chief Brunskill in 1927, he had refused to testify because he was a newspaperman. The Kasherman murder became an important issue in the 1945 Minneapolis mayoral race, which launched the career of Democrat–Farmer-Labor candidate Hubert H. Humphrey.

In his third term as governor Floyd Olson ridiculed McCormick's exaggerated charges. Olson, who was dying of cancer, chided the Colonel's posturing as a champion of freedom of the press, observing to the Minneapolis *Tribune:* "Dozens of papers have been suppressed because of economic views expressed without one word from Bertie. It is only when a scandal sheet has difficulty that Bertie comes to the rescue. That is because he is the owner of the world's leading scandal sheet."

There were those in Minnesota Farmer-Labor circles who claimed that McCormick had pumped money into the *Saturday Press* when Near attempted to re-establish it in 1932, but there is no evidence to support this allegation. To be sure, Near's fondest dream was that the notoriety resulting from the Court victory would induce the Colonel to invest in the new *Saturday Press*. There is correspondence from Near proving that he had extended such solicitations, but McCormick never bit. Also, Jay M. Near's will, which noted that evidence of ownership could be found in the law offices of Kirkland, Fleming, Green and Martin, established that sole ownership of the *Saturday Press* remained with Mrs. Near. Similarly, McCormick's charge that Governor Olson had played any role, even indirectly, in the murders of Guilford and Liggett lacks any substantiating evidence.

Olson's charismatic personality and political savvy made him presidential timber, and many of his supporters had urged him to run as a third-party candidate, with a view to clinching a vice-presidential nomination. But ill health ended this dream; Olson, now a revered legend in Minnesota history, died of cancer on August 22, 1936.

In all, three Minnesota newspapermen died by assassination. The three cases (Guilford, Liggett, Kasherman) remain unsolved, and in only one was there an indictment. Gangster, bootlegger, club boxer Kidd Cann (Isadore Blumenfeld) was indicted for first-degree murder in the Liggett case and later acquitted, even though Liggett's widow identified Cann as the man who fired the machine gun. Colonel McCormick blamed the politicians and the press of Minneapolis for not vigorously pursuing these crimes. McCormick insisted that the jurors were openly intimidated in the Liggett case and that Kidd Cann's alibi (he said he was in Garfinkle's, a downtown barbershop) was "ludicrously flawed." Despite such allegations, Kidd Cann's guilt was never established beyond a reasonable doubt. However, the mobster was later convicted of white slavery and of bribing a juror, and served time in a federal penitentiary.

In January of 1945 John Mahan, publisher of a monthly political newspaper called the *Republican Register,* was sentenced to six months in jail, having been convicted nearly a year earlier of publishing an "unregistered paper." Mahan's failure to register under the 1931 law was prosecuted because there had been complaints about his methods of soliciting advertising by giving the impression that the money was to be used by the Republican Party. Judge Arthur W. Selover offered to reduce Mahan's sentence if he disposed of his interest in the paper. Thirty days later, with no potential buyers, Mahan announced that he had gone out of business. It seems that the *Register* has been the only victim of the newspaper-registry law, which remains on the books in Minnesota.

Robert Rutherford McCormick, who eventually shed his riding britches and military attire for elegant tweeds, continued to rule the *Tribune* with irascible vigor. Reporters knew that a story marked "Special" was one which the publisher, who himself had no flair for writing, had specifically requested, and which, if they wanted to keep their jobs, should be handled in the publisher's "special" way. He ruled his newspaper kingdom from on high in the Tribune Tower, growing more aloof, and perhaps lonely, as the years passed. The story has been widely told that McCormick had such an aversion to people that he drove to work in a coupé rather than a limousine in order to avoid offering a ride to any of his neighbors.

But McCormick's aversion to human contact did not

keep him out of the center of controversy, whether it was charging Franklin D. Roosevelt and the New Deal with "creeping communism" or, later as an isolationist, declaring that Lend-Lease was a Roosevelt-Churchill plot to drag America into "an undeclared war." When a friend and former *Tribune* employee wrote the Colonel that he felt the *Tribune*'s isolationist politics were hurting the morale of the nation, McCormick replied:

> You do not know it but the fact is that I introduced the ROTC into the schools; that I introduced machine guns into the army; that I introduced mechanization; I introduced automatic rifles; I was the first ground officer to go up in the air and observe artillery fire. Now I have succeeded in making that regular practice in the army.
>
> I did get the marines out of Shanghai, but was unsuccessful in trying to get the army out of the Philippines.
>
> Campaigns such as I have carried on inevitably meet resistance and great persistence is necessary to achieve results. The opposition resorts to such tactics as charging me with hatred and so forth, but in view of the accomplishments, I can bear up under it.

When the Chicago poet Carl Sandburg read this, he quipped, "And on the seventh day he rested."

But McCormick *did* bear up under it. He thrived on the enmity of Frank Knox (his rival at the Chicago *Daily News* and President Roosevelt's wartime Secretary of the Navy), who ridiculed him in a series of devastating cartoons depicting a bumbling "Colonel McCosmic." No matter what the Colonel lacked, he had confidence that he was always right.

On April 1, 1955, McCormick died of a heart ailment and cirrhosis of the liver at the age of seventy-four. Disillusioned about the Republican Party, which his grandfather had helped found, and about an America he could no longer understand, he always looked back on his role in *Near* v. *Minnesota* as his shining hour. His friend and lawyer, Weymouth Kirkland, had died two months earlier at the age of eighty-seven. One of Kirkland's favorite recollections was about "that S.O.B. Near whose case we won."

Charles Evans Hughes served as Chief Justice until 1941, when he retired at the age of seventy-nine after leading the Court through the tests of the constitutionality of various New Deal programs and helping defeat Roosevelt's Court-packing plan. Having had the painful task of telling Justice Holmes that it was time to retire, Hughes was acutely sensitive about senility. "He felt that any Justice on the Court, especially the Chief, must be as sharp as ever," Hughes's daughter Elizabeth Gossett explained. "He was so fearful that he might be slipping that he had made a pact with Mother and us all that we would tell him if he were, even slightly. He never did." Mrs. Gossett relates that her father was suffering from a duodenal ulcer. In March of 1939, while speaking at the 150th assembly of Congress, Hughes's ulcer was bleeding. "He was pale and weak . . . we listened on the radio and we could tell there was something wrong . . . He didn't think he'd make it through, but somehow he did." Not only did he make it through the speech but he also insisted that the Justices finish their conference that Saturday afternoon, but the strain of the ordeal put him in bed for weeks. He spent the spring and summer recuperating, but the worry over senility and his weakened health helped him to make his decision to retire on July 1, 1941. He was succeeded by his junior colleague Harlan Fiske Stone.

Hughes always relished talking about his role in *Near* v.

Minnesota, referring to it as a "striking development in the jurisprudence of the Supreme Court of the United States" and in the due process clause of the Fourteenth Amendment's relation to freedom of speech and press.

Chief Justice Hughes died on August 17, 1948. Of the eight Justices who sat with him on the Near case, only Owen Roberts survived him; he died in 1955. A partner from his Philadelphia law firm who knew him well said, "Knowing Roberts and the times and the issues in *Near v. Minnesota,* I would have given a hundred-to-one odds that Roberts would have voted the other way. Well, maybe ten to one."

Iz Cohen, the eleven-year-old newsboy who hawked the *Rip-saw* on Superior Street in Duluth in 1924, has just retired from the news business. A reporter for the Duluth *News-Tribune* for thirty-five years, Cohen only recently discovered the role that the *Rip-saw* played in the Near case.

Epilogue:
From the Saturday Press to the New York Times

JUDGE MURRAY GURFEIN: What good would it do for the
public to read in the New York *Times* in 1971 what the
American Ambassador to the Soviet Union had
thought in 1968?

ALEXANDER BICKEL: I think, Your Honor, the First Amendment forecloses [you] from asking that question.

—*In camera* proceedings:
United States v. *New York Times (1971)*

A LTHOUGH his name is hardly a household word, the
ghost of Jay M. Near still stalks most U.S. courtrooms.
There exists no plaque that bears his name, and even Colonel McCormick's marble memorial to Chief Justice
Hughes's opinion omits the name of the case. Near is truly
the unknown soldier in the continuing struggle between
the powers of government and the power of the press to
publish the news.

Near v. *Minnesota* placed freedom of the press "in the
least favorable light"; as Minnesota and New York newspapers and lawyers viewed the litigation, it was the worst
possible case. But perhaps it is just because Near's cause
did not at first appear to be significant, except to Colonel
McCormick and Roger Baldwin, that it created such sturdy
law. So indestructible has it proved that its storied progeny,

the Pentagon Papers case, was able to survive the political firestorms of 1971. If "great cases like hard cases make bad law," as the Holmes proverb warns, it may follow that since few knew or cared about Near's cause, freedom of the press was transformed successfully from an eighteenth- and nineteenth-century ideal into a twentieth-century constitutional bulwark.

By his admonition, Holmes meant that volatile national confrontations which appeal to prejudices and distort judgment can be counterproductive in shaping the law of the future. Such emotional conflicts as slavery, as in the Dred Scott decision, and child-labor laws, as in *Adkins,* Holmes suggested seventy-seven years ago, "exercise a kind of hydraulic pressure which makes what previously was clear seem doubtful, and before which even well-settled principles of law will bend." In 1931 an American public plagued by economic panic, unemployment, Prohibition and the likes of Al Capone cared little about the civil rights of a scandalmonger from Minnesota. To paraphrase Holmes, Near's case embodied all the underwhelming interests required to shape the grand law of the future. His success was based not in frenzied national debate, but in quirks-of-fate delays in the Minnesota courts, the deaths of two conservative Justices, and Hoover's subsequent appointments. It was the new Chief Justice who made the difference, not simply because he added one more vote to Near's side, but because of his unexpected passion for the First Amendment and his intellectual capacity to lead others, especially Justice Roberts.

The precedent of *Near* v. *Minnesota* has withstood onslaughts from Presidents, legislatures and even the judiciary itself in its attempts to enforce basic rights which seemed to clash with the First Amendment. It demonstrated the latent strengths for an amendment which had gone untested for 150 years. That five-to-four decision achieved far more than simply asserting Near's rights. Like Yetta Stromberg's case, announced two weeks earlier in 1931, it marked the beginning of a concerted process "to plug the holes punched in the Bill of Rights," and what Mencken had called in 1926 "the most noble opportunity that the Supreme Court, in all its history, ever faced."

Another gaping hole was repaired in 1937 when the Hughes court, with Benjamin N. Cardozo having replaced Holmes, established in *De Jonge* v. *Oregon* for free speech and assembly what *Near* had established for freedom of the press. The case involved syndicalism, a Portland streetcar conductor's right to attend a Communist meeting in a public hall. Again Hughes contributed the majority opinion: "The greater the importance of safeguarding the community from incitement . . . by force and violence, the more imperative is the need to preserve inviolate the constitutional rights of free speech, free press and free assembly . . . Therein lies the security of the Republic, the very foundation of constitutional government."

There have been hundreds of other press cases before the Court since 1931—some won, some lost. Perhaps the seminal judgment was the 1964 decision in *New York Times Co.* v. *Sullivan,* which prevented Southern courts from using the law of libel to thwart national news coverage of the civil rights battle. Although not a prior-restraint case, *Sullivan* freed the press from the threat of chilling damages in reporting the conduct of public officials in Alabama in the explosive sixties. Associate Justice William Brennan's majority opinion established that officials, and later public figures, could not recover libel damages for reports concerning their official actions without proving "malice," that is, deliberate lying or "reckless disregard for the truth."

But *Near*'s ultimate legacy was finally realized forty years later, almost to the day, in the clash between the power of the presidency of the United States and two powerful newspapers, the New York *Times* and the Washington *Post.* Its official name was *New York Times Co.* v. *United States,* but it is remembered as the Pentagon Papers case. It began when the New York *Times* obtained a forty-seven-volume secret history of the Vietnam war from Daniel Ellsberg, a former analyst of the Rand Corporation; it ended with a major victory for the press in the Supreme Court. On June 13, 1971, the New York *Times* began publishing its synopsis and analysis of the secret documents, and two days later the Nixon Administration began legal efforts to restrain it. Later that week the government also sought to enjoin the Washington *Post* from publishing the same classified material. In a "frenzied train of events," as one Justice described it, the cases bobbed back and forth between district and appeals courts until, eleven days later, the Supreme Court agreed to try to untangle the conflicting and confusing opinions.

What dominated all the arguments in all briefs and opinions, from district court to Supreme Court, was the theory of no previous restraint, codified by Blackstone and incorporated by Madison, but made concrete in *Near.*

The Court met hastily on Saturday morning, June 25, and five days later announced its six-to-three decision. Leaning heavily on *Near* v. *Minnesota,* the Court held that the heavy burden of justifying the imposition of prior restraint had not been met by the government. It required nine opinions for the Supreme Court to explain its votes, and *Near* was cited ten times.

Justice William O. Douglas, in an opinion joined by Justice Hugo Black, quoted long passages from Chief Justice Hughes's majority opinion in *Near.* Believing that the government had no power to punish or restrain "material that is embarrassing to the powers-that-be," Douglas and Black reiterated Hughes's opinion: "The fact that liberty of the press may be abused . . . does not make any less necessary the immunity of the press." But it was Douglas' concluding statement that emphasized the tremendous strength of *Near:* "The stays in these cases that have been in effect for more than a week constitute a flouting of the principles of the First Amendment as interpreted in *Near* v. *Minnesota.*"

Justice Black's language, in an opinion joined by Justice Douglas, also echoed some of the discussion during oral arguments in *Near*:

> Both the history and language of the First Amendment support the view that the press must be left free to publish news, whatever the source, without censorship, injunctions or prior restraints . . . Only a free and unrestrained press can effectively expose deception in government . . . [T]he New York *Times,* the Washington *Post,* and other newspapers should be commended for serving the purpose that the Founding Fathers saw so clearly. In revealing the workings of government that led to the Vietnam War, the newspapers did precisely what the founders hoped and trusted they would do.

Even in the dissents in the Pentagon Papers case, *Near* was ubiquitous. Chief Justice Warren Burger, Justice John Harlan and Justice Harry Blackmun in their dissenting opinions also cited Hughes's exceptions to the prohibitions against prior restraint such as interfering with recruiting during wartime and publishing troopship sailing dates. As in *Near,* the Court's judgment in the Pentagon Papers case did not establish the absolutism of the First Amendment (as some journalists still contend) against *all* prior restraints. Justice Byron White wrote: "I do not say that in no circumstances would the First Amendment permit an injunction against publishing information about government plans and operations."

Although it was the judgment of the divided Court that lifted the prior restraint on the New York *Times,* the Washington *Post* and twenty other newspapers,* which were prepared to publish sections of the Pentagon Papers, five sentences by District Court Judge Murray Gurfein endure. It is the kind of quotation Colonel McCormick might have had chiseled in his hall:

> The security of the Nation is not at the ramparts alone. Security also lies in the value of our free institutions. A cantankerous press, an obstinate press, a ubiquitous press must be suffered by those in authority in order to preserve the even greater values of freedom of expression and the right of the people to know . . . These are troubled times. There is no greater safety valve for discontent and cynicism about the affairs of Government than freedom of expression in any form.

---

*The Justice Department brought injunctions against the Boston *Globe* and the St. Louis *Post-Dispatch* in addition to the actions against the New York *Times* and the Washington *Post.* Among the other newspapers that obtained and published copies of the documents leaked by Daniel Ellsberg were the *Christian Science Monitor,* the Los Angeles *Times* and the Chicago *Sun-Times.*

In an uncharacteristic response the Chicago *Tribune,* unable to obtain copies of the Pentagon Papers, editorialized against the Court's permitting some newspapers "to publish documents in the official custody of a public agency . . . until the entire record is studied by an impartial group of editors and government officials skilled in sorting out the perils that indiscriminate publication of classified documents would entail." The same newspaper which, in 1942, stunned the nation and infuriated President Roosevelt by revealing that U.S. Navy intelligence had broken the Japanese code, now cautioned in a front-page editorial that "a few more days' delay will cause no harm either to the government or the people's right to know." The editorial was headed "Sorry about this." Colonel McCormick might have shared the sentiment, but for the opposite reasons.

Gurfein said that he scribbled his opinion "in the light of *Near* with Hughes' opinion in front of me." The Chief Justice had composed his judgment in the light of Madison, who certainly had Blackstone's four-volume commentaries beside him when such concepts as "the freedom of speech and of the press" and "due process" were written into the Bill of Rights.*

Near v. *Minnesota,* that yarn stretching from the *Rip-saw* to the *Saturday Press* to a split court in Washington, reminds us of what great law emerged from those noxious scandal sheets. Or *were* those publications so "malicious, scandalous and defamatory"? Mathias Baldwin, the county judge who imposed the first gag, and Sam Shapiro, the cleaner who considered Near his only champion, might still argue about that judgment. So would Justice Pierce Butler, who was convinced that Near and Guilford were blackmailers, and McCormick, who thought all Minnesota politicians were crooks.

Brandeis would have called the question irrelevant. "These editors . . . seek to expose combinations between criminals and public officials . . . ," he said during the oral arguments. "Now if that campaign was not privileged, if that is not one of the things for which the press exists, then for what does it exist?"

Near was a perilously close case, but "a morsel of genuine history," as Jefferson described such events, "a thing so rare as to be always valuable."

On that afternoon in 1931, few could have predicted the impact that *Near* would have on the half century that fol-

---

*Even before the Declaration of Independence, 2,500 copies of Blackstone's commentaries had been sold in the Colonies, prompting Edmund Burke to observe that "a prominent bookseller . . . tells me that they have sold nearly as many of Blackstone's commentaries in America as in England."

lowed, particularly the last two decades with the civil rights struggle and the antiwar movement. No other nation on earth has a constitutional tradition against prior restraints comparable to those which sprang from Hughes's sweeping opinion.

But the Constitution is not a self-executing document. The free-press clause and the rest of the Bill of Rights could have remained a benign exhortation, "impossible . . . of literal interpretation . . . as counsels of moderation rather than as parts of our constituent law . . ."

But history, fate or whatever force it is that provides the unlikely champion, or the subtle, improbable turn of events that leaves its indelible stamp upon the course of human events, intervened. It was one such incident that ultimately empowered five Supreme Court Justices to infuse with life and spirit an amendment which for 150 years had existed only as a bare skeleton.

Victories such as *Near* often pass almost without notice, obscured by the crush of daily events until time affords them their proper stature. Yet the pendulum swings; *Near*'s landmark status will continually be reread in the context of history. Whether its significance is to be upheld or eroded is a question whose answer lies chapters ahead in American law and liberty, in our newsrooms no less than in our courtrooms.

Acknowledgments

"THE historian is like the giant of the fairy tale. He knows that wherever he catches the scent of human flesh, there his quarry lies." So Marc Bloch defined his craft. The instincts of journalists are similar, although they usually work in a different time frame. In broadcast journalism, a teacher and partner of mine always searched for the "little picture," convinced that the self-generating narrative was the most satisfactory reporting instrument. The scenario of *Near* v. *Minnesota* is traced from its obscure headwaters in northern Minnesota to its mighty terminus in that old Supreme Court chamber in Washington in the hope that it will illuminate the way this nation's Constitution writes, rewrites and revitalizes itself.

With no formal claims as either a constitutional authority or state historian, I have leaned on a battery of colleagues and friends. They range from Professor Paul Freund of Harvard Law School, who two decades ago tutored me in preparation for a television broadcast, and in so doing, first made me aware of the significance of *Near* v. *Minnesota;* to Floyd Abrams, who as a litigator for major news organizations and individual reporters never permits judges to forget what the Hughes court declared in 1931; to my son, Richard Mark, whose legal education at Columbia Law School ran concurrently with the three years it took me to write this book. Benno Schmidt, Jr., a professor of law at Columbia and teaching partner in our "Journalism and the First Amendment" course, kept me on track and off hyperbole—most of the time. All of the above read some or all of the chapters and provided insightful critiques.

If this were a broadcast documentary, its primary credits would include two associate producers, Martha Elliott and John Guthmann. Ms. Elliott, a former student, teaching assistant and television producer, who has been my associate in other writing projects, including *The Good Guys, the Bad Guys and the First Amendment,* took a leave of absence for the birth of her first child and continued her sabbatical to work on this book. Her mark is on every page. John Guthmann, suggested by Russell Fridley, director of the Minnesota Historical Society, to assist with some of the early digging in their archives, signed on for the duration. Combining a love of Minnesota history and a legal mind, Mr. Guthmann was an inexhaustible scout through musty court records and Hennepin County, Duluth and Mesabi lore.

Minnesota takes its historical societies seriously and invests generously in its county societies as well as its statewide facility in St. Paul, which is superbly administered by Russell Fridley. John Hartman's article, "The Minnesota Gag Law and the Fourteenth Amendment," which was published in *Minnesota History,* the magazine of the Historical Society, is of special value to anyone writing about this period. Professor Hyman Berman has written extensively on anti-Semitism in Minnesota during the Great Depression, and conversations with him helped to reconstruct the backdrop of life in the Twin Cities during the 1920s and 1930s.

Whether it was details of the giant Yellowstone mallet locomotives or back issues of the *Rip-saw,* the St. Louis County Historical Society is a mother lode for researchers interested in the history of the Iron Range. I am particularly indebted to Donald B. Shank, vice president, and Lawrence J. Sommer, director, of that society, who were hospitable and indispensable pathfinders during my numerous explorations of the north country.

The Interpretative Center in the Mesabi Iron Range is a living museum of the opening of that territory, and its staff was most helpful.

The archives of the Chicago *Tribune* not only are the repository of Colonel Robert R. McCormick's correspondence, in-house memos and public speeches on press freedom, but also contain communications from Jay M. Near, Weymouth Kirkland and a broad variety of newspaper publishers. I owe a special debt to Lee Major, the archivist of that collection, and to Stanton Cooke, publisher of the Chicago *Tribune* and chairman of the Tribune Company, for making the *Near* v. *Minnesota* file available. One of the people who understands the case and knew Colonel McCormick is the *Tribune*'s longtime lawyer, Don Reuben. A storied litigator and constitutional authority, he opened many doors for me, as did Clayton Kirkpatrick, president of the Chicago *Tribune,* who also walked me through the Colonel's office, a route he had traveled as a cub reporter many years earlier. One of the others who helped me understand the character of Colonel McCormick was John S. Knight, who built the Knight-Ridder newspaper organization.

Jonathan Landman, Columbia Graduate School of Journalism, 1978, and Karen Gannett, 1979, each stayed on for a year as teaching assistants and made substantial contributions to the research and reporting in the manuscript. Even after his tenure expired, Landman continued to help.

Among my other constructive second-guessers are Stuart Sucherman, James Cornell and Richard Friedman, whose thesis on Chief Justice Charles Evans Hughes deserves to be published.

I owe a special debt to the late Judge Harold Leventhal of the U.S. Court of Appeals, D.C. Circuit, who encouraged me to start work on this project and goaded me to continue when abstract theories of constitutional law threatened to overwhelm me. After Leventhal's untimely death in 1979, his colleague Chief Justice J. Skelly Wright and Judge Arlin Adams of the Third Circuit tutored me, as did Professor Herbert Wechsler of Columbia Law School. Harold Leventhal also led me to George MacKinnon, a former U.S. Attorney from Minnesota and now a judge on the D.C. Circuit Court of Appeals. His first-hand knowledge and experience in prosecuting crime in the Twin Cities provided me with a one-man storage and retrieval system on the laws and lawlessness of that period. Chief Judge Robert Sheran of the Minnesota Supreme Court spent many hours clarifying the intricacies of the state court system.

Irving Shapiro, chief executive officer of E.I. du Pont de Nemours, was an eyewitness to the violent attempts by the Minneapolis mob to extort money from his father, Samuel. His first-person knowledge of Near and the *Saturday Press* and of life during that roaring period in Minnesota history provided insights that no reference books or faded news clips could offer.

To write about *Near* v. *Minnesota,* it was essential to understand the characters of the two Justices who wrote the majority and minority opinions. I was fortunate to be able to interview Elizabeth Hughes Gossett, daughter of Chief Justice Hughes; her husband, William Gossett; and Pierce Butler III, grandson of Justice Butler, who also helped in my comprehension of Minnesota and its laws.

An author in search of such historical quarry is dependent on libraries, museums and the scholars who preserve, protect and defend them from errant writers such as me. I am particularly grateful to:

Philip Oxley, Barbara Kessler and Francis Gates, Columbia Law School Library

Wade Dores and Jonathan Beard, Columbia Journalism School Library

Susan Newman and Mary Harding, Ford Foundation Library

Roger Jacobs, Supreme Court Library

Erika Chadbourn, Harvard Law School Library, Manuscript Division

David Wigdor, Library of Congress

Gail Galloway and Suzanne Owens, Office of the Curator, The Supreme Court

Florian Thane, Office of the Architect of the Capitol

Stuart A. Beck, District Administrator, Duluth Courthouse, Sixth Judicial District

Stephen Isaacs and Laurel J. Paauwe, Minneapolis *Star & Tribune*

Jerry Friedheim, ANPA

Al Zdon, managing editor of the Hibbing *Daily Tribune*
Bodleian Library, Oxford University
the New York *Times*
the Washington *Post*

Although this endeavor was not funded by the Ford Foundation, it was nurtured there. Two presidents, McGeorge Bundy and Franklin A. Thomas, encouraged its growth.

Lorraine Belgrave, who was involved in the typing and proofing of this manuscript from scribblings on lined yellow pages to galley proofs, was an invaluable ally.

This is the third time that Joe Fox and Barbara Willson of Random House have attempted to transform an incorrigible storyteller into a careful writer. They mean much to this book and to me.

My meaningful associate and wife, Ruth Friendly, has lived with me and therefore this book for 1001 nights and days. She makes the difference.

FRED W. FRIENDLY
October 30, 1980
Bronx, New York

Select Bibliography

Allen, Frederick Lewis. *Only Yesterday.* New York: Harper & Brothers, 1931.

Baker, Leonard. *Back to Back.* New York: Macmillan, 1967.

Banning, Margaret Culkin. *Mesabi.* New York: Harper & Row, 1969.

Barron, Jerome A. *Freedom of the Press For Whom.* Bloomington: Indiana University Press, 1973.

Barth, Alan. *Prophets with Honor.* New York: Knopf, 1974.

Barzun, Jacques, and Graff, Henry. *The Modern Researcher.* New York: Harcourt, 1957.

Berger, Raoul. *Government by Judiciary.* Cambridge, Mass.: Harvard University Press, 1977.

Bickel, Alexander M. *The Morality of Consent.* New Haven: Yale University Press, 1975.

Blackstone, William. *Commentaries on the Law of England,* Vol. IV. Chicago: University of Chicago Press, 1979.

Blegen, Theodore C. *Minnesota: A History of the State.* 2nd ed. St. Paul: University of Minnesota Press, 1963, 1975.

Bowen, Catherine Drinker. *Yankee from Olympus.* Boston: Little, Brown, 1944.

Cahn, Lenore L., ed. *Confronting Injustice—The Edmond Cahn Reader.* Boston: Little, Brown & Co., 1962, 1966.

Cappon, Lester, J., ed. *The Adams-Jefferson Letters,* Vols. I and II. Chapel Hill: University of North Carolina Press, 1959.

Chafee, Zechariah, Jr. *Free Speech in the United States.* New York: Atheneum, 1969.

Chicago Tribune. *A Century of Tribune Editorials.* Chicago: Tribune Company Archives, 1847–1947.

Coffey, Thomas M. *The Long Thirst: Prohibition in America 1920–1933.* New York: Norton, 1975.

Cox, Archibald. *The Role of the Supreme Court in American Government.* New York: Oxford University Press, 1976.

Curtis, Charles P., Jr. *Lions Under the Throne.* Boston: Houghton Mifflin, 1947.

Danelski, David J. *A Supreme Court Justice Is Appointed.* (Pierce Butler.) New York: Random House, 1964.

———, and Tulchin, Joseph S., eds. *The Autobiographical Notes of Charles Evans Hughes.* Cambridge, Mass.: Harvard University Press, 1973.

Dunham, Allison, and Kurland, Philip B., eds. *Mr. Justice.* Chicago: University of Chicago Press, 1956.

Edwards, Jerome E. *The Foreign Policy of Colonel McCormick's Tribune (1929–1941).* Reno: University of Nevada Press, 1971.

Emerson, Thomas I. *The System of Freedom of Expression.* New York: Random House; Vintage Books, 1970.

Emery, Edwin. *The Press and America.* 3rd ed. Englewood Cliffs, N.J.: Prentice-Hall, 1954.

Folwell, William Watts. *A History of Minnesota,* Vol. IV. St. Paul: Minnesota Historical Society, 1969.

Frankfurter, Felix, ed. *Mr. Justice Holmes.* New York: Coward-McCann, 1931.

———, and Landis, James M. *The Business of the Supreme Court.* New York: Macmillan, 1927.

Freund, Paul A. *On Understanding the Supreme Court.* Boston: Little, Brown, 1949.

Friedman, Leon, and Israel, Fred, eds. *The Justices of the U.S. Supreme Court 1789–1969.* Vol. III. New York: Chelsea House, 1969.

Fritzen, John. *The History of Fond du Lac and Jay Cooke Park.* Duluth, Minn.: St. Louis County Historical Society, July 1978.

Gies, Joseph. *The Colonel of Chicago: A Biography of the Chicago Tribune's Legendary Publisher, Colonel Robert McCormick.* New York: Dutton, 1979.

Guilford, Howard A. *A Tale of Two Cities: Memoirs of Sixteen Years Behind a Pencil.* Robbinsdale, Minn., 1929.

Hand, Learned. *The Spirit of Liberty,* 3rd ed. Collected, with introduction and notes, by Irving Dilliard. Chicago: University of Chicago Press, 1952, 1953, 1960.

Harrell, Mary Ann. *Equal Justice Under the Law: The Supreme Court in American Life.* The Foundation of the Federal Bar Association/National Geographic Society, 1965, 1975.

Hershkowitz, Leo. *Tweed's New York: Another Look.* Garden City, N.Y.: Doubleday, 1977.

Hughes, Charles Evans. *The Supreme Court of the United States.* New York: Columbia University Press, 1928.

Ickes, Harold L. *The Autobiography of a Curmudgeon.* Chicago: Quadrangle Books, 1969.

Jackson, Percival E. *The Wisdom of the Supreme Court.* Norman: University of Oklahoma Press, 1962.

King, Frank A. *The Missabe Road: The Duluth, Missabe and Iron Range Railway.* San Marino, Calif.: Golden West Books, 1972.

Kinsley, Philip. *The Chicago Tribune—Its First Hundred Years,* Vol. II, 1865–1880. Chicago: The Chicago Tribune, 1945.

———. *Liberty and the Press.* Chicago: Chicago Tribune Co., 1944.

Kluger, Richard. *Simple Justice.* New York: Random House; Vintage Books, 1975.

Kobler, John. *Ardent Spirits: The Rise and Fall of Prohibition.* New York: Putnam's, 1973.

Konefsky, Samuel J. *The Legacy of Holmes and Brandeis.* New York: Macmillan, 1956.

Lee, Henry. *How Dry We Were: Prohibition Revisited.* Englewood Cliffs, N.J.: Prentice-Hall, 1963.

Lewis, Anthony. *Gideon's Trumpet.* New York: Random House, 1967.

Lewis, Sinclair. *Babbitt.* New York: Signet, 1922.

———. *Main Street.* New York: Signet, 1920.

Lockmiller, David A. *Sir William Blackstone.* Chapel Hill: University of North Carolina, 1938.

Lofton, John. *The Press as Guardian of the First Amendment.* Columbia: University of South Carolina Press, 1980.

Lynch, Denis Tilden. *"Boss" Tweed: The Story of a Grim Generation.* New York: Boni and Liveright, 1927.

Macdonald, Dora Mary. *This Is Duluth.* Duluth, Minn.: 1950.

McCormick, Robert R. *The Freedom of the Press: A History and an Argument.* New York: Appleton-Century, 1936.

Mandelbaum, Seymour J. *Boss Tweed's New York.* New York: Wiley, 1965.

Martin, Ralph G. *Cissy: The Extraordinary Life of Eleanor Medill Patterson.* New York: Simon & Schuster, 1979.

Mason, Alpheus Thomas. *Brandeis: Lawyer and Judge in the Modern State.* Princeton: Princeton University Press, 1933.

———. *Harlan Fiske Stone: Pillar of the Law.* New York: Viking, 1956.

Mayer, George H. *The Political Career of Floyd B. Olson.* Minneapolis: University of Minnesota Press, 1951.

Meiklejohn, Alexander. *Free Speech and Its Relation to Self-Government.* New York: Harper & Brothers, 1948.

Meiklejohn, Donald. *Freedom and the Public: Public and Private Morality in America.* Syracuse: Syracuse University Press, 1965.

Mencken, H. L. *The American Language.* Raven I. McDavid, Jr., ed. New York: Knopf, 1963.

———. *The Bathtub Hoax and Other Blasts and Bravos from the Chicago Tribune,* Robert McHugh, ed. New York: Knopf, 1958.

———. *A Mencken Chrestomathy.* New York: Knopf, 1949.

Merz, Charles. *The Dry Decade.* Garden City, N.Y.: Doubleday, 1930, 1931.

Mock, James R. *Censorship 1917.* Princeton: Princeton University Press, 1941.

Morrison, John L. *The Booster Book: West Duluth in 1916.* Duluth, Minn., July 1, 1916.

Nevins, Allan, and Hill, Frank Ernest. *Ford: Expansion and Challenge 1915–1933.* New York: Scribner's, 1957.

The New York Times Company v. *United States,* Vols. I and II (The Pentagon Papers). New York: Arno Press (A N.Y. Times Company), 1971.

Phillips, Harlan B. *Felix Frankfurter Reminisces.* New York: Reynal, 1960.

Practising Law Institute. *Communications Law II.* New York: Practising Law Institute, 1974.

Pringle, Henry F. *The Life and Times of William Howard Taft.* Vol. II. New York: Farrar & Rinehart, 1939.

Pusey, Merlo J. *Charles Evans Hughes,* Vols. I and II. New York: Columbia University Press, 1963.

Reitman, Alan. *The Pulse of Freedom: American Liberties 1920–1970s.* New York: Norton, 1975.

Rembar, Charles. *The Law of the Land.* New York: Simon & Schuster, 1980.

Rodell, Fred. *Nine Men: A Political History of the Supreme Court from 1790 to 1955.* New York: Random House, 1955.

Siebert, Frederick Seaton. *A Belated Diary.* Unpublished ms. Copyright 1976.

————. *The Rights and Privileges of the Press.* New York: Appleton-Century, 1934.

Smith, James Morton. *Freedom's Fetters.* Ithaca: Cornell University Press, 1956.

Steffens, Lincoln. *The Shame of the Cities.* New York: McClure, Phillips, 1904.

Stone, Harlan Fiske. *Law and Its Administration* (Columbia University Lectures). New York: Columbia University Press, 1915.

Supreme Court Historical Society. *1976 Yearbook.* Washington, D.C.

Tebbel, John. *An American Dynasty.* Garden City, N.Y.: Doubleday, 1927.

Todd, A. L. *Justice on Trial: The Case of Louis D. Brandeis.* New York: McGraw-Hill, 1964.

Ungar, Sanford J. *The Papers and the Papers.* New York: Dutton, 1972.

Villard, Oswald Garrison. *The Disappearing Daily.* New York: Knopf, 1944.

Waldrop, Frank C. *McCormick of Chicago.* Englewood Cliffs, N.J.: Prentice-Hall, 1966.

Warren, Charles. *Congress, the Constitution and the Supreme Court.* Boston: Little, Brown, 1925.

Wechsler, Herbert M. *The Nationalization of Civil Liberties and Civil Rights.* Austin: University of Texas. Supplement to *Texas Quarterly,* Vol. XII (1968).

————. *Principles, Politics and Fundamental Law.* Cambridge, Mass.: Harvard University Press, 1961.

Welch, Joseph N. *The Constitution.* Boston: Houghton Mifflin, 1956.

Wendt, Lloyd. *The Chicago Tribune: The Rise of a Great American Newspaper.* New York: Rand McNally, 1979.

————, and Kogan, Herman. *Big Bill of Chicago.* Indianapolis: Bobbs-Merrill, 1953.

White, G. Edward. *The American Judicial Tradition.* New York: Oxford University Press, 1976.

Wyzanski, Charles E., Jr. *Whereas: A Judge's Premises.* Boston: Little, Brown, 1965.

NEWSPAPERS AND PUBLICATIONS

Cass County *Pioneer*
Chicago *Daily News*
Chicago *Tribune*
Christian Science Monitor
Duluth *Herald*
Duluth *News-Tribune*
Duluth *Rip-saw*
Editor and Publisher
Hibbing *Daily News*
Literary Digest
Mankato *Free Press*
Minneapolis *Evening Tribune*
Minneapolis *Journal*
Minneapolis *Morning Tribune*

Minneapolis *Star*
Minneapolis *Tribune*
New York *Daily News*
New York *Herald Tribune*
New York *Times*
The New Yorker
Pine River *Sentinel-Blaze*
Saturday Press
St. Paul *Pioneer Press*
Time magazine
Twin City Reporter
Walker *Pilot*
Washington *Post*

INTERVIEWS

Judge Arlin Adams, Third Circuit, U.S. Court of Appeals
Ray Anderson, Minnesota state legislator for eight years
H. Thomas Austern, law clerk for Louis D. Brandeis in 1931
Roger Baldwin, American Civil Liberties Union founder
Dr. Hyman Berman, Minnesota Historical Society and professor at University of Minnesota
Eleanor Kirkland Brogan, daughter of Weymouth Kirkland
James Buchanan, Supreme Court Historical Society
Warren E. Burger, Chief Justice of the United States and former resident of St. Paul, Minnesota
Pierce Butler III, grandson of Associate Justice Pierce Butler and attorney
Isadore Cohen, newsboy for the Duluth *Rip-saw* and reporter for the Duluth *News-Tribune*
Evelyn Danahy, resident of Hibbing in the 1920s
Orlin Folnick, Minneapolis reporter during the 1920s
Paul A. Freund, Professor Emeritus, Harvard Law School
Gladys Gansey, resident of Hibbing in 1920s
Walter Gellhorn, Professor Emeritus, Columbia Law School, and law clerk for Justice Harlan Fiske Stone, 1931–1932
Elizabeth Hughes Gossett, daughter of Charles Evans Hughes and former president of the Supreme Court Historical Society

William T. Gossett, son-in-law and associate of Charles Evans Hughes, and Detroit attorney

Judge Thomas Griesa, Southern District Court, New York

Dick Griggs, son of Eli Zelotys Griggs, who was an Iron Range banker

Erwin Griswold, former Solicitor General and former Dean of Harvard Law School

Mel Harney, Minneapolis law enforcement official of the 1920s and 1930s

John C. Hogan, former fireman and lineman, lumberjack and bartender in the Iron Range

Norman Isaacs, Editor in Residence, Columbia Graduate School of Journalism, and chairman of the National News Council

Francis R. Kirkham, law clerk for Charles Evans Hughes, 1933–1935

Weymouth Kirkland, Jr., son of Weymouth Kirkland

Clayton Kirkpatrick, president and chief executive officer of the Chicago *Tribune*

John S. Knight, Editor Emeritus of the Knight-Ridder Newspapers

Judge George MacKinnon, former U.S. Attorney in Minneapolis and now judge of Washington (D.C.) Circuit Court of Appeals

John. E. Manthey, lawyer who lived in Eveleth during the 1920s

Arthur Markve, former attorney for the State of Minnesota

Frieda Monger, retired editor of the Duluth *Publicity*

Herb Palmer, former editor of the Duluth *Budgeter*

Burt D. Pearson, former editor of the Virginia *Daily Enterprise,* which became the Mesabi *Daily News*

Veda Ponikvar, publisher of the Chisholm *Tribune and Free Press*

Merlo Pusey, author and biographer of Charles Evans Hughes

Don Reuben, attorney and long-time associate of Colonel McCormick

H. Chapman Rose, law clerk for Oliver Wendell Holmes, 1932–1933

Ed Ryan, former Chief of Police of Minneapolis

Donald B. Shank, vice president of the St. Louis County Historical Society and vice president & general manager of the Duluth, Missabe and Iron Range Railway Company

Irving Shapiro, son of Samuel Shapiro

Jonas Shapiro, son of Samuel Shapiro

Robert J. Sheran, Chief Justice, Minnesota Supreme Court

Frederick S. Siebert, journalism professor and author

Gerald Thomas, former mayor of Hibbing and agent for Hibbing DMIR Railway Company

Robert Tresler, former associate of Owen J. Roberts

David Vaughn, Duluth resident during the 1920s

Arthur Veysey, general manager of Cantigny (Colonel McCormick's estate) in Wheaton, Illinois

Robert Wales, law clerk for Oliver Wendell Holmes, 1931–1932

Herbert M. Wechsler, Harlan Fiske Stone Professor Emeritus of Constitutional Law at Columbia Law School, and law clerk for Harlan Fiske Stone, 1932–1933

J. Howard Wood, Tribune Company executive and colleague of Robert R. McCormick

ARTICLES

American Civil Liberties Union. Select correspondence, on file at Princeton University and the Chicago *Tribune* Archives.

American Newspaper Publishers Association. Select correspondence.

Berger, Raoul. "The Scope of Judicial Review: An Ongoing Debate," *Hastings Constitutional Law Quarterly,* Vol. 6 (Winter 1979).

Berman, Hyman. "Political Anti-Semitism in Minnesota During the Great Depression," *Jewish Social Studies* (Summer-Fall 1976).

Birkeland, Harold. "Floyd B. Olson in the First Kidnapping–Murder in Gangster-Ridden Minnesota," Pamphlet. Minneapolis (October 1934).

Brandeis, Louis D. Letters and notes, on file at Harvard University Law School, Manuscript Division.

Frankfurter, Felix. "Chief Justices I Have Known," *Virginia Law Review* (1953).

————. "The Administrative Side of Chief Justice Hughes," 63 *Harvard Law Review* (1949).

Friedman, Richard P. "Charles Evans Hughes as Chief Justice, 1930–1941." Unpublished D. Phil. thesis. Oxford University, 1978.

Griswold, Erwin J. "Owen J. Roberts as a Judge," 104 *University of Pennsylvania Law Review* (December 1955).

Guilford, Howard A. "Gill's Pocket Book—Society Number." Pamphlet. Minneapolis (September 15, 1919).

Hartman, John E. "The Minnesota Gag Law and the Fourteenth Amendment," 37 *Minn. History* 161 (December 1960).

"Symposium on the Press Clause," *Hofstra Law Review,* Vol. 7, No. 3 (Spring 1979). Dedicated to Justice Potter Stewart.

Hughes, Charles Evans. Select correspondence.

Janey, John. "The Minnesota Enigma," *American Magazine,* Vol. 120, No. 3 (September 1935).

McCormick, Robert R. "An Address." Yale, November 18, 1930. Reprinted by the Tribune Company, 1931.

———. "Addresses." Broadcasts: April 18, 1942, to September 26, 1942. Chicago *Tribune* Archives, 1942.

———. Selected correspondence, Chicago *Tribune* Archives.

———. "The Freedom of the Press." Speech: Chicago, October 18, 1933. Reprinted by the Tribune Company, 1933.

———. "The Rights of Americans." Radio broadcasts: January 16 to March 13, 1943. Chicago *Tribune* Archives, 1943.

———. "What is a Newspaper?" Speech: Chicago, October 27, 1924. Reprinted by the Tribune Company, 1927.

McElwain, Edwin. "The Business of the Supreme Court as Conducted by Chief Justice Hughes," 63 *Harvard Law Review* 5 (1949).

Near, Jay M. Select correspondence.

Siebert, Frederick. "Contempt of Court and the Press," *Journalism Quarterly,* Vol. V. (June 1928).

Stassen, Harold. "Bench and Bar, the Show Window of the Bar," 20 *Minnesota Law Review* 577 (1935–1936).

Taft, William Howard. Select correspondence on file at Library of Congress.

Trapp, William Oscar. "The Constitutional Doctrines of Owen J. Roberts." Ph.D. thesis. Cornell University, May 1943.

United States Senate Commission on Art and Antiquities, "The Senate Chamber 1810–1859."

Source Notes

PAGE

ix   Epigraph: H. L. Mencken, *The Bathtub Hoax and Other Blasts and Bravos*, p. 31.

Chapter 1 · The Trail from *Rip-saw*

3   Newsboy quote: Interview with Isadore Cohen, April 12, 1979.

3   Copies of the *Rip-saw* are on file at the Minnesota Historical Society, St. Paul, Minnesota, and the St. Louis County Historical Society, Duluth, Minnesota.

4   "There was no holding Duluth . . .": Macdonald, *This is Duluth*, p. 102.

4   "The zenith city . . .": King, *The Missabe Road*, p. 46.

4   Mark Twain quote, "coldest winter . . .": Macdonald, *op. cit.*, p. 13.

5   "We are going to build . . .": King, *op. cit.*, p. 46.

6   "The range towns . . .": Interview with Richard L. Griggs, son of Eli Zelotys Griggs, early Duluth banker, April 12, 1979.

9   Description of prohibition on range: Siebert, *A Belated Diary* (unpublished).

PAGE

9   Prohibition quotes: Kobler, *Ardent Spirits,* pp. 12, 223.

10   Mencken quote: *Ibid.,* p. 199.

8–9   "We had the stuff . . .": Letter to Hibbing News Agency from John L. Morrison, August 12, 1921.

Chapter 2 · The Issue of October 25

Epigraph   Swift quote, "Swift's Journal to Stella," August 7, 1712 (Pickering Edition).

16   "Glandular troubles . . .": Jamison affidavits (advertisement), Walker *Pilot,* (October 30, 1924); Cass County *Pioneer* (October 31, 1924).

16   Election results: Pine River *Sentinel-Blaze,* November 7, 1924.

17   "I don't . . . damn desk": Walker *Pilot* (June 25, 1925).

17   Quotes about Vic Power: Interviews with Evelyn Danahy and Gladys Gansey, April 13, 1979.

19   Quotes from Morrison's Hibbing trial: Hibbing *Daily News* (December 4, 1924).

21   C. L. Butler quote: Letter to Colonel McCormick, June 11, 1931.

22   Senate House Bill, "Gag Law," Act of April 20, 1925, Chapter 285, 1925 Minnesota Law, p. 358.

22   "the House also passed . . .": St. Paul *Pioneer Press* (April 17, 1925).

24   "I'm not going to stand . . .": Minneapolis *Morning Tribune* (May 15, 1926).

24   "had injured his character . . .": Duluth *Herald* (May 12, 1926).

25   "The circumstances . . .": Duluth *News-Tribune* (May 18, 1926).

27   "Unlike the current magazines . . .": Letter to Editor from Harriette Wilbur Porter, Duluth *Herald* (May 21, 1926).

Chapter 3 · The Birth of Another Rag

30   "Reflections from Nate Bomberg": Reprinted in the St. Paul *Pioneer Press* (August 28, 1979).

30   Account of illegal activities in Minneapolis from interview

PAGE

Chapter 5 · Rogues and Prophets under Siege

56   Three Kasherman questions: *In re Arthur Kasherman,* File No. 26284 (Minnesota Fourth District Court), February 10, 1928; *State* v. *Kasherman,* 177 Minn. 200, 224 N. W. 838, *cert. denied,* 280 U.S. 602 (1929).

56   "Leach didn't get his cut . . .": Interview with Orlin Folwick, April 14, 1979.

57   *In re disbarment of Philip Moses,* 186 Minn. 357, 243 N. W. 386 (1932).

57   *State* v. *Barnett,* 193 Minn. 336, 258 N.W. 508 (1935).

58   Birkeland scandal: Interview with Orlin Folwick, April 14, 1979.

59   Deposition of Philip De Lage, File No. 28324 (Minnesota Fourth District Court).

59–60 Petition of Howard A. Guilford, January 9, 1928, *State ex rel Olson* v. *Guilford,* 174 Minn. 457, 219 N.W. 770 (1928).

60   *State ex rel. Olson* v. *Guilford,* 174 Minn. 457, 219 N.W. 770 (1928).

63ff. Information on ACLU involvement from interview with Roger Baldwin and ACLU correspondence on file at Princeton University.

63–64 ACLU announcement: Minneapolis *Evening Tribune* (July 20, 1928).

64   "If the Minnesota law . . .": Letter to Forrest Bailey (director of the ACLU) from Carole King, June 22, 1928.

64   "the decision of the state court . . .": Minneapolis *Evening Tribune* (July 20, 1928).

Chapter 6 · The Daddy Warbucks of the First Amendment

66–67 "He had his megalomaniac side . . .": Gies, *The Colonel of Chicago,* p. 237.

68   "If the Ku Klux Klan . . .": Villard, *The Disappearing Daily,* p. 136.

69   "Thus as to policy . . .": Ickes, *Autobiography of a Curmugeon,* p. 149.

70   "fairly temperate . . .": Letter to ANPA from Robert R. McCormick, September 21, 1928.

PAGE

71   "Flivver Patriotism" editorial and headline: Chicago *Tribune* (June 22 and 23, 1916).

72–73   Quotes from Ford trial, Nevins and Hill, *Ford 1916–1933*, p. 135.

73   "Bob McCormick represents the trust press . . .": Wendt and Kogan, *Big Bill of Chicago*, p. 75.

73   "Tammany government . . .": *City of Chicago* v. *The Chicago Tribune*, 307 Ill. 595, 597, 139 N.E. 86 (1920).

74–75   Information on suit: *Ibid.;* Kogan and Wendt, *Big Bill of Chicago;* archives of the Chicago *Tribune* and other Chicago dailies.

75–76   "People ask me how . . .": Waldrop, *McCormick of Chicago*, p. 182.

76   Anecdote about McCormick's office door: Interview with Clayton Kirkpatrick, April 10, 1980.

76   "The Colonel was . . .": Interview with Frederick Siebert, October 11, 1979.

77   "It is only recently . . .": Siebert, "Contempt of Court and the Press," *Journalism Quarterly,* Vol. 5 (June 1928). p. 22.

78   "Minnesota was dominated . . .": Memo of Robert R. McCormick, June 1, 1931.

78   ". . . the mere statement . . .": Letter to Robert R. McCormick from Weymouth Kirkland, September 14, 1928.

78   "It was feared . . .": An address by Robert R. McCormick, Monticello, Va., October 20, 1931.

79   "Our interest . . .": Memo of Robert R. McCormick, June 1, 1931.

80   Latimer's argument: Record, *State ex rel. Olson* v. *Guilford,* 179 Minn. 40, 228 N.W. 326 (1929).

Chapter 7 · Grumbling in the Ranks

Epigraph   Letter to Robert R. McCormick from Jay M. Near, December 14, 1929.

83   "if we were to resort . . .": Letter to the Chicago *Tribune* from Forrest Bailey (ACLU Director), December 20, 1928.

83   "I am advised . . .": Letter to Forrest Bailey from E. S. Beck, January 11, 1929.

85–86   Letter to Robert R. McCormick from Jay M. Near, December 14, 1929.

PAGE

87   Letter to Robert R. McCormick from Weymouth Kirkland, January 27, 1930.

87–88   "We see no reason . . .": *State ex. rel. Olson* v. *Guilford,* 179 Minn. 40, 228 N.W. 326 (1929).

88   Appeal procedure: Act of February 13, 1925, ch. 299, 43 Stat. 936.

88   "You will have seen . . .": Letter to Harry Chandler from Robert R. McCormick, December 23, 1929.

88   "If we go . . .": Letter to Robert R. McCormick from Harry Chandler, January 1, 1930.

89   "they would like to see . . .": Letter to Robert R. McCormick from S. Emory Thompson, February 14, 1930.

90   "the politicians will begin . . .": Letter to S. Emory Thompson from Robert R. McCormick, February 18, 1930.

90   "We will all . . .": Letter to Robert R. McCormick from Harry Chandler, March 20, 1930.

Chapter 8 · Death Holds Two Wild-Card Seats on the Supreme Court

93   "Damn you . . .": Pringle, *The Life and Times of William Howard Taft,* p. 852.

93–94   "I love judges . . .": David Burner, *The Justices of the U.S. Supreme Court,* Vol. III, p. 2105.

94   "I would not think . . .": Pringle, *Taft,* p. 1049.

94   "A good fellow . . .": *Ibid.,* p. 971.

95   "near breakdown": Letter to Justice Stone from Chief Justice Taft, January 26, 1927.

95   "he is so completely . . .": Letter to Henry L. Stimson from William Howard Taft, May 18, 1928. (Taft Letters on file at Manuscript Division, Library of Congress.)

95   "I think we can hold our six . . .": Letter to Horace Taft from William Howard Taft, December 1, 1929.

95   "What you say . . . Stone's promotion . . .": Letter to Pierce Butler from William Howard Taft, September 14, 1929.

96   *Gitlow* v. *New York,* 268 U.S. 652 (1925).

100   Footnote: *The Federalist,* #78.

101–105 Taft successor information: Letters of William Howard Taft; letter of Willis Van Devanter; interview with James Buchanan, Supreme Court Historical Society, May 10,

PAGE

113 "You tell the Chief...": Interview with William T. Gossett, March 10, 1980.

113 "The splenetic Tennessean": Pusey, *Charles Evans Hughes,* p. 671.

113 Cardozo story: Interview with Herbert Wechsler, February 4, 1980.

114–115 *Adkins* v. *Childrens Hospital,* 261 U.S. 525 (1923).

116 "I rather forced the President . . .": Letter to Robert A. Taft from William Howard Taft, July 2, 1925.

116 "a very sad spectacle": Mason, *Stone,* p. 211.

116 "As a practising lawyer . . ."; "the skepticism . . .": *Ibid.,* pp. 211–212.

116 "the sober second thought . . .": Stone, "The Common Law in the U.S.," 50 *Harv. Law Rev.* 24 (1936).

117 "a learned lawyer . . .": Letter to Charles P. Taft, II, from William Howard Taft, May 12, 1929.

117 "Are we to go . . .": *Congressional Record,* Vol. 65, part III, and New York *Times* (February 16, 1923).

118 "on the pristine powers . . .": Keedy, "Owen J. Roberts and the Law School," 104 *U. Pa. Law Rev.* 318 (1955).

118 "I have no illusions . . .": Felix Frankfurter, "Mr. Justice Roberts," 104 *U. Pa. Law Rev.* 311 (1955).

120 "I shall not resign . . .": Bowen, *Yankee from Olympus,* p. 406.

Chapter 9 · Argument Day in the Supreme Court

121–122 Brandeis notes to H. Thomas Austern from Louis D. Brandeis, October 16, 1930.

123 "this unique and hallowed spot": Pusey, *Charles Evans Hughes,* Vol. II, p. 688.

123 "Almost bombastically pretentious": Mason, *Stone,* p. 406.

124 "I presume . . .": Interview with William Gossett, March 10, 1980.

124 "To see him preside . . .": Frankfurter, "Chief Justices I Have Known," 31 *Va. Law Rev.* 7 (1953).

125 "It has been reported . . .": McElwain, "The Business of the Supreme Court," 63 *Harv. Law Rev.* 5 (1949).

125–133 Note: There is no written record or transcript of the complete oral arguments; this account has been pieced together, from Chicago *Tribune* and New York *Times* (February 1, 1931); *Editor and Publisher* (February 7, 1931); appellants and responds briefs; interviews with law clerks and other observers.

132   "I was much younger . . .": McCormick, *Freedom of the Press;* Kinsley, *Liberty and the Press.*

133   "I have been gagged . . .": Letter to George Lommen from Jay M. Near, January 20, 1931.

134   "the possibilities for abuse . . .": Chicago *Tribune* (January 14, 1931).

134   Lommen quotations: Letter to Railroad Brotherhoods' State Legislative Board from George Lommen, October 7, 1930.

Chapter 10 · The Barest of Margins

136   "The country's business . . .": Walter Lippmann, "To Justice Holmes on his Seventy-Fifth Birthday," from *Mr. Justice Holmes,* ed. Felix Frankfurter.

137   "He is the most important . . .": Hughes, *Supreme Court of the United States,* p. 56.

137–138   "In making assignments . . .": McElwain, "The Supreme Court's Business Under Hughes," 63 *Harv. Law Rev.* 1 (1949).

138ff.   By the very nature of the Justices conference on *Near v. Minnesota,* the explicit evidence available for this chapter is limited. Elsewhere it has been possible to find direct evidence from documents or witnesses for every quotation and to respect the most demanding criteria of evidence for conclusions of fact. The account of the Justices conference on *Near* is necessarily different. There can be no direct quotations and indeed no contemporary evidence on the moods of individuals or the other details of such a closed debate. In much of the author's description there are statements that are only probably true. Those probabilities are as high as one who was not there fifty years ago can make them. I have not traced for the reader all the reasons for inferences. I have not cluttered the account with "probably" or "surely" or "must have argued." Nonetheless, what appears is no more—though also no less—than as

Chapter 11 · Judgment Day

Chapter 12 · The Forgotten Champion

Source Notes

PAGE

173   "great cases . . .": *Northern Securities Co.* v. *United States,* 193 U.S. 197 (1904).

174   *De Jonge* v. *Oregon,* 299 U.S. 353 (1937).

174   *New York Times Co.* v. *Sullivan,* 376 U.S. 254 (1964).

175   *New York Times Co.* v. *United States,* 403 U.S. 713 (1971).

177   "The security . . .": *United States* v. *New York Times Co.,* 328 F. Supp. 324 (S.D.N.Y. 1971).

178   "a morsel of genuine . . .": Letter from Thomas Jefferson to John Adams, September 8, 1814, from *The Adams-Jefferson Letters,* Vol. II, p. 520, ed. L. Cappon.

179   "impossible . . . of literal . . .": Learned Hand, *The Spirit of Liberty,* p. 179.

J. M. Near v. State of Minnesota, 283 U.S. 697 (1931)

NEAR *v.* MINNESOTA EX REL. OLSON, COUNTY ATTORNEY.

APPEAL FROM THE SUPREME COURT OF MINNESOTA.

No. 91.   Argued January 30, 1931.—Decided June 1, 1931.

MR. CHIEF JUSTICE HUGHES delivered the opinion of the Court.

Chapter 285 of the Session Laws of Minnesota for the year 1925[1] provides for the abatement, as a public nuisance, of a "malicious, scandalous and defamatory newspaper, magazine or other periodical." Section one of the Act is as follows:

"Section 1. Any person who, as an individual, or as a member or employee of a firm, or association or organization, or as an officer, director, member or employee of a corporation, shall be engaged in the business of regularly or customarily producing, publishing or circulat-

[1]Mason's Minnesota Statutes, 1927, 10123-1 to 10123-3.

ing, having in possession, selling or giving away.

(a) an obscene, lewd and lascivious newspaper, magazine, or other periodical, or

(b) a malicious, scandalous and defamatory newspaper, magazine or other periodical,

is guilty of a nuisance, and all persons guilty of such nuisance may be enjoined, as hereinafter provided.

"Participation in such business shall constitute a commission of such nuisance and render the participant liable and subject to the proceedings, orders and judgments provided for in this Act. Ownership, in whole or in part, directly or indirectly, of any such periodical, or of any stock or interest in any corporation or organization which owns the same in whole or in part, or which publishes the same, shall constitute such participation.

"In actions brought under (b) above, there shall be available the defense that the truth was published with good motives and for justifiable ends and in such actions the plaintiff shall not have the right to report *(sic)* to issues or editions of periodicals taking place more than three months before the commencement of the action."

Section two provides that whenever any such nuisance is committed or exists, the County Attorney of any county where any such periodical is published or circulated, or, in case of his failure or refusal to proceed upon written request in good faith of a reputable citizen, the Attorney General, or upon like failure or refusal of the latter, any citizen of the county, may maintain an action in the district court of the county in the name of the State to enjoin perpetually the persons committing or maintaining any such nuisance from further committing or maintaining it. Upon such evidence as the court shall deem sufficient, a temporary injunction may be granted. The defendants have the right to plead by demurrer or answer, and the plaintiff may demur or reply as in other cases.

The action, by section three, is to be "governed by the practice and procedure applicable to civil actions for injunctions," and after trial the court may enter judgment permanently enjoining the defendants found guilty of violating the Act from continuing the violation and, "in and by such judgment, such nuisance may be wholly abated." The court is empowered, as in other cases of contempt, to punish disobedience to a temporary or permanent injunction by fine of not more than $1,000 or by imprisonment in the county jail for not more than twelve months.

Under this statute, (section one, clause (b)), the County Attorney of Hennepin County brought this action to enjoin the publication of what was described as a "malicious, scandalous and defamatory newspaper, magazine and periodical," known as "The Saturday Press," published by the defendants in the city of Minneapolis. The complaint alleged that the defendants, on September 24, 1927, and on eight subsequent dates in October and November, 1927, published and circulated editions of that periodical which were "largely devoted to malicious, scandalous and defamatory articles" concerning Charles G. Davis, Frank W. Brunskill, the Minneapolis Tribune, the Minneapolis Journal, Melvin C. Passolt, George E. Leach, the Jewish Race, the members of the Grand Jury of Hennepin County impaneled in November 1927, and then holding office, and other persons, as more fully appeared in exhibits annexed to the complaint, consisting of copies of the articles described and constituting 327 pages of the record. While the complaint did not so allege, it appears from the briefs of both parties that Charles G. Davis was a special law enforcement officer employed by a civic organization, that George E. Leach was Mayor of Minneapolis, that Frank W. Brunskill was its Chief of Police, and that Floyd B. Olson (the relator in this action) was County Attorney.

Without attempting to summarize the contents of the voluminous exhibits attached to the complaint, we deem it sufficient to say that the articles charged in substance that a Jewish gangster was in control of gambling, bootlegging and racketeering in Minneapolis, and that law enforcing officers and agencies were not energetically performing their duties. Most of the charges were directed against the Chief of Police; he was charged with gross neglect of duty, illicit relations with gangsters, and with participation in graft. The County Attorney was charged with knowing the existing conditions and with failure to take adequate measures to remedy them. The Mayor was accused of inefficiency and dereliction. One member of the grand jury was stated to be in sympathy with the gangsters. A special grand jury and a special prosecutor were demanded to deal with the situation in general, and, in particular, to investigate an attempt to assassinate one Guilford, one of the original defendants, who, it appears from the articles, was shot by gangsters after the first issue of the periodical had been published. There is no question but that the articles made serious accusations against the public officers named and others in connection with the prevalence of crimes and the failure to expose and punish them.

At the beginning of the action, on November 22, 1927, and upon the verified complaint, an order was made directing the defendants to show cause why a temporary injunction should not issue and meanwhile forbidding the defendants to publish, circulate or have in their possession any editions of the periodical from September 24, 1927, to November 19, 1927, inclusive, and from publishing, circulating, or having in their possession, "any future editions of said The Saturday Press" and "any publication, known by any other name whatsoever containing malicious, scandalous and defamatory matter of the kind alleged in plaintiff's complaint herein or otherwise."

The defendants demurred to the complaint upon the ground that it did not state facts sufficient to constitute a cause of action, and on this demurrer challenged the constitutionality of the statute. The District Court overruled the demurrer and certified the question of constitutionality to the Supreme Court of the State. The Supreme Court sustained the statute (174 Minn. 457, 219 N. W. 770), and it is conceded by the appellee that the Act was thus held to be valid over the objection that it violated not only the state constitution but also the Fourteenth Amendment of the Constitution of the United States.

Thereupon, the defendant Near, the present appellant, answered the complaint. He averred that he was the sole owner and proprietor of the publication in question. He admitted the publication of the articles in the issues described in the complaint but denied that they were malicious, scandalous or defamatory as alleged. He expressly invoked the protection of the due process clause of the Fourteenth Amendment. The case then came on for trial. The plaintiff offered in evidence the verified complaint, together with the issues of the publication in question, which were attached to the complaint as exhibits. The defendant objected to the introduction of the evidence, invoking the constitutional provisions to which his answer referred. The objection was overruled, no further evidence was presented, and the plaintiff rested. The defendant then rested, without offering evidence. The plaintiff moved that the court direct the issue of a permanent injunction, and this was done.

The District Court made findings of fact, which followed the allegations of the complaint and found in general terms that the editions in question were "chiefly devoted to malicious, scandalous and defamatory articles," concerning the individuals named. The court further found that the defendants through these publications "did engage in the business of regularly and customarily producing, publishing and circulating a malicious, scandalous and defamatory newspaper," and that "the said publication" "under said name of The Saturday Press, or any other name, constitutes a public nuisance under the laws of the State." Judgment was thereupon entered adjudging that "the newspaper, magazine and periodical known as The Saturday Press," as a public nuisance, "be and is hereby abated." The judgment perpetually enjoined the defendants "from producing, editing, publishing, circulating, having in their possession, selling or giving away any publication whatsoever which is a malicious, scandalous or defamatory newspaper, as defined by law," and also "from further conducting said nuisance under the name and title of said The Saturday Press or any other name or title."

The defendant Near appealed from this judgment to the Supreme Court of the State, again asserting his right under the Federal Constitution, and the judgment was affirmed upon the authority of the former decision. 179 Minn. 40; 228 N. W. 326. With respect to the contention that the judgment went too far, and prevented the defendants from publishing any kind of a newspaper, the court observed that the assignments of error did not go to the form of the judgment and that the lower court had not been asked to modify it. The court added that it saw no reason "for defendants to construe the judgment as restraining them from operating a newspaper in harmony with the public welfare, to which all must yield," that the allegations of the complaint had been found to be true, and, though this was an equitable action, defendants had not indicated a desire "to conduct their business in the usual and legitimate manner."

From the judgment as thus affirmed, the defendant Near appeals to this Court.

This statute, for the suppression as a public nuisance of a newspaper or periodical, is unusual, if not unique, and raises questions of grave importance transcending the local interests involved in the particular action. It is no longer open to doubt that the liberty of the press, and of speech, is within the liberty safeguarded by the due process clause of the Fourteenth Amendment from invasion by state action. It was found impossible to conclude that this essential personal liberty of the citizen was left unprotected by the general guaranty of fundamental rights of person and property. *Gitlow* v. *New York,* 268 U. S. 652, 666; *Whitney* v. *California,* 274 U. S. 357, 362, 373; *Fiske* v. *Kansas,* 274 U. S. 380, 382; *Stromberg* v. *California, ante,* p. 359. In maintaining this guaranty, the authority of the State to enact laws to promote the health, safety, morals and general welfare of its people is necessarily admitted. The limits of this sovereign power must always be determined with appropriate regard to the particular subject of its exercise. Thus, while recognizing the broad discretion of the legislature in fixing rates to be charged by those undertaking a public service, this Court has decided that the owner cannot constitutionally be deprived of his right to a fair return, because that is deemed to be of the essence of ownership. *Railroad Commission Cases,* 116 U. S. 307, 331; *Northern Pacific Ry. Co.* v. *North Dakota,* 236

U. S. 585, 596. So, while liberty of contract is not an absolute right, and the wide field of activity in the making of contracts is subject to legislative supervision (*Frisbie* v. *United States,* 157 U. S. 161, 165), this Court has held that the power of the State stops short of interference with what are deemed to be certain indispensable requirements of the liberty assured, notably with respect to the fixing of prices and wages. *Tyson Bros.* v. *Banton,* 273 U. S. 418; *Ribnik* v. *McBride,* 277 U. S. 350; *Adkins* v. *Children's Hospital,* 261 U. S. 525, 560, 561. Liberty of speech, and of the press, is also not an absolute right, and the State may punish its abuse. *Whitney* v. *California, supra; Stromberg* v. *California, supra.* Liberty, in each of its phases, has its history and connotation and, in the present instance, the inquiry is as to the historic conception of the liberty of the press and whether the statute under review violates the essential attributes of that liberty.

The appellee insists that the questions of the application of the statute to appellant's periodical, and of the construction of the judgment of the trial court, are not presented for review; that appellant's sole attack was upon the constitutionality of the statute, however it might be applied. The appellee contends that no question either of motive in the publication, or whether the decree goes beyond the direction of the statute, is before us. The appellant replies that, in his view, the plain terms of the statute were not departed from in this case and that, even if they were, the statute is nevertheless unconstitutional under any reasonable construction of its terms. The appellant states that he has not argued that the temporary and permanent injunctions were broader than were warranted by the statute; he insists that what was done was properly done if the statute is valid, and that the action taken under the statute is a fair indication of its scope.

With respect to these contentions it is enough to say that in passing upon constitutional questions the court has regard to substance and not to mere matters of form, and that, in accordance with familiar principles, the statute must be tested by its operation and effect. *Henderson* v. *Mayor,* 92 U. S. 259, 268; *Bailey* v. *Alabama,* 219 U. S. 219, 244; *United States* v. *Reynolds,* 235 U. S. 133, 148, 149; *St. Louis Southwestern Ry. Co.* v. *Arkansas,* 235 U.S. 350, 362; *Mountain Timber Co.* v. *Washington,* 243 U. S. 219, 237. That operation and effect we think is clearly shown by the record in this case. We are not concerned with mere errors of the trial court, if there be such, in going beyond the direction of the statute as construed by the Supreme Court of the State. It is thus important to note precisely the purpose and effect of the statute as the state court has construed it.

First. The statute is not aimed at the redress of individual or private wrongs. Remedies for libel remain available and unaffected. The statute, said the state court, "is not directed at threatened libel but at an existing business which, generally speaking, involves more than libel." It is aimed at the distribution of scandalous matter as "detrimental to public morals and to the general welfare," tending "to disturb the peace of the community" and "to provoke assaults and the commission of crime." In order to obtain an injunction to suppress the future publication of the newspaper or periodical, it is not necessary to prove the falsity of the charges that have been made in the publication condemned. In the present action there was no allegation that the matter published was not true. It is alleged, and the statute requires the allegation, that the publication was "malicious." But, as in prosecutions for libel, there is no requirement of proof by the State of malice in fact as distinguished from malice inferred from the mere publication of the defamatory matter.[2] The judgment in this case proceeded upon the mere proof of publication. The statute permits the defense, not of the truth alone, but only that the truth was published with good motives and for justifiable ends. It is apparent that under the statute the publication is to be regarded as defamatory if it injures reputation, and that it is scandalous if it circulates charges of reprehensible conduct, whether criminal or otherwise, and the publication is thus deemed to invite public reprobation and to constitute a public scandal. The court sharply defined the purpose of the statute, bringing out the precise point, in these words: "There is no constitutional right to publish a fact merely because it is true. It is a matter of common knowledge that prosecutions under the criminal libel statutes do not result in efficient repression or suppression of the evils of scandal. Men who are the victims of such assaults seldom resort to the courts. This is especially true if their sins are exposed and the only question relates to whether it was done with good motives and for justifiable ends. This law is not for the protection of the person attacked nor to punish the wrongdoer. It is for the protection of the public welfare."

Second. The statute is directed not simply at the circulation of scandalous and defamatory statements with regard to private citizens, but at the continued publication by newspapers and periodicals of charges against public officers of corruption, malfeasance in office, or serious neglect of duty. Such charges by their very nature create a public scandal. They are scandalous and defamatory within the meaning of the statute, which has

[2]Mason's Minn. Stats. 10112, 10113; *State* v. *Shipman,* 83 Minn. 441, 445; 86 N. W. 431; *State* v. *Minor,* 163 Minn. 109, 110; 203 N. W. 596.

its normal operation in relation to publications dealing prominently and chiefly with the alleged derelictions of public officers.[3]

Third. The object of the statute is not punishment, in the ordinary sense, but suppression of the offending newspaper or periodical. The reason for the enactment, as the state court has said, is that prosecutions to enforce penal statutes for libel do not result in "efficient repression or suppression of the evils of scandal." Describing the business of publication as a public nuisance, does not obscure the substance of the proceeding which the statute authorizes. It is the continued publication of scandalous and defamatory matter that constitutes the business and the declared nuisance. In the case of public officers, it is the reiteration of charges of official misconduct, and the fact that the newspaper or periodical is principally devoted to that purpose, that exposes it to suppression. In the present instance, the proof was that nine editions of the newspaper or periodical in question were published on successive dates, and that they were chiefly devoted to charges against public officers and in relation to the prevalence and protection of crime. In such a case, these officers are not left to their ordinary remedy in a suit for libel, or the authorities to a prosecution for criminal libel. Under this statute, a publisher of a newspaper or periodical, undertaking to conduct a campaign to expose and to censure official derelictions, and devoting his publication principally to that purpose, must face not simply the possibility of a verdict against him in a suit or prosecution for libel, but a determination that his newspaper or periodical is a public nuisance to be abated, and that this abatement and suppression will follow unless he is prepared with legal evidence to prove the truth of the charges and also to satisfy the court that, in addition to being true, the matter was published with good motives and for justifiable ends.

This suppression is accomplished by enjoining publication and that restraint is the object and effect of the statute.

Fourth. The statute not only operates to suppress the offending newspaper or periodical but to put the publisher under an effective censorship. When a newspaper or periodical is found to be "malicious, scandalous and defamatory," and is suppressed as such, resumption of

---

[3]It may also be observed that in a prosecution for libel the applicable Minnesota statute (Mason's Minn. Stats., 1927, §§ 10112, 10113), provides that the publication is justified "whenever the matter charged as libelous is true and was published with good motives and for justifiable ends," and also "is excused when honestly made, in belief of its truth, and upon reasonable grounds for such belief, and consists of fair comments upon the conduct of a person in respect to public affairs." The clause last mentioned is not found in the statute in question.

publication is punishable as a contempt of court by fine or imprisonment. Thus, where a newspaper or periodical has been suppressed because of the circulation of charges against public officers of official misconduct, it would seem to be clear that the renewal of the publication of such charges would constitute a contempt and that the judgment would lay a permanent restraint upon the publisher, to escape which he must satisfy the court as to the character of a new publication. Whether he would be permitted again to publish matter deemed to be derogatory to the same or other public officers would depend upon the court's ruling. In the present instance the judgment restrained the defendants from "publishing, circulating, having in their possession, selling or giving away any publication whatsoever which is a malicious, scandalous or defamatory newspaper, as defined by law." The law gives no definition except that covered by the words "scandalous and defamatory," and publications charging official misconduct are of that class. While the court, answering the objection that the judgment was too broad, saw no reason for construing it as restraining the defendants "from operating a newspaper in harmony with the public welfare to which all must yield," and said that the defendants had not indicated "any desire to conduct their business in the usual and legitimate manner," the manifest inference is that, at least with respect to a new publication directed against official misconduct, the defendant would be held, under penalty of punishment for contempt as provided in the statute, to a manner of publication which the court considered to be "usual and legitimate" and consistent with the public welfare.

If we cut through mere details of procedure, the operation and effect of the statute in substance is that public authorities may bring the owner or publisher of a newspaper or periodical before a judge upon a charge of conducting a business of publishing scandalous and defamatory matter—in particular that the matter consists of charges against public officers of official dereliction—and unless the owner or publisher is able and disposed to bring competent evidence to satisfy the judge that the charges are true and are published with good motives and for justifiable ends, his newspaper or periodical is suppressed and further publication is made punishable as a contempt. This is of the essence of censorship.

The question is whether a statute authorizing such proceedings in restraint of publication is consistent with the conception of the liberty of the press as historically conceived and guaranteed. In determining the extent of the constitutional protection, it has been generally, if not universally, considered that it is the chief purpose of the guaranty to prevent previous restraints upon publication. The struggle in England, directed against the legislative power of the licenser, resulted in renunciation of the censorship of the press.[4] The liberty deemed to be established was thus described by Blackstone: "The liberty of the press is indeed essential to the nature of a free state; but this consists in laying no *previous* restraints upon publications, and not in freedom from censure for criminal matter when published. Every freeman has an undoubted right to lay what sentiments he pleases before the public; to forbid this, is to destroy the freedom of the press; but if he publishes what is improper, mischievous or illegal, he must take the consequence of his own temerity." 4 Bl. Com. 151, 152; see Story on the Constitution, §§ 1884, 1889. The distinction was early pointed out between the extent of the freedom with respect to censorship under our constitutional system and that enjoyed in England. Here, as Madison said, "the great and essential rights of the people are secured against legislative as well as against executive ambition. They are secured, not by laws paramount to prerogative, but by constitutions paramount to laws. This security of the freedom of the press requires that it should be exempt not only from previous restraint by the Executive, as in Great Britain, but from legislative restraint also." Report on the Virginia Resolutions, Madison's Works, vol. IV, p. 543. This Court said, in *Patterson* v. *Colorado,* 205 U. S. 454, 462: "In the first place, the main purpose of such constitutional provisions is 'to prevent all such *previous restraints* upon publications as had been practiced by other governments,' and they do not prevent the subsequent punishment of such as may be deemed contrary to the public welfare. *Commonwealth* v. *Blanding,* 3 Pick. 304, 313, 314; *Respublica* v. *Oswald,* 1 Dallas, 319, 325. The preliminary freedom extends as well to the false as to the true; the subsequent punishment may extend as well to the true as to the false. This was the law of criminal libel apart from statute in most cases, if not in all. *Commonwealth* v. *Blanding, ubi sup.;* 4 Bl. Com. 150."

The criticism upon Blackstone's statement has not been because immunity from previous restraint upon publication has not been regarded as deserving of special emphasis, but chiefly because that immunity cannot be deemed to exhaust the conception of the liberty guaranteed by state and federal constitutions. The point of criticism has been "that the mere exemption from previous restraints cannot be all that is secured by the constitutional provisions"; and that "the liberty of the press might be rendered a mockery and a delusion, and the phrase itself

---

[4]May, Constitutional History of England, vol. 2, chap. IX, p. 4; DeLolme, Commentaries on the Constitution of England, chap. IX, pp. 318, 319

a by-word, if, while every man was at liberty to publish what he pleased, the public authorities might nevertheless punish him for harmless publications." 2 Cooley, Const. Lim., 8th ed., p. 885. But it is recognized that punishment for the abuse of the liberty accorded to the press is essential to the protection of the public, and that the common law rules that subject the libeler to responsibility for the public offense, as well as for the private injury, are not abolished by the protection extended in our constitutions. *id.* pp. 883, 884. The law of criminal libel rests upon that secure foundation. There is also the conceded authority of courts to punish for contempt when publications directly tend to prevent the proper discharge of judicial functions. *Patterson* v. *Colorado, supra; Toledo Newspaper Co.* v. *United States,* 247 U. S. 402, 419.[5] In the present case, we have no occasion to inquire as to the permissible scope of subsequent punishment. For whatever wrong the appellant has committed or may commit, by his publications, the State appropriately affords both public and private redress by its libel laws. As has been noted, the statute in question does not deal with punishments; it provides for no punishment, except in case of contempt for violation of the court's order, but for suppression and injunction, that is, for restraint upon publication.

The objection has also been made that the principle as to immunity from previous restraint is stated too broadly, if every such restraint is deemed to be prohibited. That is undoubtedly true; the protection even as to previous restraint is not absolutely unlimited. But the limitation has been recognized only in exceptional cases: "When a nation is at war many things that might be said in time of peace are such a hindrance to its effort that their utterance will not be endured so long as men fight and that no Court could regard them as protected by any constitutional right." *Schenck* v. *United States,* 249 U. S. 47, 52. No one would question but that a government might prevent actual obstruction to its recruiting service or the publication of the sailing dates of transports or the number and location of troops.[6] On similar grounds, the primary requirements of decency may be enforced against obscene publications. The security of the community life may be protected against incitements to acts of violence and the overthrow by force of orderly government. The constitutional guaranty of free speech does

[5]See *Huggonson's Case,* 2 Atk. 469; *Respublica* v. *Oswald,* 1 Dallas 319; *Cooper* v. *People,* 13 Colo. 337, 373; 22 Pac. 790; *Nebraska* v. *Rosewater,* 60 Nebr. 438; 83 N. W. 353; *State* v. *Tugwell,* 19 Wash. 238; 52 Pac. 1056; *People* v. *Wilson,* 64 Ill. 195; *Storey* v. *People,* 79 Ill. 45; *State* v. *Circuit Court,* 97 Wis. 1; 72 N. W. 193.

[6]Chafee, Freedom of Speech, p. 10.

not "protect a man from an injunction against uttering words that may have all the effect of force. *Gompers* v. *Buck Stove & Range Co.,* 221 U. S. 418, 439." *Schenck* v. *United States, supra.* These limitations are not applicable here. Nor are we now concerned with questions as to the extent of authority to prevent publications in order to protect private rights according to the principles governing the exercise of the jurisdiction of courts of equity.[7]

The exceptional nature of its limitations places in a strong light the general conception that liberty of the press, historically considered and taken up by the Federal Constitution, has meant, principally although not exclusively, immunity from previous restraints or censorship. The conception of the liberty of the press in this country had broadened with the exigencies of the colonial period and with the efforts to secure freedom from oppressive administration.[8] That liberty was especially cherished for the immunity it afforded from previous restraint of the publication of censure of public officers and charges of official misconduct. As was said by Chief Justice Parker, in *Commonwealth* v. *Blanding,* 3 Pick. 304, 313, with respect to the constitution of Massachusetts: "Besides, it is well understood, and received as a commentary on this provision for the liberty of the press, that it was intended to prevent all such *previous restraints* upon publications as had been practiced by other governments, and in early times here, to stifle the efforts of patriots towards enlightening their fellow subjects upon their rights and the duties of rulers. The liberty of the press was to be unrestrained, but he who used it was to be responsible in case of its abuse." In the letter sent by the Continental Congress (October 26, 1774) to the Inhabitants of Quebec, referring to the "five great rights" it was said:[9] "The last right we shall mention, regards the freedom of the press. The importance of this consists, besides the advancement of truth, science, morality, and arts in general, in its diffusion of liberal sentiments on the administration of Government, its ready communication of thoughts between subjects, and its consequential promotion of union among them, whereby oppressive officers are shamed or intimidated, into more honourable and just modes of conducting affairs." Madison, who was the leading spirit in the preparation of the First Amendment of the Federal Constitution, thus described the practice and sentiment which led to the

[7]See 29 Harvard Law Review, 640.
[8]See Duniway "The Development of Freedom of the Press in Massachusetts," p. 123; Bancroft's History of the United States, vol. 2, 261.
[9]Journal of the Continental Congress, 1904 ed., vol. I, pp. 104, 108.

guaranties of liberty of the press in state constitutions:[10]

"In every State, probably, in the Union, the press has exerted a freedom in canvassing the merits and measures of public men of every description which has not been confined to the strict limits of the common law. On this footing the freedom of the press has stood; on this footing it yet stands. . . . Some degree of abuse is inseparable from the proper use of everything, and in no instance is this more true than in that of the press. It has accordingly been decided by the practice of the States, that it is better to leave a few of its noxious branches to their luxuriant growth, than, by pruning them away, to injure the vigour of those yielding the proper fruits. And can the wisdom of this policy be doubted by any who reflect that to the press alone, chequered as it is with abuses, the world is indebted for all the triumphs which have been gained by reason and humanity over error and oppression; who reflect that to the same beneficent source the United States owe much of the lights which conducted them to the ranks of a free and independent nation, and which have improved their political system into a shape so auspicious to their happiness? Had 'Sedition Acts,' forbidding every publication that might bring the constituted agents into contempt or disrepute, or that might excite the hatred of the people against the authors of unjust or pernicious measures, been uniformly enforced against the press, might not the United States have been languishing at this day under the infirmities of a sickly Confederation? Might they not, possibly, be miserable colonies, groaning under a foreign yoke?"

The fact that for approximately one hundred and fifty years there has been almost an entire absence of attempts to impose previous restraints upon publications relating to the malfeasance of public officers is significant of the deep-seated conviction that such restraints would violate constitutional right. Public officers, whose character and conduct remain open to debate and free discussion in the press, find their remedies for false accusations in actions under libel laws providing for redress and punishment, and not in proceedings to restrain the publication of newspapers and periodicals. The general principle that the constitutional guaranty of the liberty of the press gives immunity from previous restraints has been approved in many decisions under the provisions of state constitutions.[11]

[10]Report on the Virginia Resolutions, Madison's Works, vol. iv, 544.

[11]*Dailey* v. *Superior Court,* 112 Cal. 94, 98; 44 Pac. 458; *Jones, Varnum & Co.* v. *Townsend's Admx.,* 21 Fla. 431, 450; *State ex rel. Liversey* v. *Judge,* 34 La. 741, 743; *Commonwealth* v. *Blanding,* 3 Pick, 304, 313; *Lindsay* v. *Montana Federation of Labor,*

The importance of this immunity has not lessened. While reckless assaults upon public men, and efforts to bring obloquy upon those who are endeavoring faithfully to discharge official duties, exert a baleful influence and deserve the severest condemnation in public opinion, it cannot be said that this abuse is greater, and it is believed to be less, than that which characterized the period in which our institutions took shape. Meanwhile, the administration of government has become more complex, the opportunities for malfeasance and corruption have multiplied, crime has grown to most serious proportions, and the danger of its protection by unfaithful officials and of the impairment of the fundamental security of life and property by criminal alliances and official neglect, emphasizes the primary need of a vigilant and courageous press, especially in great cities. The fact that the liberty of the press may be abused by miscreant purveyors of scandal does not make any the less necessary the immunity of the press from previous restraint in dealing with official misconduct. Subsequent punishment for such abuses as may exist is the appropriate remedy, consistent with constitutional privilege.

In attempted justification of the statute, it is said that it deals not with publication *per se,* but with the "business" of publishing defamation. If, however, the publisher has a constitutional right to publish, without previous restraint, an edition of his newspaper charging official derelictions, it cannot be denied that he may publish subsequent editions for the same purpose. He does not lose his right by exercising it. If his right exists, it may be exercised in publishing nine editions, as in this case, as well as in one edition. If previous restraint is permissible, it may be imposed at once; indeed, the wrong may be as serious in one publication as in several. Characterizing the publication as a business, and the business as a nuisance, does not permit an invasion of the constitutional immunity against restraint. Similarly, it does not matter that the newspaper or periodical is found to be "largely" or "chiefly" devoted to the publication of such derelictions. If the publisher has a right, without

---

37 Mont. 264, 275, 277; 96 Pac. 127; *Howell* v. *Bee Publishing Co.,* 100 Neb. 39, 42; 158 N. W. 358; *New Yorker Staats-Zeitung* v. *Nolan,* 89 N. J. Eq. 387; 105 Atl. 72; *Brandreth* v. *Lane,* 8 Paige 24; *New York Juvenile Guardian Society* v. *Roosevelt,* 7 Daly 188; *Ulster Square Dealer* v. *Fowler,* 111 N. Y. Supp. 16; *Star Co.* v. *Brush,* 170 *id.* 987; 172 *id.* 320; 172 *id.* 851; *Dopp* v. *Doll,* 9 Ohio Dec. Rep. 428; *Republica* v. *Oswald,* 1 Dall. 319, 325; *Republica* v. *Dennie,* 4 Yeates 267, 269; *Ex parte Neill,* 32 Tex. Cr. 275; 22 S. W. 923; *Mitchell* v. *Grand Lodge,* 56 Tex. Civ. App. 306, 309; 121 S. W. 178; *Sweeney* v. *Baker,* 13 W. Va. 158, 182; *Citizens Light, Heat & Power Co.* v. *Montgomery Light & Water Co.,* 171 Fed. 553, 556; *Willis* v. *O'Connell,* 231 Fed. 1004, 1010; *Dearborn Publishing Co.* v. *Fitzgerald,* 271 Fed. 479, 485.

previous restraint, to publish them, his right cannot be deemed to be dependent upon his publishing something else, more or less, with the matter to which objection is made.

Nor can it be said that the constitutional freedom from previous restraint is lost because charges are made of derelictions which constitute crimes. With the multiplying provisions of penal codes, and of municipal charters and ordinances carrying penal sanctions, the conduct of public officers is very largely within the purview of criminal statutes. The freedom of the press from previous restraint has never been regarded as limited to such animadversions as lay outside the range of penal enactments. Historically, there is no such limitation; it is inconsistent with the reason which underlies the privilege, as the privilege so limited would be of slight value for the purposes for which it came to be established.

The statute in question cannot be justified by reason of the fact that the publisher is permitted to show, before injunction issues, that the matter published is true and is published with good motives and for justifiable ends. If such a statute, authorizing suppression and injunction on such a basis, is constitutionally valid, it would be equally permissible for the legislature to provide that at any time the publisher of any newspaper could be brought before a court, or even an administrative officer (as the constitutional protection may not be regarded as resting on mere procedural details) and required to produce proof of the truth of his publication, or of what he intended to publish, and of his motives, or stand enjoined. If this can be done, the legislature may provide machinery for determining in the complete exercise of its discretion what are justifiable ends and restrain publication accordingly. And it would be but a step to a complete system of censorship. The recognition of authority to impose previous restraint upon publication in order to protect the community against the circulation of charges of misconduct, and especially of official misconduct, necessarily would carry with it the admission of the authority of the censor against which the constitutional barrier was erected. The preliminary freedom, by virtue of the very reason for its existence, does not depend, as this Court has said, on proof of truth. *Patterson* v. *Colorado, supra.*

Equally unavailing is the insistence that the statute is designed to prevent the circulation of scandal which tends to disturb the public peace and to provoke assaults and the commission of crime. Charges of reprehensible conduct, and in particular of official malfeasance, unquestionably create a public scandal, but the theory of the constitutional guaranty is that even a more serious public evil would be caused by authority to prevent publication. "To prohibit the intent to excite those unfavorable sentiments against those who administer the Government, is equivalent to a prohibition of the actual excitement of them; and to prohibit the actual excitement of them is equivalent to a prohibition of discussions having that tendency and effect; which, again, is equivalent to a protection of those who administer the Government, if they should at any time deserve the contempt or hatred of the people, against being exposed to it by free animadversions on their characters and conduct."[12] There is nothing new in the fact that charges of reprehensible conduct may create resentment and the disposition to resort to violent means of redress, but this well-understood tendency did not alter the determination to protect the press against censorship and restraint upon publication. As was said in *New Yorker Staats-Zeitung* v. *Nolan,* 89 N. J. Eq. 387, 388; 105 Atl. 72: "If the township may prevent the circulation of a newspaper for no reason other than that some of its inhabitants may violently disagree with it, and resent its circulation by resorting to physical violence, there is no limit to what may be prohibited." The danger of violent reactions becomes greater with effective organization of defiant groups resenting exposure, and if this consideration warranted legislative interference with the initial freedom of publication, the constitutional protection would be reduced to a mere form of words.

For these reasons we hold the statute, so far as it authorized the proceedings in this action under clause (b) of section one, to be an infringement of the liberty of the press guaranteed by the Fourteenth Amendment. We should add that this decision rests upon the operation and effect of the statute, without regard to the question of the truth of the charges contained in the particular periodical. The fact that the public officers named in this case, and those associated with the charges of official dereliction, may be deemed to be impeccable, cannot affect the conclusion that the statute imposes an unconstitutional restraint upon publication.

Judgment reversed.

MR. JUSTICE BUTLER, dissenting.

The decision of the Court in this case declares Minnesota and every other State powerless to restrain by injunction the business of publishing and circulating among the people malicious, scandalous and defamatory periodicals that in due course of judicial procedure has been adjudged to be a public nuisance. It gives to freedom of the press a meaning and a scope not heretofore recognized and construes "liberty"

---

[12]Madison, *op. cit.* p. 549

in the due process clause of the Fourteenth Amendment to put upon the States a federal restriction that is without precedent. Confessedly, the Federal Constitution prior to 1868, when the Fourteenth Amendment was adopted, did not protect the right of free speech or press against state action. *Barron* v. *Baltimore,* 7 Pet. 243, 250. *Fox* v. *Ohio,* 5 How. 410, 434. *Smith* v. *Maryland,* 18 How. 71, 76. *Withers* v. *Buckley,* 20 How. 84, 89–91. Up to that time the right was safeguarded solely by the constitutions and laws of the States and, it may be added, they operated adequately to protect it. This Court was not called on until 1925 to decide whether the "liberty" protected by the Fourteenth Amendment includes the right of free speech and press. That question has been finally answered in the affirmative. Cf. *Patterson* v. *Colorado,* 205 U. S. 454, 462. *Prudential Ins. Co.* v. *Cheek,* 259 U. S. 530, 538, 543. See *Gitlow* v. *New York,* 268 U. S. 652. *Fiske* v. *Kansas,* 274 U. S. 380. *Stromberg* v. *California, ante,* p. 359.

The record shows, and it is conceded, that defendants' regular business was the publication of malicious, scandalous and defamatory articles concerning the principal public officers, leading newspapers of the city, many private persons and the Jewish race. It also shows that it was their purpose at all hazards to continue to carry on the business. In every edition slanderous and defamatory matter predominates to the practical exclusion of all else. Many of the statements are so highly improbable as to compel a finding that they are false. The articles themselves show malice.[1]

[1]The following articles appear in the last edition published, dated November 19, 1927:

"FACTS NOT THEORIES.

" 'I am a bosom friend of Mr. Olson,' snorted a gentleman of Yiddish blood, 'and I want to protest against your article,' and blah, blah, blah, ad infinitum, ad nauseam.

"I am not taking orders from men of Barnett faith, at least right now. There have been too many men in this city and especially those in official life, who HAVE been taking orders and suggestions from JEW GANGSTERS, therefore we HAVE Jew Gangsters, practically ruling Minneapolis.

"It was buzzards of the Barnett stripe who shot down my buddy. It was Barnett gunmen who staged the assault on Samuel Shapiro. It is Jew thugs who have 'pulled' practically every robbery in this city. It was a member of the Barnett gang who shot down George Rubenstein (Ruby) while he stood in the shelter of Mose Barnett's ham-cavern on Hennepin avenue. It was Mose Barnett himself who shot down Roy Rogers on Hennepin avenue. It was at Mose Barnett's place of 'business' that the '13 dollar Jew' found a refuge while the police of New York were combing the country for him. It was a gang of Jew gunmen who boasted that for five hundred dollars they would kill any man in the city. It was Mose Barnett, a

The defendant here has no standing to assert that the statute is invalid because it might be construed so as to violate the Constitution. His right

---

Jew, who boasted that he held the chief of police of Minneapolis in his hand—had bought and paid for him.

"It is Jewish men and women—pliant tools of the Jew gangster, Mose Barnett, who stand charged with having falsified the election records and returns in the Third ward. And it is Mose Barnett himself, who, indicted for his part in the Shapiro assault, is a fugitive from justice today.

"Practically every vendor of vile hooch, every owner of a moonshine still, every snake-faced gangster and embryonic yegg in the Twin Cities is a JEW.

"Having these examples before me, I feel that I am justified in my refusal to take orders from a Jew who boasts that he is a 'bosom friend' of Mr. Olson.

"I find in the mail at least twice per week, letters from gentlemen of Jewish faith who advise me against 'launching an attack on the Jewish people.' These gentlemen have the cart before the horse. I am launching, nor is Mr. Guilford, no attack against any race, BUT:

"When I find men of a certain race banding themselves together for the purpose of preying upon Gentile or Jew; gunmen, KILLERS, roaming our streets shooting down men against whom they have no personal grudge (or happen to have); defying OUR laws; corrupting OUR officials; assaulting business men; beating up unarmed citizens; spreading a reign of terror through every walk of life, then I say to you in all sincerity, that I refuse to back up a single step from that 'issue'—if they choose to make it so.

"If the people of Jewish faith in Minneapolis wish to avoid criticism of these vermin whom I rightfully call 'Jews' they can easily do so BY THEMSELVES CLEANING HOUSE.

"I'm not out to cleanse Israel of the filth that clings to Israel's skirts. I'm out to 'hew to the line, let the chips fly where they may.'

"I simply state a fact when I say that ninety per cent. of the crimes committed against society in this city are committed by Jew gangsters.

"It was a Jew who employed JEWS to shoot down Mr. Guilford. It was a Jew who employed a Jew to intimidate Mr. Shapiro and a Jew who employed JEWS to assault that gentleman when he refused to yield to their threats. It was a JEW who wheedled or employed Jews to manipulate the election records and returns in the Third ward in flagrant violation of law. It was a Jew who left two hundred dollars with another Jew to pay to our chief of police just before the last municipal election, and:

"It is Jew, Jew, Jew, as long as one cares to comb over the records.

"I am launching no attack against the Jewish people AS A RACE. I am merely calling attention to a FACT. And if the people of that race and faith wish to rid themselves of the odium and stigma THE RODENTS OF THEIR OWN RACE HAVE BROUGHT UPON THEM, they need only to step to the front and help the decent citizens of Minneapolis rid the city of these criminal Jews.

"Either Mr. Guilford or myself stand ready to do battle for a MAN, regardless of his race, color or creed, but neither of us will step one inch out of our chosen path to avoid a fight IF the Jews want to battle.

"Both of us have some mighty loyal friends among the Jewish people but not is limited solely to the inquiry whether, having regard to the points properly raised in his case, the effect of applying the statute is to deprive him of his liberty without due process of law. This Court should not reverse the judgment below upon the ground that in some other case the statute may be applied in a way that is repugnant to the freedom of the press protected by the Fourteenth Amendment. *Castillo* v. *McConnico*, 168 U. S. 674, 680. *Williams* v. *Mississippi*, 170 U. S. 213, 225. *Yazoo & Miss. R. Co.* v. *Jackson Vinegar Co.*, 226 U. S. 217, 219–220. *Plymouth Coal Co.* v. *Pennsylvania*, 232 U. S. 531, 544–546.

This record requires the Court to consider the statute as applied to the business of publishing articles that are in fact malicious, scandalous and defamatory.

The statute provides that any person who "shall be engaged in the

---

one of them comes whining to ask that we 'lay off' criticism of Jewish gangsters and none of them who comes carping to us of their 'bosom friendship' for any public official now under our journalistic guns."

"GIL'S [Guilford's] CHATTERBOX.

"I headed into the city on September 26th, ran across three Jews in a Chevrolet; stopped a lot of lead and won a bed for myself in St. Barnabas Hospital for six weeks. . . .

"Whereupon I have withdrawn all allegiance to anything with a hook nose that eats herring. I have adopted the sparrow as my national bird until Davis' law enforcement league or the K.K.K. hammers the eagle's beak out straight. So if I seem to act crazy as I ankle down the street, bear in mind that I am merely saluting MY national emblem.

"All of which has nothing to do with the present whereabouts of Big Mose Barnett. Methinks he headed the local delegation to the new Palestine-for-Jews-only. He went ahead of the boys so he could do a little fixing with the Yiddish chief of police and get his twenty-five per cent. of the gambling rake-off. Boys will be boys and 'ganefs' will be ganefs."

"GRAND JURIES AND DITTO.

"There are grand juries, and there are grand juries. The last one was a real grand jury. It acted. The present one is like the scion who is labelled 'Junior.' That means not so good. There are a few mighty good folks on it—there are some who smell bad. One petty peanut politician whose graft was almost pitiful in its size when he was a public official, has already shot his mouth off in several places. He is establishing his alibi in advance for what he intends to keep from taking place.

"But George, we won't bother you. [Meaning a grand juror.] We are aware that the gambling syndicate was waiting for your body to convene before the big crap game opened again. The Yids had your dimensions, apparently, and we always go by the judgment of a dog in appraising people.

"We will call for a special grand jury and a special prosecutor within a short time, as soon as half of the staff can navigate to advantage, and then we'll show you what a real grand jury can do. Up to the present we have been merely tapping on the window. Very soon we shall start smashing glass."

business of regularly or customarily producing, publishing or circulating" a newspaper, magazine or other periodical that is (a) "obscene, lewd and lascivious" or (b) "malicious, scandalous and defamatory" is guilty of a nuisance and may be enjoined as provided in the Act. It will be observed that the qualifying words are used conjunctively. In actions brought under (b) "there shall be available the defense that the truth was published with good motives and for justifiable ends."

The complaint charges that defendants were engaged in the business of regularly and customarily publishing "malicious, scandalous and defamatory newspapers" known as the Saturday Press, and nine editions dated respectively on each Saturday commencing September 25 and ending November 19, 1927, were made a part of the complaint. These are all that were published.

On appeal from the order of the district court overruling defendants' demurrer to the complaint the state supreme court said (174 Minn. 457, 461; 219 N. W. 770):

"The constituent elements of the declared nuisance are the customary and regular dissemination by means of a newspaper which finds its way into families, reaching the young as well as the mature, of a selection of scandalous and defamatory articles treated in such a way as to excite attention and interest so as to command circulation. . . . The statute is not directed at threatened libel but at an existing business which, generally speaking, involves more than libel. The distribution of scandalous matter is detrimental to public morals and to the general welfare. It tends to disturb the peace of the community. Being defamatory and malicious, it tends to provoke assaults and the commission of crime. It has no concern with the publication of the truth, with good motives and for justifiable ends. . . . In Minnesota no agency can hush the sincere and honest voice of the press; but our constitution was never intended to protect malice, scandal and defamation when untrue or published with bad motives or without justifiable ends. . . . It was never the intention of the constitution to afford protection to a publication devoted to scandal and defamation. . . . Defendants stand before us upon the record as being regularly and customarily engaged in a business of conducting a newspaper sending to the public malicious, scandalous and defamatory printed matter."

The case was remanded to the district court.

Near's answer made no allegations to excuse or justify the business or the articles complained of. It formally denied that the publications were malicious, scandalous or defamatory, admitted that they were made as alleged, and attacked the statute as unconstitutional. At the trial the plaintiff introduced evidence unquestionably sufficient to support the complaint. The defendant offered none. The court found the facts as alleged in the complaint and specifically that each edition "was chiefly devoted to malicious, scandalous and defamatory articles" and that the last edition was chiefly devoted to malicious, scandalous and defamatory articles concerning Leach (mayor of Minneapolis), Davis (representative of the law enforcement league of citizens), Brunskill (chief of police), Olson (county attorney), the Jewish race and members of the grand jury then serving in that court; that defendants in and through the several publications "did thereby engage in the business of regularly and customarily producing, publishing and circulating a malicious, scandalous and defamatory newspaper."

Defendant Near again appealed to the supreme court. In its opinion (179 Minn. 40; 228 N. W. 326) the court said: "No claim is advanced that the method and character of the operation of the newspaper in question was not a nuisance if the statute is constitutional. It was regularly and customarily devoted largely to malicious, scandalous and defamatory matter. . . . The record presents the same questions, upon which we have already passed."

Defendant concedes that the editions of the newspaper complained of are "defamatory *per se.*" And he says: "It has been asserted that the constitution was never intended to be a shield for malice, scandal, and defamation when untrue, or published with bad motives, or for unjustifiable ends. . . . The contrary is true; every person *does* have a constitutional right to publish malicious, scandalous, and defamatory matter though untrue, and with bad motives, and for unjustifiable ends, *in the first instance,* though he is subject to responsibility therefor *afterwards.*" The record, when the substance of the articles is regarded, requires that concession here. And this Court is required to pass on the validity of the state law on that basis.

No question was raised below and there is none here concerning the relevancy or weight of evidence, burden of proof, justification or other matters of defense, the scope of the judgment or proceedings to enforce it or the character of the publications that may be made notwithstanding the injunction.

There is no basis for the suggestion that defendants may not interpose any defense or introduce any evidence that would be open to them in a libel case, or that malice may not be negatived by showing that the publication was made in good faith in belief of its truth, or that at the time and under the circumstances it was justified as a fair comment on public affairs or upon the conduct of public officers in respect of their duties as such. See Mason's Minnesota Statutes, §§ 10112, 10113.

The scope of the judgment is not reviewable here. The opinion of the state supreme court shows that it was not reviewable there, because defendants' assignments of error in that court did not go to the form of the judgment, and because the lower court had not been asked to modify the judgment.

The Act was passed in the exertion of the State's power of police, and this court is by well established rule required to assume, until the contrary is clearly made to appear, that there exists in Minnesota a state of affairs that justifies this measure for the preservation of the peace and good order of the State. *Lindsley* v. *Natural Carbonic Gas Co.,* 220 U. S. 61, 79. *Gitlow* v. *New York, supra,* 668–669. *Corporation Commission* v. *Lowe,* 281 U. S. 431, 438. *O'Gorman & Young* v. *Hartford Ins. Co.,* 282 U. S. 251, 257–258.

The publications themselves disclose the need and propriety of the legislation. They show:

In 1913 one Guilford, originally a defendant in this suit, commenced the publication of a scandal sheet called the Twin City Reporter; in 1916 Near joined him in the enterprise, later bought him out and engaged the services of one Bevans. In 1919 Bevans acquired Near's interest, and has since, alone or with others, continued the publication. Defendants admit that they published some reprehensible articles in the Twin City Reporter, deny that they personally used it for blackmailing purposes, admit that by reason of their connection with the paper their reputation did become tainted and state that Bevans, while so associated with Near, did use the paper for blackmailing purposes. And Near says it was for that reason he sold his interest to Bevans.

In a number of the editions defendants charge that, ever since Near sold his interest to Bevans in 1919, the Twin City Reporter has been used for blackmail, to dominate public gambling and other criminal activities and as well to exert a kind of control over public officers and the government of the city.

The articles in question also state that, when defendants announced their intention to publish the Saturday Press, they were threatened, and that soon after the first publication Guilford was waylaid and shot down before he could use the firearm which he had at hand for the purpose of defending himself against anticipated assaults. It also appears that Near apprehended violence and was not unprepared to repel it. There is much more of like significance.

The long criminal career of the Twin City Reporter—if it is in fact as described by defendants—and the arming and shooting arising out of the publication of the Saturday Press, serve to illustrate the kind of conditions, in respect of the business of publishing malicious, scandalous and defamatory periodicals, by which the state legislature presumably was moved to enact the law in question. It must be deemed appropriate to deal with conditions existing in Minnesota.

It is of the greatest importance that the States shall be untrammeled and free to employ all just and appropriate measures to prevent abuses of the liberty of the press.

In his work on the Constitution (5th ed.) Justice Story, expounding the First Amendment which declares: "Congress shall make no law abridging the freedom of speech or of the press," said (§ 1880):

"That this amendment was intended to secure to every citizen an absolute right to speak, or write, or print whatever he might please, without any responsibility, public or private, therefor, is a supposition too wild to be indulged by any rational man. This would be to allow to every citizen a right to destroy at his pleasure the reputation, the peace, the property, and even the personal safety of every other citizen. A man might, out of mere malice and revenge, accuse another of the most infamous crimes; might excite against him the indignation of all his fellow-citizens by the most atrocious calumnies; might disturb, nay, overturn, all his domestic peace, and embitter his parental affections; might inflict the most distressing punishments upon the weak, the timid, and the innocent; might prejudice all a man's civil, and political, and private rights; and might stir up sedition, rebellion, and treason even against the government itself, in the wantonness of his passions or the corruption of his heart. Civil society could not go on under such circumstances. Men would then be obliged to resort to private vengeance to make up for the deficiencies of the law; and assassination and savage cruelties would be perpetrated with all the frequency belonging to barbarous and brutal communities. It is plain, then, that the language of this amendment imports no more than that every man shall have a right to speak, write, and print his opinions upon any subject whatsoever, without any prior restraint, so always that he does not injure any other person in his rights, person, property, or reputation; and so always that he does not thereby disturb the public peace, or attempt to subvert the government. It is neither more nor less than an expansion of the great doctrine recently brought into operation in the law of libel, *that every man shall be at liberty to publish what is true, with good motives and for justifiable ends.* And with this reasonable limitation it is not only right in itself, but it is an inestimable privilege in a free government. Without such a limitation, it might become the scourge of the republic, first denouncing the principles of liberty, and then, by rendering the most virtuous patriots odious through the terrors of the press, introducing despotism in its worst form." (Italicizing added.)

The Court quotes Blackstone in support of its condemnation of the statute as imposing a previous restraint upon publication. But the *previous restraints* referred to by him subjected the press to the arbitrary will of an administrative officer. He describes the practice (Book IV, p. 152): "To subject the press to the restrictive power of a licenser, as was formerly done, both before and since the revolution [of 1688], is to subject all freedom of sentiment to the prejudices of one man, and make him the arbitrary and infallible judge of all controverted points in learning, religion, and government."[2]

Story gives the history alluded to by Blackstone (§ 1882):

"The art of printing soon after its introduction, we are told, was looked upon, as well in England as in other countries, as merely a matter of state, and subject to the coercion of the crown. It was, therefore, regulated in England by the king's proclamations, prohibitions, charters of privilege, and licenses, and finally by the decrees of the Court of Star-Chamber, which limited the number of printers and of presses which each should employ, and prohibited new publications, unless previously approved by proper licensers. On the demolition of this odious jurisdiction, in 1641, the Long Parliament of Charles the First, after their rupture with that prince, assumed the same powers which the Star-Chamber exercised with respect to licensing books; and during the Commonwealth (such is human frailty and the love of power even in republics!) they issued their ordinances for that purpose, founded principally upon a Star-Chamber decree of 1637. After the restoration of Charles the Second, a statute on the same subject was passed, copied, with some few alterations, from the parliamentary ordinances. The act expired in 1679, and was revived and continued for a few years after the revolution of 1688. Many attempts were made by the government to keep it in force; but it was so strongly resisted by Parliament that it expired in 1694, and has never since been revived."

It is plain that Blackstone taught that under the common law liberty

---

[2]May, Constitutional History of England, c. IX. Duniway, Freedom of the Press in Massachusetts, cc. I and II. Cooley, Constitutional Limitations (8th ed.) Vol. II, pp. 880–881. Pound, Equitable Relief against Defamation, 29 Harv. L. Rev. 640, 650 et seq. Madison, Letters and Other Writings (1865 ed.) Vol. IV, pp. 542, 543. *Republica* v. *Oswald,* 1 Dall. 319, 325. Rawle, A View of the Constitution (2d ed. 1829) p. 124. Paterson, Liberty of the Press, c. III.

of the press means simply the absence of restraint upon publication in advance as distinguished from liability, civil or criminal, for libelous or improper matter so published. And, as above shown, Story defined freedom of the press guaranteed by the First Amendment to mean that "every man shall be at liberty to publish what is true, with good motives and for justifiable ends." His statement concerned the definite declaration of the First Amendment. It is not suggested that the freedom of press included in the liberty protected by the Fourteenth Amendment, which was adopted after Story's definition, is greater than that protected against congressional action. And see 2 Cooley's Constitutional Limitations, 8th ed., p. 886. 2 Kent's Commentaries (14th ed.) Lect. XXIV, p. 17.

The Minnesota statute does not operate as a *previous* restraint on publication within the proper meaning of that phrase. It does not authorize administrative control in advance such as was formerly exercised by the licensers and censors but prescribes a remedy to be enforced by a suit in equity. In this case there was previous publication made in the course of the business of regularly producing malicious, scandalous and defamatory periodicals. The business and publications unquestionably constitute an abuse of the right of free press. The statute denounces the things done as a nuisance on the ground, as stated by the state supreme court, that they threaten morals, peace and good order. There is no question of the power of the State to denounce such transgressions. The restraint authorized is only in respect of continuing to do what has been duly adjudged to constitute a nuisance. The controlling words are "All persons guilty of such nuisance may be enjoined, as hereinafter provided. . . . Whenever any such nuisance is committed . . . an action in the name of the State" may be brought "to perpetually enjoin the person or persons committing, conducting or maintaining any such nuisance, *from further committing, conducting or maintaining any such nuisance.* . . . The court may make its order and judgment permanently enjoining . . . defendants found guilty . . . from committing or continuing the acts prohibited hereby, and in and by such judgment, such nuisance may be wholly abated. . . ." There is nothing in the statute[3] purporting

---

[3] § 1. Any person who, as an individual, or as a member or employee of a firm, or association or organization, or as an officer, director, member or employee of a corporation, shall be engaged in the business of regularly or customarily producing, publishing or circulating, having in possession, selling or giving away.

(a) an obscene, lewd and lascivious newspaper, magazine, or other periodical, or

to prohibit publications that have not been adjudged to constitute a nuisance. It is fanciful to suggest similarity between the granting or enforcement of the decree authorized by this statute to prevent *further* publication of malicious, scandalous and defamatory articles and the *previous restraint* upon the press by licensers as referred to by Blackstone and described in the history of the times to which he alludes.

The opinion seems to concede that under clause (a) of the Minnesota law the business of regularly publishing and circulating an obscene periodical may be enjoined as a nuisance. It is difficult to perceive any distinction, having any relation to constitutionality, between clause (a) and clause (b) under which this action was brought. Both nuisances are offensive to morals, order and good government. As that resulting from lewd publications constitutionally may be enjoined it is hard to understand why the one resulting from a regular business of malicious defamation may not.

It is well known, as found by the state supreme court, that existing libel

---

(b) a malicious, scandalous and defamatory newspaper, magazine, or other periodical,
is guilty of a nuisance, and all persons guilty of such nuisance may be enjoined, as hereinafter provided.

*   *   *   *   *

In actions brought under (b) above, there shall be available the defense that the truth was published with good motives and for justifiable ends and in such actions the plaintiff shall not have the right to report [resort] to issues or editions of periodicals taking place more than three months before the commencement of the action.

§ 2. Whenever any such nuisance is committed or is kept, maintained, or exists, as above provided for, the County Attorney of any county where any such periodical is published or circulated . . . may commence and maintain in the District Court of said county, an action in the name of the State of Minnesota . . . to perpetually enjoin the person or persons committing, conducting or maintaining any such nuisance, from further committing, conducting, or maintaining any such nuisance. . . .

§ 3. The action may be brought to trial and tried as in the case of other actions in such District Court, and shall be governed by the practice and procedure applicable to civil actions for injunctions.

After trial the court may make its order and judgment permanently enjoining any and all defendants found guilty of violating this Act from further committing or continuing the acts prohibited hereby, and in and by such judgment, such nuisance may be wholly abated.

The court may, as in other cases of contempt, at any time punish, by fine of not more than $1,000, or by imprisonment in the county jail for not more than twelve months, any person or persons violating any injunction, temporary or permanent, made or issued pursuant to this Act.

laws are inadequate effectively to suppress evils resulting from the kind of business and publications that are shown in this case. The doctrine that measures such as the one before us are invalid because they operate as previous restraints to infringe freedom of press exposes the peace and good order of every community and the business and private affairs of every individual to the constant and protracted false and malicious assaults of any insolvent publisher who may have purpose and sufficient capacity to contrive and put into effect a scheme or program for oppression, blackmail or extortion.

The judgment should be affirmed.

Mr. Justice Van Devanter, Mr. Justice McReynolds, and Mr. Justice Sutherland concur in this opinion.

Index

About the Author

Born in New York City and reared in Providence, Rhode Island, FRED W. FRIENDLY has spent virtually all his life in journalism: practicing it, shaping it, teaching it and writing about it.

With his partner, Edward R. Murrow, Mr. Friendly was responsible for many of television's most distinguished moments, including *See It Now* and *CBS Reports*. After serving as president of CBS News from 1964 to 1966, Mr. Friendly joined the Ford Foundation and was named the Edward R. Murrow Professor of Journalism at Columbia University. Through his work at the Foundation, he was instrumental in the growth of public television and in creating seminars designed to encourage dialogue and ease tensions between journalists and other elements of society.

Mr. Friendly continues to write and comment on media issues.